1482

THE JOURNAL OF INDUSTRIAL ECONOMICS

VOLUME XVII

1968–69

BASIL BLACKWELL

OXFORD

CONTENTS

VOLUME XVII

Number 1, *November* 1968

PAGE

The Financial Prospects of Shipbuilding after Geddes, by J. R. PARKINSON — 1

Making Micro-Economics Multi-Dimensional, by KENNETH SIMMONDS — 18

On Relative Fuel Efficiency and the Output Elasticity of Energy Consumption in Western Europe, by F. GERARD ADAMS and PETER MIOVIC — 41

Cost Functions, Concentration, and Barriers to Entry in Twenty-nine Manufacturing Industries of India, by VINOD E. GUPTA — 57

Sales Revenue Maximization—A Note, by LEONARD WAVERMAN — 73

Sales Revenue Maximization—A Reply, by MARSHALL HALL — 78

Number 2, *April* 1969

Optimal Plant under Conditions of Risk, by T. M. WHITIN — 81

Measuring the Profitability of Advertising: An Empirical Study, by JEAN-JACQUES LAMBIN — 86

Market Structure and Industrial Performance: Relation of Profit Rates to Concentration, Advertising Intensity, and Diversity, by RICHARD A. MILLER — 104

The Behavior of the Firm with a Financial Restriction, by GUIDO DI TELLA — 119

Stock Market Valuation and Acquisitions: An Empirical Test on one Component of Managerial Utility, by D. A. KUEHN — 132

Tests of Market Share Stability in the Cigarette Industry, 1950–66, by THOMAS HAVRILESKY and RICHARD BARTH — 145

The Organization of the Ceramic Industry around the Nagoya Area of Japan, by TSUTOMU NAKAMURA — 151

Number 3, July 1969

Pricing Pioneering Products, by JOEL DEAN 165

Some Managerial Influences on a Firm's Pricing Policy, by A. J. BURKART 180

The U.S. Tanker Industry: A Structural and Behavioral Analysis, by RAN HETTENA and HIRSCH S. RUCHLIN 188

Liner Nationality and Steamship Conference Rate-making, by JOHN A. WALGREEN 205

Television Station Profitability and FCC Regulatory Policy, by EDWARD GREENBERG 210

The Computer Utility: Market Entry in Search of Public Policy, by MANLEY R. IRWIN 239

Printed in Great Britain by
Alden & Mowbray Ltd
at the Alden Press, Oxford

THE FINANCIAL PROSPECTS OF SHIPBUILDING AFTER GEDDES*

by J. R. Parkinson

Devaluation of sterling ought to do more for the shipbuilding industry than the writing of the Geddes Report. The underlying difficulties of the industry are real: inefficient organization, unwilling labour and loss of comparative advantage; but the immediate difficulties are financial. Profitability will have to be restored rapidly if respite is to be gained for the Geddes recommendations to be effective. The conclusions reached in the Report have been widely discussed and they are reviewed here only briefly with the object of trying to relate them to the financial position of the industry as it appears from company accounts.

THE GEDDES RECOMMENDATIONS

The most striking recommendation of the Report was that the industry should henceforward look to the expanding world demand for ships for its market and not confine its attention to the needs of nationally based shipowners. Devaluation may give a new edge to this exhortation. The market for United Kingdom shipbuilders was previously thought of as being confined to the British flag plus some export of ships on balance not because the industry was not export-minded (though it was not sales-minded) but because it was not fully capable of meeting competition in the open market.

In some measure the Geddes proposals for financial assistance to the industry are linked to the existence of an expanding market. How far is such a view justified? If the criterion for giving public assistance to an industry were the existence of expanding markets, it would be difficult to know where to draw the line. Many industries can look to growing world demand. Their markets may be more protected than those of flags of convenience, but protection is not an insuperable barrier and in spite of setbacks is a declining factor in world trade. It would be difficult to single out shipbuilding as presenting greater opportunities than other industries, on the ground of expanding markets alone. Indeed it might be better to advocate the concentration of industrial endeavour in those fields where our share of the market had been expanding, or declining at a rate no more than in proportion to our general decline in economic importance and affluence. Competition, contrary to a popularly held belief, may not

* I gratefully acknowledge the assistance of Mr. B. Buckley in the preparation of this article, and Mr. J. Buckley in the preparation of the diagrams.

be any easier to master in an expanding market than in a declining one. Supply from other countries may expand at least as rapidly as the increase in demand without large profits being made. It is competitive ability that leads to sales opportunities in the world market, not the other way round. But the Geddes arguments must not be distorted. The justification for spending public money on the industry is that the industry can become efficient. The availability of an expanding market is a reason helping to justify the efforts needed to reorganize the industry, no more.

The major European shipbuilding countries could, of course, be exhorted to reorganize on similar grounds. It is Japan and to a less extent Sweden and Norway that have taken full advantage of the growing market for ships in the post-war period. The recession of the late 'fifties was scarcely felt by these countries. Figures of the tonnage of ships launched may be misleading in the indications they give of the work content of output but they seem to show that it affected nearly every other producer. Germany has fared much the same as the United Kingdom and the Netherlands even worse. France and Italy continue to keep their yards occupied with ½ million gross tons output per year while Norwegian output has not continued its advance in recent years. All these countries could have been advised by the Geddes Committee, had it been considering their position, that the world market for ships was wide open to them and that there was no reason why their costs should not be reduced and the decline in their market shares arrested. In fact this view has not always been taken, France at least has laid stress on the conversion to other activities of wage-earners in shipbuilding.[1] Devaluation by the United Kingdom hardly affects this conclusion, for the standard of reference is Japan not the United Kingdom.

Having established that the world market for ships is likely to expand the Report dismissed the view that fluctuations in orders are likely to be so severe as to make it undesirable for the United Kingdom to expand its activities in shipbuilding. Fluctuations in orders it is argued are reflected not in fluctuations in output so much as in fluctuations in order books. Moreover it is claimed that orders for replacement of the home fleet are more subject to fluctuation than orders for expanding the world fleet, and it is safer therefore to look farther afield.

It may be safer to do so but this does not mean that fluctuations will not occur as the Report recognized. Fluctuations are likely to fall less hardly on competitive producers like Japan than on United Kingdom producers working on small margins even in times of

[1] See *The Situation in the Shipbuilding Industry*, O.E.C.D., Paris 1965, p. 63.

prosperity. They could be so great as to affect Japanese shipyards which are vulnerable because their productive capacity is large in relation to that of the world. They are bound to affect United Kingdom shipyards in present circumstances; and it would not be realistic to think that government subsidies could be used on a scale to offset the effects of a world slump in orders.

It is true that post-war statistics of output show, as Geddes maintained, that disequilibria between capacity and demand were absorbed more by the queue of orders than by the queue of unemployed. Fluctuations in order books were much greater than fluctuations in output; but the course of output was not invariably upwards. It fell from 9 million gross tons in 1958 to 8 million in 1961 and did not recover until 1963 after five years of stagnation. For some countries the fall was much greater; in the case of the United Kingdom from nearly $1\frac{1}{2}$ g.r.t. millions in 1955 to less than 1 million g.r.t. in 1963. For Italy there were also appreciable ups and downs and for the Netherlands very considerable fluctuations. It is the marginal producers that are most affected by downward fluctuations and it is difficult for them to increase output once demand rises, because workers leave the industry permanently. It is surprising how easily a fall in shipyard employment can be absorbed by even a development area, sometimes with benefit from the release of men with scarce skills who may provide a nucleus for the development of other, often export, industries and the absorption of men previously unemployed. When men are lost to the shipbuilding industry an increase in productivity may not always suffice to build up output to previous or higher levels.

Present circumstances give point to the likelihood of fluctuations in output in the next few years. The output of ships amounted to 14 million g.r.t. in 1966 and 15 million g.r.t. in 1967, a figure that the Geddes Report suggested would not be attained before 1972. New orders in 1966 amounted to 17 million g.r.t. and to 22 million g.r.t. in 1967 compared with a world fleet of 180 million g.r.t. at the end of 1967. When these figures are set against increases in non-tanker and tanker tonnage of 47 and 114 per cent respectively from 1957 to 1967 the danger of a decline in output between now and 1972–73 is evident.

The large inflow of orders in 1966 and 1967 continued in the first half of 1968. Over half of the 40 million g.r.t. of shipping on order in June 1968 consisted of tankers and 124 of those on order exceeded 100,000 g.r.t. The trend towards the use of large tankers has been a feature of the whole post-war period, but the closure of the Suez Canal gave a new momentum to it. It does not seem that the 200–

300 thousand d.w.t. tanker represents the limit of size; transport costs are thought to continue to fall, though less strikingly, for larger tankers and it may be that some of 500,000 d.w.t. or even 750,000 d.w.t. will supersede the largest so far built.

If such vessels become usual for trunk hauls, there will be considerable repercussions in all shipbuilding countries. Competition will be greatly intensified, for rather few orders for the largest sizes of tankers are likely to be placed each year, not many more perhaps than the number of sites that are currently being equipped to build them. It is true that many building docks will be flexible in operation, capable of being used to build two or more smaller vessels or for repair. But this will serve only to intensify competition for orders for smaller vessels including those for dry cargo as well as tankers.

When orders come in chunks of £10 million or quite possibly multiples of this figure, large financial groupings are needed. It may be asked whether, if this were to be the future pattern, the shipbuilding industry would be able to manage without government help in getting orders. There were already the first signs of this happening in the placing of orders for tankers over 200,000 deadweight before devaluation. Would these orders have come to the United Kingdom without government assistance and pressure on the oil company concerned? So long as the United Kingdom shipbuilding industry is less than competitive it is to be expected that its market will reflect at least as much the need of the United Kingdom for shipping services as world demand. In the home market some stop can be put to the loss of orders by the exercise of countervailing power.

It follows from this that the precise form that groupings take is of importance. Only thorough-going control of all operations will produce the results required and as the Upper Clyde Shipbuilders have rightly recognized there is no escaping concentration of production in the most suitable yards and the closure of those that would be only a drain on the group's resources. One of the most difficult operations will be to establish and develop the new management teams that are needed. Traditionally, shipbuilders are a race of individualists and it will not come easily to accustom themselves to working under the direction of a larger entity.

One of the advantages of larger groups urged by the Geddes Report was that it would give scope for staff specializing in modern management and functions. It would be quite wrong to view this as the furnishing only of common services from some central point covering perhaps design, purchasing or some form of internal management consultancy. Some of the advantages of the groupings will be felt not in these ways but in the development of good industrial relations which will pave the way for the adoption of new systems of management. It is possible also that on a larger scale it will be easier to integrate good yard management to the adoption of efficient production processes. Staff teams might be established to examine all the implications of adopting new production methods and to eliminate in advance of their adoption all technical, financial or labour difficulties likely to be encountered; if necessary by carrying out pilot projects. The adoption of such new methods might then become not only easy but obligatory in a new setting establishing its own code of professional expertise.

These are high hopes. The danger is that they may be over-optimistic in assuming that problems of yard management can be easily overcome by superior organization induced by grouping. The basic need is to increase output per man until it is as high as in efficient yards elsewhere, to use capital much more effectively and to ensure that the simple things are well done. It is the need to get on top of yard management that stands out in the first spell of reorganization at Fairfields (accompanied by an appropriate choice of ships) far more than out-of-date design or even the lack of a world sales organization.

THE EFFICIENCY OF THE INDUSTRY

For the United Kingdom, as for other less successful shipbuilding countries, there is no alternative to increasing productivity.[2] The Geddes checklist of ways to do this is comprehensive. It starts with the need for establishing larger shipbuilding units. Such a conclusion might seem inevitable at a time when scale of operation is assuming a new importance, but it is not obvious that difficulties experienced in running a small unit can be eliminated by attempting to run a much larger unit. In this respect the Geddes Report propounds its own solution, reflecting a basic philosophy:

> There must be executive direction of high quality. The job cannot be done on a part-time basis, and yet the business arising from a single yard of the normal economic size will not give adequate scope and employment to top management of the quality required. (Para. 285)

[2] It appears from figures given in *The Situation in the Shipbuilding Industry* (O.E.C.D., 1965) that Japanese yards do not employ many more men in new building than United Kingdom yards, yet the tonnage they produce may be four times as much. Presumably the comparison in terms of value of output would be less favourable to the Japanese because the Parliamentary Secretary, Ministry of Technology has said that productivity in Japanese yards was 40 per cent higher than British yards (*The Times*, January 11th, 1968).

Typical shipyards employ 2/3000 men if they are efficient, 5000 if they are not. It is arguable that the future of United Kingdom industry depends on the outstanding qualities of a few men thinly spread over their fellow human beings and that such men are found only occasionally in organizations employing less than 10,000 workers, for that is what Geddes seems to imply. If so, such men are very few in number, perhaps as few as 100 are born in the United Kingdom each year. This may be so; it is easy to suppose that qualities of management are log-normally distributed amongst individuals and outstanding men consequently rare, and to conclude that what the shipbuilding industry has lacked above all these past fifty years has been leaders of quite exceptional talent, rather than economic opportunity. But it is a view that must be submitted to examination. Can entrepreneurs bring their talents to bear in the industrial committee as once they did in the industrial revolution and do they really have the talent to transform the performance of the many other managers on whom the brunt of the task of organizing the industry will fall?

If the question of reorganization of shipbuilding firms had been left to merchant bankers investing their own money in the venture, they might well not have taken it on. But if they had done so they would almost certainly have concentrated on salvaging those firms that they judged to be relatively efficient and which held out the prospect of making a market rate of return on the money invested in them. Other firms would have been excluded from the exercise and the better yards developed to a point where they could take advantage of economies of scale. There are no giants like G.E.C. or A.E.I. in shipbuilding whose services cannot be dispensed with and for whom there is no alternative to the throes of rationalization. Reduction in the number of yards engaged in the industry is not going to mean any less competition in a world market dominated by Japan, except for Admiralty work and orders tied to United Kingdom yards by loans below market rates of interest. But the prospect of receiving government assistance conditional on amalgamation offers not only an incentive to firms to come together but considerable bargaining power to those who would be better left out of the exercise altogether. There is no room for fair shares in rationalization. The loans available from the Shipbuilding Board to assist with rationalization are little enough for the job they are expected to do; there is nothing to spare for meeting the aspirations of disgruntled shareholders of any shipyards that are likely to be a liability rather than an asset to the group.

The Geddes list of vital changes in management practice is very long and will take many years to complete. It will take time and not be easy for the groups to build up expert staffs capable of covering marketing, development, design, drawing office work, purchasing, progressing, personnel, training, accounting, systems analysis and computer services. Most of this one would expect to find in a modern organization; it should not be implied that it is completely absent in shipbuilding. But there is hardly any aspect of professional management that the Geddes Report does not find it necessary to spell out in much of the detail of a management course primer. The remarks on how to reduce costs are models of their kind: the essence of budgetary control is outlined, the value of the computer in many spheres set out; and many other devices are described. There are not many management techniques that the Committee failed to list. Those in the shipbuilding industry cannot say that they have not been informed. They know there is plenty of scope for improvement; so much so that it may be overwhelming. Does the Report not ask for more than a backward industry can reasonably find?

In some instances answers are being found to long-standing difficulties. Labour relations are improving even if there are still signs of trouble. Modern management methods do not automatically make the labour force respond. The magic wand of state ownership or the much more relevant application of modern management techniques to the work force at Fairfields has not transformed the situation over-night; but progress is being made and there is a breath of optimism in the air. More widely labour relations are becoming less rigid. There are signs of the breaking down of demarcation practices and a greater understanding that flexibility is essential to survival.

It is not intended to discuss the recommendations made about shipyard operations in any detail here; it is for shipbuilders themselves to do this and to get on with the job. Nor will the Geddes Report itself stand or fall on the detail of its recommendations. The purpose of writing the Report was to reach certain conclusions about the potentialities of the industry and the policies needed for it to realize its potentiality.

The conclusions were positive. There was a market which could absorb expanding production; there were many ways in which the industry could improve its performance; and it was possible to suggest action that could assist in bringing about the changes needed. The assistance proposed was to be dependent on the industry accepting the course of action outlined and so was in no sense an unconditional use of public funds. A report of this nature is as much as can be expected from a committee. In fact the Committee wrote a good

Report. It could scarcely have been expected to have suggested that the industry's future was hopeless, for it was not; or to have preached non-interference leaving it to the efficient firms to survive. Doubts were indeed felt about the adequacy of existing management, but this problem was not shirked and an answer proposed.

The Russian answer to the industry's problems might have been a wholesale change in management by decree or a closer link between management salaries and performance. It might have been difficult outside the command economy to have linked managers' pay to their performance in a largely unprofitable industry but once government assistance was given to specific firms management changes followed. As yet it is too early to say whether the further disbursement of government loans to the industry from the Shipbuilding Industry Board will be associated with government intervention in management structures; probably not. Nevertheless the scale of assistance presently being given to the industry is such as to render it largely dependent on public policy for its survival. This is never a comfortable position for private enterprise to be in.

THE FINANCIAL POSITION

The decline in the financial position of the industry has been gradual and it is only recently that the drain on the resources of the companies engaged became such as to threaten their existence. It is never easy to interpret those published accounts which are assumed to represent the fortunes of the industry. There are private as well as public companies, and the diverse activities of the major public companies are interwoven making it impossible fully to segregate the financial consequences of shipbuilding activities.

The picture is further complicated by the different sources that have to be used to obtain insight into the financial position at various times. From 1957, figures compiled by the Board of Trade from company accounts are probably the most reliable source of information, although as with the other sources it is almost impossible to determine how far they record the financial results of shipbuilding operations and how far the results of other activities. For investment in fixed assets the census of manufacturing is a useful (though still confusing) source of information, but the series stops short at 1962.[3] Figures collated by the *Economist* provide a working series before 1957 (and have been made available for recent years) but they are less complete in some respects than those of the Board of Trade and present a different picture at times. One problem is that investment

[3] The overlapping break in the series in 1958 is due to a change in compilation of figures from an establishment to a business unit basis.

in fixed assets is not given directly by the figures and while the change in the value of balance sheet entries for fixed assets gives some indication of the trend of investment it is subject to several adjustments, including the writing-off of capital. Under the accounting procedures followed, when an asset is written off the value of fixed investment in the balance sheet is reduced by the amount paid for the asset. If writing-off proceeds sporadically the value of fixed assets may decline in particular years for accounting reasons. Nevertheless some facts stand out and there are some useful impressions to be gained from the figures about the general financial position of the industry. In the diagrams, certain of these are brought out for the period 1948–56 from the figures prepared by the *Economist* and the estimates of fixed investment given in the Census. For the period 1957 onwards, the Board of Trade figures, though compiled on a different basis, enable a general impression to be formed of the financial position of the industry for more recent years.

It appears from a study of these sources that the immediate post-war years were years of comparative financial prosperity, at a time when there was not much pressure to generate funds for investment in fixed assets. Fixed assets of companies whose accounts were collated in the *Economist* rose only slowly; and in the first half of the nineteen-fifties less than £5 million was spent on the average each year. The coverage of the figures given in the *Economist* is less complete than those recorded in the Census of Manufacturing, but the difference between the figures at this period was not very great in absolute terms.

It is known that restrictions limited investment much more than the cash flow, and this is borne out in the *Economist's* analysis from which it appears that there was ample long-term finance available to cover investment in fixed capital. Depreciation provisions alone covered about half the cost incurred, and retained profits more than made up the difference. The finance of stocks and debtors came to more than that of fixed investment, but the amount owed by debtors to the companies rose much less rapidly than the amount due to creditors, and on balance cash balances changed little.

Towards the end of the 1950s the position was beginning to change. The level of investment in fixed assets had built up sharply and in the second half of the 1950s, census of manufacturing figures show it as having risen from £5 to £10 million per year to £10 to £20 million, as investment programmes became more ambitious and easier of implementation. Depreciation provided less than half the funds needed for investment in fixed capital but retained profits were at least as important, and a number of companies supplemented their

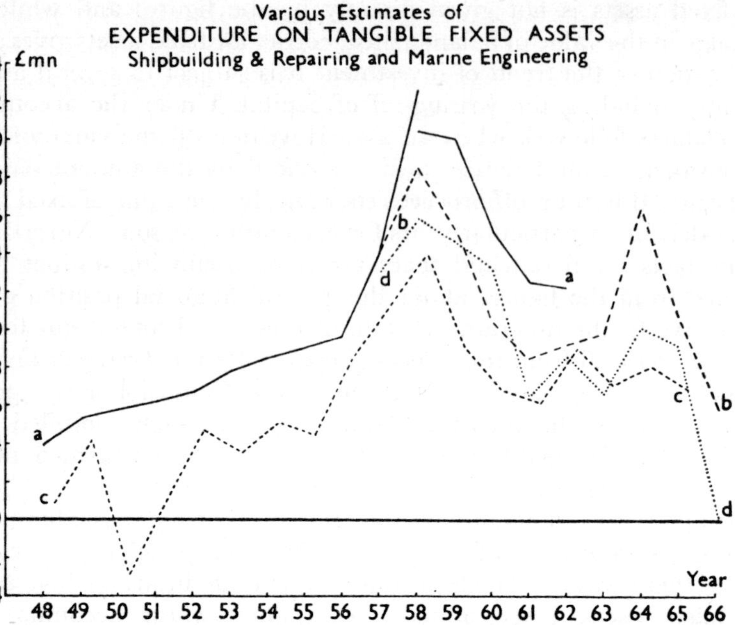

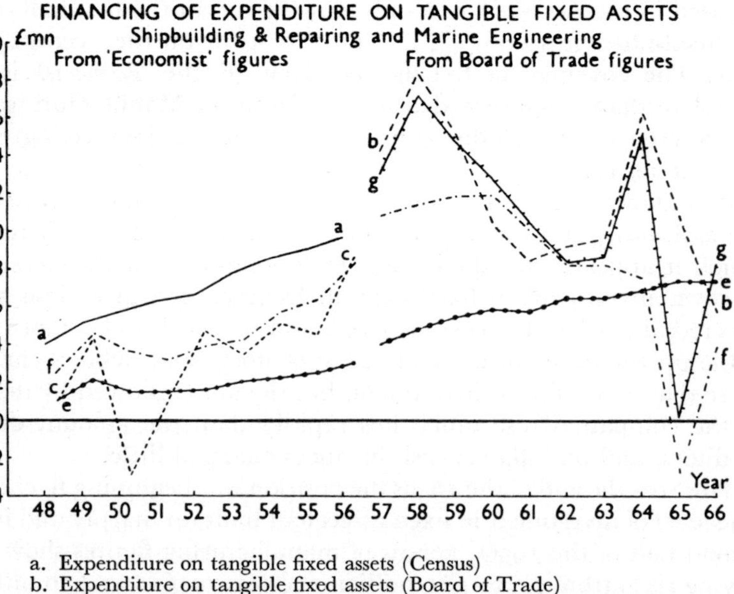

a. Expenditure on tangible fixed assets (Census)
b. Expenditure on tangible fixed assets (Board of Trade)
c. Difference in gross value of tangible fixed assets ('Economist')
d. Difference in gross value of tangible fixed assets (Board of Trade)
e. Depreciation provision.
f. Depreciation provision plus retained profit.
g. Depreciation provision plus retained profit plus long-term loans.

funds by mainly small capital issues. Stocks fluctuated from year to year but changed little on balance, and the finance of debtors was not a drain on the industry, being more than matched by sums owing to creditors. Cash holdings continued to increase, to some extent at the expense of gilt-edged holdings.

In the 1960s the position developed differently. The rate of investment in fixed assets fell, averaging for the company accounts analysed by the Board of Trade a little more than £10 million per annum, which presented of itself no great financial problem so long as profits continued to be made. With depreciation allowances running at about £6–£7 million and some sums available from retained profits and long-term loans, £10 million a year was within the financial resources of the industry until 1965. In that year a loss of £3½ million was made before providing for depreciation and although companies seem to have fared a little better in 1966, trading profits failed to cover depreciation (see Table). The industry was finding difficulty in generating the cash flow needed for its survival.

It is difficult to assess how many firms could have withstood these financial pressures without the actuality or prospect of government assistance. Contracts in 1964 had been taken at prices offering little prospect of profit and since costs rose substantially large losses resulted. Some companies fell by the wayside but the performance of others was capable of improvement. Both Swan Hunter and Fairfields estimated before devaluation was announced that they would return to a reasonable level of profitable working in 1968. But then Fairfields, which had failed under private enterprise, had been reorganized through government intervention and given financial assistance. Harland & Wolff likewise survived only with the assistance of government finance.

It is difficult to apportion the losses made in 1965 and 1966 between the various types of work undertaken by the shipyards. Hawthorn Leslie, for example, sustained a loss of £1 million on prefabricated houses in a single year.[4] Even within the allied fields of shipbuilding, repairing and marine engineering, losses may have been made on repair or naval construction as well as on new building. There is also the problem of apportioning overhead costs to these various types of output. Nevertheless, although there are exceptions, it may be reasonable to suppose that repair for the most part has been making some contribution to overhead costs rather than leading to losses. Refitting or lengthening a ship can be a time-consuming and expensive job resulting in substantial losses. But the general run of

[4] The loss on housing was £2m. in 1967 and Hawthorn Leslie decided to sell their industrialized building subsidiary.

APPROPRIATION OF INCOME BY SHIPBUILDING COMPANIES
(£ thousand)

	1957	1958	1959	1960	1961	1962	1963	1964	1965	1966
Number of companies	30	30	29	29	28	27	26	29	28	25
Trading profit (before depreciation and other provisions)	23,096	22,538	21,292	22,272	19,110	13,596	13,322	10,534	3,553	6,616
Less provision for depreciation	3,990	4,829	5,504	5,788	5,651	6,369	6,407	6,785	7,419	7,724
Less other provisions[a]	−147	474	413	367	520	118	142	...	...	...
Trading profit	19,253	17,235	15,375	16,117	12,939	7,109	6,773	3,749	−10,972	−1,108
Plus income from investments	1,786	1,922	1,872	2,284	2,117	2,232	2,079	2,972	3,708	2,244
Plus other income	10	10	9	−40	10	11	12	−37	−40	−13
Less interest on long-term liabilities	50	414	591	340	377	399	399	971	1,385	1,714
Net income (before taxation)	20,999	18,753	16,665	18,021	14,689	8,953	8,465	5,713	−9,319	−591
Less taxation	10,926	9,319	6,999	8,381	7,637	4,572	3,370	2,167	−1,574	3,010
Net income (after taxation)	10,073	9,434	9,666	9,640	7,052	4,381	5,095	3,546	−7,745	−3,601
Plus prior year adjustments:										
Tax	229	286	608	191	1,060	769	371	599	343	1,836
Other	292	266	146	48	78	91	23	154	−19	11
Disposable income	10,594	9,986	10,420	9,879	8,190	5,241	5,489	4,229	−7,421	−1,754
Less dividends (net):										
Ordinary	3,157	3,055	3,714	3,274	3,323	2,964	3,203	3,135	2,505	1,903
Preference, etc.	334	335	338	365	324	351	343	330	320	274
Less share due to minority interest[b]	236	27	42	143	98	105	156	...	...	...
Balance retained in reserves	6,867	6,569	6,326	6,097	4,445	1,821	1,787	834	−10,246	−3,931

[a] From 1964 on, 'other provisions' were treated partly as expenses and partly as reserves.
[b] From 1964 on, 'share due to minority interest' was treated partly as dividends and partly as reserve.

repair jobs can be fairly expeditiously completed, indeed must be so, and charges can be related to costs with some accuracy. Naval building may also be assumed to be generally profitable since so much of it has the character of prototype construction and tends to be on 'time and lime'. In annual reports shipbuilders refer to losses on shipbuilding and it is almost certainly on merchant shipbuilding that the bulk of losses was incurred. The profit and loss accounts themselves also seem to support the conclusions reached in this paragraph so far as they can be analysed.[5] Thus losses of the order of £10 million per annum after providing for depreciation sustained in 1965 and continued losses in 1966 (see Table) may be attributed in large measure to building new ships and related in a rough and ready manner to an output in 1964 of some £100 million per year and to the higher production costs of the industry relative to Japanese competitors as they appeared before devaluation. It is always difficult to compare production costs in different countries and comparisons can be misleading. But the Geddes Report leaves little room for doubt that production costs in the United Kingdom were well above those of Japan at the time it reported. For tankers, costs may have been as much as 30 per cent greater; for other vessels the difference was less but significant, and it may well have averaged 10 per cent. The general impression (it can be no more) to be gained from this is that United Kingdom shipyards were not able to charge much more than Japanese yards for the orders they took and that at these prices their comparative inefficiency was reflected in losses. It should not be inferred that the position was vastly better in Japan; profits there too were low, higher productivity in part being offset by low prices.

If this view of the position is generally correct, the cost advantage given by devaluation will restore some measure of profitability to the industry. It will not restore previous levels of profitability without further effort, though as we shall see other forms of assistance might on a superficial examination seem to have this effect. There is no escape from implementing the Geddes proposals concerned with the rationalization of production facilities. Even so it is not clear how far the aim should be to extend and develop the industry.

The industry is now by normal standards heavily subsidized. There are special investment grants available to it by reason of its location, and wages are reduced below the level of other areas by the regional employment premium. Exports will continue to attract the special

[5] Some give separate figures of profits and losses for different types of operations; some companies also are concerned almost exclusively with repair or marine engineering and their results also provide confirmation.

rebate which will be withdrawn from other industries; banks offer special credits to the industry's customers; there is a special fund of £32½ million for the reorganization of the industry and a disturbance allowance of £5 million, which it is now proposed to raise to £20 million; research is assisted and consultants subsidized. Only the price of steel is or was artificially high, another act of public policy.

Not all will agree as to how far these various measures should be regarded as specific assistance and therefore as subsidizing the shipbuilding industry. The regional employment premium in particular is given to all industries not just to shipbuilding. But is there really so much in this distinction? The development areas would certainly be much less in need of assistance if the shipbuilding industry had been fully competitive.

What do all these subsidies add up to? First the regional employment premium applies to most, though not all, shipyards engaged in new construction. It applies to a lesser extent to ship repairing which is partly conducted outside development areas. About 50,000 men are generally engaged in building merchant vessels and about the same number in marine engineering which contributes to repair as well as new construction. In addition over 10,000 men are generally engaged in naval construction by private firms and there are about 20,000 non-operatives employed by the industry. If it is assumed that half of those employed in marine engineering are engaged on repair it appears that total employment on new building might be of the order of 100,000, which with a regional employment premium of about £100 per man per year comes to roughly £10 million. Thus it might be said that the industry is receiving a subsidy of £10 million per year on the construction of new ships and a much greater sum in respect of all types of work carried out. If £10 million per year were to be invested in new plant and machinery in development areas where the highest level of grants are payable, about £4 million would be received per year (though it will, of course, be offset by the loss of depreciation allowances amounting to roughly half this amount).

The provision by the banks of a line of credit of £200 million to British shipowners for the purchase of ships from British yards can be described as a commercial operation for the rate is fixed by the banks. But the rate fixed appears to be designed to match the terms offered to British shipowners ordering abroad, and since the yield is much less than that on many government stocks, it might be reasonable to regard the loans as being subsidized by the banks. If such loans were no more than 2½ per cent below the corresponding market rate and the loans were for four years the equivalent cost of a ship would be reduced by about 10 per cent (neglecting the niceties of discounted cash flows). If the full amount made available by the banks were lent this would come to a joint subsidy to shipbuilders and shipowners of some £5 million per year. The subsidy paid for export orders is, of course, less but the present intention appears to be to maintain it at 2½ per cent.

It is more difficult to appraise the effects of the sum of money to be disbursed by the Shipbuilding Industry Board. Much will depend on the terms on which the £32½ million available for reconstruction of yards is made available.[6]

The rate of interest is to be that applying to other government loans from the National Loan Fund at the time the loans are made, at present perhaps 7½ per cent. But there is a provision for giving grants in relief of any interest payable in the period up to the end of 1970. Apart from this it might still be maintained that the industry was getting an implicit subsidy, if only in the provision of money itself, thus relieving companies of what might be the difficult financial operation of raising permanent finance on the open market. This is in addition to the provision for grants up to a ceiling of £20 million.

In total these various forms of subsidy could amount to more than £20 million per year (£10 million regional premium, £4 million capital grants, £5 million cheap loans plus other benefits) for new ships and substantially more for all forms of shipyard activity. None of these is intended to be permanent. But the total assistance for even the five or so years for which they are intended to run is very large. No doubt the intention is to withdraw them gradually as the prospects for the development areas and shipbuilding improve. But subsidies once given are not easy to withdraw and may sometimes slow down the very processes that they are meant to encourage such as the more productive use of manpower.

It is true that when shipbuilding firms make profits some of the money given to firms will be returned to the government in taxation —but only after losses have been expunged as an offset against the taxation of profits. To that extent the measures will cost the taxpayer less. Yet even this is a sad reflection on the present day complications of public finance with subsidies promoting taxes and taxes promoting subsidies because there is insufficient capital to plough back or insufficient incentive to produce efficiently.

[6] It is interesting that the first commitment of the Fund was to finance a new building dock at Harland & Wolff, a use of money not advocated by Geddes. 'In our view the time to assess the desirability of constructing a building dock will be when we have more experience of large tanker construction, can see the prospect for giant tanker building and repair business more clearly than at present time and have achieved higher throughput in existing yards' (para. 247).

The assistance recommended by the Geddes Committee may now be seen to be small by comparison with what has subsequently been given. Quantitatively it is credits to shipowners and the regional employment premium that are significant. Geddes proposed £30 million not £200 million in credits. There were naturally no proposals for the regional employment premium. The total effect of all the measures now adopted may be to make it possible to reduce the cost of ships produced in United Kingdom shipyards by something of the order of 15 per cent at 1964 levels of output. On top of this devaluation will reduce the price at which sales can be made very substantially; even allowing for increases in the cost of imported materials the advantage should hardly be less than 10 per cent. The shipbuilding industry is now receiving unprecedented assistance due to an unexpected conjuncture of forces.

Of all these forces it is devaluation that makes most sense. Propping up an industry that has lagged in its adjustment to the effects of technological change on the organization of production can be an unpromising activity and a costly one not only in the money that is spent but in the diversion of resources from other potentially more profitable uses. Of course shipbuilding is not the only industry to receive government assistance; nor is the United Kingdom alone in resorting to government assistance to this industry. This again is quite a good reason for reflecting whether such money is well spent. France may be more realistic in attempting to secure the conversion of shipyards to other activities rather than an expansion of their output. One of the problems is that industries can seldom be allowed to disappear from a modern industrial state, particularly if they are of strategic significance, because the pace of technical development is such that it may be feared that once an industry begins to decline it will have no opportunity of reasserting itself. This conclusion is still of relevance to shipbuilding but not to the degree that once applied; it is not so overwhelming as to dictate a policy of supporting the shipbuilding industry. If government financial assistance is to be a feature of the promotion of industrial efficiency it might be better directed to industries where competition is less fierce and which have better prospects of success than the shipbuilding industry has shown in the postwar period. The stimulus to exports from devaluation is not confined to shipbuilding. It affects all industries. And on past performance it might be wise to direct resources into other industries which have been able to export on a satisfactory scale even without additional assistance. Nor is the location of the shipbuilding industry in the development areas an irrefutable reason for assisting it with government finance. There are other industries that might thrive even better with the aids currently given to the shipbuilding industry in those areas.

Yet withal, the shipbuilding industry has probably a better chance of survival with the accident of circumstances that has given it unprecedented potential competitive advantage. By themselves the Geddes proposals were not enough to do the job. More government assistance would have been called for by the industry in a few years time. The net effect might have been no more than to slow the attrition of the industry. Now the industry has the opportunity to break through—or squander the large resources within its grasp.

Speed is essential. As time goes on many present advantages will prove to be temporary. The regional employment premium can easily be taken out in higher wages or slower improvement in productivity; the advantages of devaluation may not be sustained; the Japanese are still formidable competitors; and orders for ships will not be so plentiful until present order books are worked through. Above all the industry must not grow to rely on subsidies.

The present level of assistance to the industry should be sufficient to enable losses to be extinguished and some modest contribution to profits to be made as is already occurring. But restoration of a market return on the capital employed in the industry will depend on the competitive advantage to be obtained from devaluation and the extent to which prices have to be cut in an era when it is more difficult to secure orders for new ships. This makes it all the more important either to increase output of existing yards or to concentrate available orders in a limited number of yards in order to use capital more intensively. This is, of course, what controlled grouping is intended to accomplish. Perhaps it will succeed, but as in other examples of promoting economic development there is something to be said for concentrating on natural growth points. This is what government can seldom do, only merchant bankers.

THE QUEEN'S UNIVERSITY OF BELFAST

MAKING MICRO-ECONOMICS MULTI-DIMENSIONAL

by Kenneth Simmonds

It has long been acknowledged that the usefulness of the theory of the firm cannot be measured solely from its ability to explain the behaviour of particular firms.[1] For its prime purpose in explaining the behaviour of markets, industries or economies, economists have even argued on occasion for a theory that should not be testable against individual real-world firms.[2] Nevertheless, the theory of the firm is widely used as a basis for analysing the price and output decisions of individual firms—a use for which it has major limitations.[3]

One aspect of the theory that produces problems in application to the real world is its assumption of a fixed set of products as the units of output in terms of which price and volume actions are taken. Now in the real world, a firm is likely to change continually the basis on which it defines units for action—and to use different units for different actions. A firm might take price action on a geographical slice of output on one day, on a slice defined by some physical attribute on another, or on the output going through a particular type of outlet on a third. Then again it might base price actions on units determined by a characteristic of the customer, say the customer's income, and base actions to adjust volume on another dimension, say the amount of a limiting factor required in its production.

Over time, many dimensions of output are used as the basis for separating out units to be the subject of management actions. The reality of adjustment of the firm is thus multi-dimensional. The conventional theory of the firm, on the other hand, is uni-dimensional. It is an economics that can 'explain' economic behaviour in terms of only one classification of product units at a time. Moreover, although the units chosen will influence the predictions, verifications and conclusions that result from conventional analysis, the theory gives little guide as to which way the units should be defined. Firms engaged in multi-dimensional reality thus have no adequate theory on which to draw for multi-dimensional analysis and have had to build their own heuristic methods for deciding actions *and* the units on which these should be based. The growing literature on segmen-

[1] See for example Wm. J. Baumol, 'What Can Economic Theory Contribute to Managerial Economics?', *American Economic Review*, May 1961, pp. 144, 145; Edith T. Penrose, *The Theory of the Growth of the Firm*, Basil Blackwell, London, p. 26.

[2] Milton Friedman, *Essays in Positive Economics*, The University of Chicago Press, Chicago, 1953, Part 1.

[3] A good summary of some of the limitations is presented by Avery B. Cohan, 'The Theory of the Firm: A View on Methodology', *Journal of Business*, July 1963, pp. 316–24.

tation in marketing for example has evolved partly to fill this gap.[4]

This paper is an attempt to show how different the problems of economic adjustment of the firm become when fixed units are rejected and the additional complication is added of selecting the units along which the adjustment should be taken. To begin with, the multi-dimensional shape of such an economics is established, showing that it is not simply a matter of extending the analysis to more narrowly defined product units. Units become the row and column totals of a multi-dimensional classification of output. In order to select units on which actions are required from amongst the vectors of this multi-dimensional matrix, the different dimensional influences within any vector need to be isolated. Further complicating the selection, a different grouping of competing firms may be relevant for each vector, and reactions by competitors may be based on units that do not completely coincide but include some of the components of the vector. While such problems do not arise with conventional fixed units, a multi-dimensional extension would greatly increase the value of micro-economics to the decision maker in the real firm. For the first time it would provide a theoretical basis for the selection of the action unit in a given situation.

THE UNITS OF A MULTI-DIMENSIONAL THEORY

The basic element of a multi-dimensional micro-theory will be termed an *attribute*. And an attribute will be defined as any aspect or quality of output that can be differentiated by management as separately adjustable—whether it be a physical characteristic of the output or a characteristic of the customer, the order, or the method of distribution.

To build a closed system the attributes to be included for any firm must be specified. As every possible attribute could not be included without making analysis completely unwieldy, however, some criteria are needed against which to make the selection. Materiality, action significance and independence seem most appropriate. Materiality would rule out some attributes for which the demand represented does not justify separate consideration; action significance would rule out those which are not likely to be the

[4] Wendell R. Smith, 'Product Differentiation and Market Segmentation as Alternative Marketing Strategies', *Journal of Marketing*, July 1956, p. 4; Daniel Yankelovich, 'New Criteria for Market Segmentation', *Harvard Business Review*, March–April 1964, pp. 83–90; Wm. H. Reynolds, 'More Sense about Market Segmentation', *Harvard Business Review*, September–October 1965, pp. 107–14; R. E. Frank and Wm. F. Massy, 'Market Segmentation and the Effectiveness of a Brand's Price and Dealing Policies', *Journal of Business*, April 1965, pp. 186–200; Purnell H. Benson, 'Analysis of Irregular Two-Dimensional Distributions of Consumer Buying Choices', *Journal of Marketing Research*, August 1966, pp. 279–88.

focus of any action; and independence would eliminate attributes that always coincide with attributes already included.

Attributes taken into account in the past in setting price, choosing customers, preparing sales brochures, advertising, classifying production, comparing sales achievement, and so on, could be included straight away. Each of these is separately adjustable. So too are attributes that have been the focus of discussion by management but have not been the target of any action. And the experience and judgment of management steeped in the background and peculiarities of the particular business will produce other attributes that might be separately adjusted.

Attributes that are mutually exclusive, i.e. that cannot exist in the same segment of output, can now be grouped into *attribute classes.* Examples of attribute classes might be type of outlet, size of order, customer industry, customer location, class of credit extended, or material used. Where an attribute class forms a continuous scale it can be broken into units sufficiently small to avoid actions being considered separately for sections of any one attribute. Attributes that the firm does not offer, but which fall within a graded attribute class out of which the firm offers some attribute units, would be included as empty units. Competitor actions on these units will affect the firm's results and they will be potential units for the firm's own actions. In like manner, attributes at either end of a class, if it can be graded, or close attributes of a non-graded class (e.g. another colour), should also be included.

Corresponding to every attribute there is a segment of output with that attribute as the common feature. This will be defined as an *attribute unit.* It is the total of all output showing that particular attribute, and the section of output directly affected by action taken with that attribute as the focus. The attribute units within any attribute class will sum to total output.

In a multi-dimensional system the units of output in terms of which actions are taken may be single attribute units, sums of attribute units, or unions of attribute units. Unions of attribute units are the segments of output in which specified attributes occur jointly. An *action unit* may thus differ from an attribute unit.

THE REJECTION OF N-DIMENSIONAL CELLS

The point must be clearly emphasized that a multi-dimensional extension of the theory of the firm is not achieved simply by more narrowly defined product units. It is not achieved by dividing output into products which are cells specified for their position in each of the n attribute classes included in an n-dimensional classification. In this respect a multidimensional extension is different from modern value theory in which products are 'completely specified, physically, temporally and spatially'.[5]

While the theory of the firm can be expressed with mathematical nicety using cells as the basic units, it breaks down in application to the real world for a number of reasons:

(*a*) The size of cells is too small, representing minute segments of output. The cost of separate consideration and the limitations on managerial time would outweigh any advantages from separate adjustment. In 1943 a National Bureau of Economic Research publication classified book paper into 40 'product' classes, 12 grades, 33 finishes, 9 sizes and trims, 8 colours, 8 quantity classes, and 19 types of packing.[6] This was calculated to give between 170 and 180 million possible products—yet still exclude many additional attributes on which actions might be based, such as size of order, size of customer, or customer location. Explanation of actions using this number of units without aggregation is virtually impossible.

(*b*) The information needed for detailed decision on individual cells would not be available. Actual sales may be easily broken into individual cells—but it would be impossible to collect information on customer preferences broken down into say, fifteen-dimensional cells. It is possible, however, to measure preferences for each attribute within an attribute class with other attributes of the segment of output held constant or considered independent.[7]

(*c*) Many actions cannot be taken in terms of more than one or two dimensions. Most firms, for example, would find it impossible to introduce pricing for individual cells based on size, quality, customer location, size of order, industry of customer, and so on.

(*d*) The interdependence of cells on both demand and cost sides would require extenuated decision concepts.

(*e*) An attribute is the basic element of management thought. Initial diagnosis is seldom made in terms of units specified by more than one attribute, and it is virtually impossible for man-

[5] Gerard Debreu, *Theory of Value: An Axiomatic Analysis of Economic Equilibrium*, John Wiley & Sons Inc., New York, 1959, p. 32. Other attempts occur in Hans Brems, *Product Equilibrium under Monopolistic Competition*, Harvard University Press, Cambridge, 1951, and P. J. Verdoorn, 'Marketing from the Producer's Point of View', *Journal of Marketing*, January 1956.

[6] National Bureau of Economic Research, *Cost Behavior and Price Policy*, New York, 1943. Appendix D.

[7] Such an approach is discussed in Alfred Kuehn and Ralph L. Day, 'Strategy of Product Quality', *Harvard Business Review*, November–December 1962, pp. 100–10.

agement to think in terms of units differentiated in n-dimensions. Policy directives can be expressed more sensibly in terms of attributes, leaving to operating staff the detailed interpretation and resolution of cases where attribute policies conflict.

Rather than commencing with cells, the approach starts with information in terms of attribute units, i.e. multi-dimensional row and column totals, and works towards action units that may involve combinations or intersections of these units. For the reasons listed, however, the number of attribute dimensions in which any action unit is defined will be less than n.

MULTI-DIMENSIONAL ADJUSTMENT WITH INTERRELATED UNITS

More is required for choosing an action unit in a multi-dimensional structure than a prescription for multi-dimensional equilibrium. Because the action units are not basic cells, action on any unit will affect the readings on others which include some of the same basic cells. It is not appropriate simply to take action on the attribute unit showing the highest profitability regardless of whether the attribute is that along which the conditions causing the opportunity for action reach the firm. Only action on units along which the environment affects the firm will adjust the entire output affected. An approach is thus needed that will differentiate endogenously and exogenously caused readings, and also provide for the elimination of alternatives without detailed consideration of each attribute unit. It would be as impractical as the use of n-dimensional cells to attempt to quantify and compare profitability for each possible action for each possible unit, including the separation of endogenous and exogenous effects.

One approach that has grown up empirically is a multi-dimensional extension of the diagnosis by exception widely written up for conventional fixed units in accounting literature. The essence of diagnosis by exception, given a conventional set of products, is the comparison of performance measurements for the different products. It usually includes measurements of sales, market share, inventory position, unfilled orders, gross margin realized, and return on investment. Using the principle of management by exception, variation from average performance is taken as indicative of potential for further attention.

Extended to multi-dimensional reality this approach starts with cross-classification of sales and market potential—broken down by a range of physical, geographical, customer and order characteristics. But once the units showing exceptions within the different classifications have been isolated the next stage of eliminating endogenous effects is carried out very imprecisely. Usually it is left to executive intuition and experience to decide whether the cause of the variation is affecting the firm along the dimension recording the variation.

Accepting this diagnosis by exception as the first stage in multi-dimensional diagnosis, it is possible to eliminate endogenous effects more rigorously. Firstly, if there is little variation in the readings for the different units in an attribute class it can be assumed that no major exogenous difference exists for any of the attributes. However, where the readings do differ significantly the difference may be caused either exogenously or endogenously. At one extreme the cause may be directly reaching the firm in terms of the attributes showing the variation in readings; at the other, the variation may be entirely caused by different proportions of other attributes making up the attribute units.

To separate out the part of any variation that is caused endogenously, the attribute composition of the unit showing the variation must be compared with the attribute composition of the other units in the class. Where the composition does differ and the variation appears to be influenced by some attribute contained in different proportions, then a further check is needed to determine which way the causation runs. This may be done by checking whether the output associated with the attribute contained in different proportions itself contains a different proportion of the first attribute than other units in its own attribute class. If there is no significant difference in composition then it can be concluded that the attribute contained in different proportions is in some degree responsible for the variation in the original reading. But if there is a significant difference in the quantity of this first attribute contained in the second unit, either the causal effect runs the other way or the combination of the two attributes attracts the exogenous difference.

Extending this sort of reasoning at length, the major endogenous effects might be eliminated. As described here it is not a mathematically precise procedure although it can be expressed precisely. The significant point, however, is that exogenously caused variation in opportunity can be diagnosed without requiring a complete breakdown of the attribute composition of all units. The procedure works backwards from the row and column totals of the n-dimensional matrix, requiring further dimensional breakdowns only for those units showing exceptions. Furthermore, it is unlikely to require data broken down into cells of more than two or three dimensions—nowhere near the requirement of all data specified for n-dimensional cells.

COMPETITIVE ANALYSIS WITH MANY DIMENSIONS

With major endogenous effects eliminated, the next stage in the process of deciding adjustment actions would be to forecast the profitability from actions on different units. This could be done through forecasting the resulting cash flows, just as for actions on conventional product units. Some added difficulties arise, however, in forecasting competitor reaction in a multi-dimensional system. A distinction between first-order and second-order reactions will be helpful. First-order reactions by competitors will be defined as those taken with the same action unit and second-order reactions as those taken with different units although caused by the initial action.

Prediction of first-order reactions draws on much of the conventional theory of the firm but requires a different grouping of competitors. The firm is placed at the centre of a competitive environment and analysis extends outwards to the competition relevant to the particular action unit. The firm is no longer one competing unit within the cradle of a conventional industry. Moreover, it will not be enough to consider solely those firms already offering an attribute. Firms that already offer the attribute will be a potential source for retaliation and firms that do not have it will offer potential competition from its competitive adoption. Instead, the ordering of competition significant to a potential action unit might be based on the expected loss from retaliation, i.e. the magnitude of sales likely to be lost through a competitor's retaliation, multiplied by the probability of retaliation. Such a probability might depend on—

(*a*) The amount of effective demand that is transferred from any one firm by the action. A firm that loses a significant amount of output will be likely to attempt to recapture it, and so too will any firm that is left with a segment that will no longer be profitable unless demand is recaptured.

(*b*) Whether after the action the total market for output containing this attribute is large enough to support a second firm with a similar offering, taking into account the investment required.

(*c*) The economic advantage on which the firm taking the action is building. A second firm will hesitate to carry competition further on the same unit where it has significant disadvantages.

(*d*) The spread of consumer preferences in the segment of demand achieved, measured along the attribute class in which the action unit fell. If the spread is wide, a second firm may more easily obtain a part of the demand by differentiating on that attribute class.

(*e*) The position that is chosen in the attribute class. This is the location problem applied to an attribute dimension. If the firm locates just to the left of the firm furthest to the left on the attribute scale, then it may be argued that it will obtain the maximum amount of demand lying to the left. But this location may make it more likely that another firm will find it profitable to locate still further to the left.

(*f*) The cost of recouping the attribute position. The initial action may build up brand loyalty that becomes much more expensive to reverse.

Second-order competitor reactions would be harder to predict. To allow for these, however, a coefficient of sales decay might be introduced. This could be set at a constant rate and based on the firm's general experience of rate of fall-off in demand after first-order reactions have taken effect.[8]

SOME IMPLICATIONS OF A MULTI-DIMENSIONAL EXTENSION TO THE THEORY OF THE FIRM

By introducing the dimension along which actions are taken, a multi-dimensional extension would give more precision to concepts such as diversification, differentiation, rationalization, standardization and closeness of substitution. It would become possible, for example, to talk about differentiation along specific attribute dimensions and rationalization through elimination of specific dimensions.

The introduction of the choice of action units can also extend the predictive scope of economic theory. With fixed units, conventional theory is limited in its explanation of economic behaviour to those situations in which the fixed units are the units of action. Thus conventional theory makes predictions only about some actions. Even price-output policy cannot be predicted if the products chosen are not those in terms of which price or output decisions are made. To test predictions of conventional theory the economist must first find situations in which the action takes place on the conventional units. With a multi-dimensional theory all situations should fit the theory, which would include the specification of units on which actions should rationally be taken.

A further advantage of a multi-dimensional approach would be the switching of emphasis in the multi-product firm from decisions concerning volume of different products to choice between attributes. Given fixed units, the main focus of conventional theory when

[8] A model employing a sales decay function is set out in M. L. Vidale and H. B. Wolfe, 'An Operations Research Study of Sales Response to Advertising', *Operations Research*, June 1957, pp. 370–81.

applied to multi-product firms became the choice of the volumes of the different units. This over-emphasized the role of volume decision in the running of a business. Few firms set limits to the amounts they will produce of a fixed product unit, leaving the demand unexhausted at a particular price level. Neither do they overcome this by adjusting price. What the firm does in practice is quite different. It makes a selection of the attributes it will offer, bearing in mind the limits of its resources. Should a firm find that the demand for the attributes that it has been offering is going to exceed its capacity, it will choose some attribute unit or units that it will dispense with. There is no restriction that says the choice must be made between products A, B, C or D. It might be more profitable to cut off sales in District X whether they be A, B, C, or D, or all sales to customer ordering under $Q, or all orders that will not bring repeat sales.

The conventional wisdom of a distinction between a single product firm and a multi-product firm vanishes once a firm can vary the attribute focus of its actions. A firm that chooses to name specific product titles is no more a multi-product firm than a firm that does not name classifications but nevertheless takes actions in terms of different attributes. Every firm is a multi-attribute firm.

A multi-dimensional approach also recasts competition into a multi-dimensional competitive environment that must be analysed by moving outwards from the firm towards the competition relevant to action on a particular attribute. This calls for major changes in concepts. It becomes possible for a firm to be a monopolist in one attribute and a fringe supplier in another. Where competition is active it will continually search for new action units on which it has an advantage over competitors. And measures of attribute changes might be the best indicators of the effectiveness of competition. Such measures would be a far cry from conventional concepts of effectiveness based on the numbers and relative sizes of firms offering the *same* attribute—that on which the product or industry is defined.

Conventional theory offers little help in the explanation of competition in a multi-dimensional setting. The only competitive actions that can be explained directly in terms of a conventional industry or other grouping are those which coincide with the basis on which the collection of firms is brought together. When competition continually changes the units on which it acts, so that it competes outside, across, or well within the boundaries of any one industry definition, then it is unlikely that to classify a firm into one industry will give any depth of insight into competition. Some economists claim that their product and industry classifications are flexible, and that there can be a different classification for each different purpose. But this has usually meant just re-classification over time and not the use of many cross classifications to analyse one situation.

The concept of an industry is also misleading because it is based on similarities of firms' output. The implicit assumption is that where firms have a number of attributes in common, the grouping will be significant for the competitive actions they choose. It would not be difficult to show, however, that competitive actions are more likely to be in terms of differences than similarities. There is already a vast literature concerned with how firms should and do build on strengths —which, by definition, are differences.[9]

EARLIER WRITING MOVING TOWARDS A MULTI-DIMENSIONAL ECONOMICS

There have been many attempts to extend micro-economic theory by relaxing the product definition. None of these writings, however, has really relaxed the initial acceptance of a fixed classification of products as the basic units of the theory. Chamberlin for example has a number of writings dealing with the product as a variable, yet he failed to acknowledge that at any one time there are many different dimensions of product differentiation between a single firm and its competitors.[10] He accepted a one-dimensional classification of products even though he allowed for each to vary. Chronologically, Triffin, Brems and Debreu can be cited as examples of attempts to increase the explanatory value of the theory by breaking the fixed classification into smaller cells. It is ironical that Triffin in accepting commodities as 'goods between which the entrepreneur himself differentiates' referred to more fully specified and hence smaller units, but failed to recognize the cross-classification of actual practice.[11] As was pointed out above, smaller units quickly become unmanageable, and do not overcome the problems of a fixed unit theory.

Outside the main stream of writing in conventional theory a number of writers have advanced strong arguments for the development of a theory that would achieve what is possible with a 'variable unit' economics. For example Clark expresses the need for a wider theoretical base that would enable the incorporation of many factual

[9] Eli W. Clemens, 'Price Discrimination and the Multiple-Product Firm', *The Review of Economic Studies*, 1950–51, p. 2; Edith T. Penrose, *The Theory of the Growth of the Firm*, Basil Blackwell, Oxford, 1959, chaps. V–VIII; Gordon R. Conrad, 'Unexplored Assets for Diversification', *Harvard Business Review*, January–February 1966; H. Igor Ansoff, *Corporate Strategy*, McGraw-Hill Book Co. Inc., New York, 1965.

[10] See for example Edward Chamberlin, *The Theory of Monopolistic Competition*, Harvard University Press, Cambridge, 1933, pp. 103–4; *Towards a More General Theory of Value*, Oxford University Press, New York, 1957, p. 61.

[11] Robert Triffin, *Monopolistic Competition and General Equilibrium Theory*, Harvard University Press, Cambridge, 1940, pp. 89–95.

observations that cannot be fitted to existing theories.[12] He even goes as far as treating competition separately on three or four different classes of attributes. Heflebower has similarly been concerned with developing a richer, more empirical theory of industrial markets and prices.[13] He seemed to be reaching for a multi-dimensional approach with his listing of 'requirements for a satisfactory theory'. While an extension of theory that allows for variation in units fits many of their specifications for what is needed, however, Clark and Heflebower also limited their own attempt at recasting theory by retaining fixed products as the basic units.

CONCLUSION

This paper introduces some aspects of the multi-dimensional micro-economics that must develop if real world actions taken along many dimensions are to be provided with a tested theoretical base. This is particularly needed for decision concerning changes in a firm's product direction. As the appropriate theory develops it should be reflected in an improvement in strategic planning and in the information systems and analysis behind it.

A range of concepts not used in uni-dimensional theory will be needed for this theory and some have been indicated here; attributes as the basic elements of thought and actions, endogenous and exogenous effects, re-orientation of competition for each attribute, first- and second-order competitor reactions, attribute rather than volume adjustment, and so on. While this paper by no means sets out a completely polished micro-economics of multi-dimensional action, these beginnings show how different a multi-dimensional approach can be from conventional micro-theory.

MANCHESTER BUSINESS SCHOOL

[12] John M. Clark, *Competition as a Dynamic Process*, Brookings Institute, Washington, 1962, p. 7.

[13] Richard B. Heflebower, 'Towards a Theory of Industrial Markets and Prices', *American Economic Review*, May 1955, p. 122.

TRADING STAMPS AND CONSUMER WELFARE[1]

by Roger Sherman

Having outlasted the controversy which surrounded their sharp rise in usage during the 1950s in the United States, trading stamps must now be regarded as an important retail marketing device. About one-half of all food sales in the U.S. and nearly a third of the gasoline sales involve trading stamps, and retailers pay stamp companies about one billion dollars for the stamps they distribute each year[7]. This seems an appropriate time to ask whether all consumers benefit from trading stamps. There have been both subjective and objective approaches to this question. Klass found that consumers attach importance to stamps because the stamps fill psychological needs[8], but most efforts have taken a more objective approach, centering on whether trading stamps lead to a rise in prices. Some price studies have compared changes in prices, between stores that give stamps and those that do not, in an effort to isolate the effect of trading stamps on price. The first reliable conclusion found a higher *increase* in price at trading stamp stores; P. Rothwell reported a greater *increase* by about 0.6 percentage points over an almost two-year study period[9]. More recently, Bromley and Wallace studied a specific store that adopted stamps when most of its competitors already had them, and found an *increase* in store prices of about 2 per cent[5]. Price increases have been shown to be higher in stores that give stamps, although differences between stamp and non-stamp stores have been modest.

But the difference in price between stores that give trading stamps and those that do not will not isolate the effect of stamps on price levels[11]. Trading stamps may affect price levels in all stores, even those that do not give stamps. Moreover, distributional and allocative effects of trading stamps have been ignored.[2] Some consumers benefit from trading stamps while others are harmed. Because they can seldom be exchanged for cash or traded, trading stamps limit the opportunities for any harmed consumers to be compensated by those who gain, and so the market can balance only imperfectly the preferences of consumers regarding the extent to which trading stamps should be used.

This paper is an attempt to clarify the possible allocative effects

[1] For their helpful comments on earlier drafts, I am indebted to James M. Buchanan, Lester B. Lave, James D. Rodgers, and a reviewer.

[2] For an exception, see [6].

of trading stamps. Section I examines some possible effects of trading stamps on the utility maximizing problems of rational and well informed consumers. Section II treats the cost conditions underlying possible consumer choice problems. Harm to some consumers from trading stamps is shown to be possible in Section III and the lack of any true market test of net benefit is demonstrated. It is argued that trading stamps can rob the market of some of its precision in responding to the intensity of consumer desires, and can produce a bias in resource allocation. Conclusions are summarized in Section IV.

I. CONSUMER CHOICE

Economic analysis of promotional devices is difficult because the devices usually affect both demand and supply functions. This is true of trading stamps. Their effect on demand may be examined using the normal utility maximizing model of a rational consumer, however, by assuming that stamps do not alter utility functions. By then concentrating on the way stamps alter consumers' income constraints, demand and supply effects can be considered separately. The consumer is assumed to be informed concerning all of his alternatives. Every store is regarded as presenting a different income constraint, so that in choosing a store the consumer selects a constraint, one that enables him to achieve the highest level of utility. In this way we can focus on the choice of store and emphasize in particular the choice between a store that gives trading stamps and one that does not. We postpone until the following section consideration of the supply costs which might underlie the possible cases that are deemed of interest here for their effect on consumer choice.

Let us first divide all commodities into two groups: those goods with which trading stamps are given, x_j, and those premium goods for which trading stamps can be redeemed, x_k. We shall assume that relative prices for a particular store are held constant although the price levels at each store may change. Prices of premium goods will be assumed unaffected by the introduction of trading stamps, and such goods can either be purchased or obtained in exchange for stamps. Without trading stamps, the consumer choice opportunities lie below and to the left of budget line MN in the x_j, x_k space shown in Figure 1. Two different consumers who have the same budget constraint but different tastes are represented by indifference curves u_1 and u_2; consumer 1 would choose point N while consumer 2 would prefer point G.

Introducing trading stamps can affect a consumer's budget constraint in two ways. First, the price of non-premium goods may change, causing the budget constraint for the store that gives stamps to rotate around point M. In Figure 1, the introduction of stamps has caused an increase in the price of goods with which stamps are given, rotating the budget constraint counter clockwise to LM. Second, any selection of goods along this new budget line also entitles the consumer to further premium items through redemption of trading stamps, which are granted in proportion to the consumer's expenditure on non-premium goods (x_j). The result is a truncated budget constraint for shopping at stores that give stamps, such as

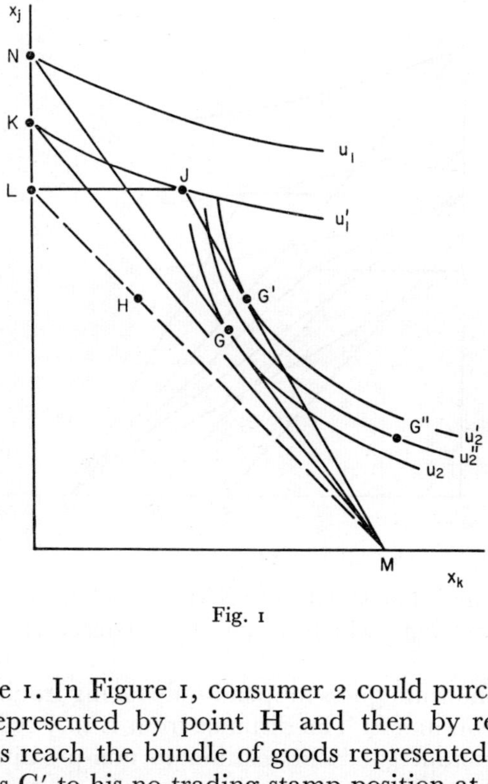

Fig. 1

LJM in Figure 1. In Figure 1, consumer 2 could purchase goods in the bundle represented by point H and then by redemption of trading stamps reach the bundle of goods represented by point G′. And he prefers G′ to his no-trading stamp position at G. Consumer 1 finds premium goods relatively less attractive than does consumer 2, however, and is not benefited in Figure 1 if all stores offer stamps or if stores that do not offer stamps raise their prices to create budget line KM, because then he could no longer reach his preferred point, N.[3]

[3] There may be other consumers who desire premium goods but not non-premium goods, although the nature of available premium goods makes this unlikely; in any case, such persons are not affected by trading stamps.

Each budget constraint can also be shifted relative to others, to represent the greater convenience of some stores than others for any given consumer. Even though prices are lower at one store, a consumer may not shop there because it is inconvenient for him and requires more of his time. The extra time he may have to devote to shopping at that store could otherwise be spent at work to generate more money income.[4] Thus, differences in shopping time may be represented as shifts in the budget constraints, which will depend in amount not only on the location of the consumer, but also on the

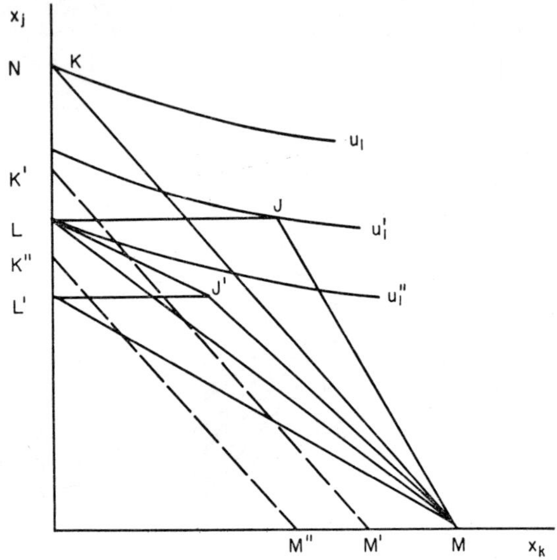

Fig. 2

value of his time.[5] The shifts from KM to K′M′ or K″M″ in Figure 2 serve as illustrations which would lead consumer 1 from utility level U_1.

Similarly, the willingness to spend time saving trading stamps may vary among consumers. The distance from L to J reflects the availability of premium goods in relation to non-premium goods purchased. But it may have to be modified to take account of time which the consumer must spend collecting and redeeming the trading stamps. Such time can shift LJM to L′J′M′ in Figure 2, again because it can reduce the time spent earning income. Various shopping and redemption alternatives can then be represented by LJ′M, since the consumer can reach LM if he shops at the stamp

[4] For a thorough analysis of this possibility, see [2]. Measurement in the context of shopping is undertaken in [4] and discussed in [1].

[5] It is not necessary that the value of the consumer's time equal his wage rate. See [10].

store but does not bother with stamps, and L′J′M if he saves and redeems them.

Consider the special case of the consumer who places a high value on his time and whose most convenient store offers trading stamps. A non-stamp store may be so inconvenient that the consumer will continue to buy from the stamp-giving store, as shown in Figure 2 when KM shifts to K″M″ and the consumer is at U''_1. Moreover, the consumer in this case does not receive enough benefit from premium goods to warrant his devoting time to collecting and redeeming stamps. This can affect all consumers who might shop at a store that gives stamps, because to the extent that stamps are not redeemed the premium offer to those who do redeem stamps can be enhanced (L higher or L′J′ longer in Figure 2, making the slope of J′M steeper). This possibility does not seem to predominate, however, for it is quite reliably estimated that in the U.S., over 90 per cent of all trading stamps are eventually redeemed[9, 12].

Nevertheless, the attractiveness of stamps to a consumer can be affected by the value of his time, and the alternative of not buying at a store that gives stamps may involve inconvenience for some consumers who do not place a high value on the premium goods. To the extent that his failure to redeem stamps can enhance the offer made to consumers who do value premium goods, it is conceivable that those consumers might be attracted to stores that give stamps. This could occur even though a store that offered stamps was less convenient to the consumer than a non-stamp store, especially if the consumer placed a low value on his time. Thus differences among consumers can affect choice in a way that favors consumers who value premium goods, who live close to stamp stores, or who place a low value on their time.

II. SUPPLY

We now turn to supply factors that may affect available combinations of stamp and non-stamp store budget constraints, ignoring at first any differences among consumers. It is conceivable that the volume of industry activity affects cost curves of individual retailer firms, but in view of the modest effect trading stamps can be expected to have on total industry volume, such an effect is unlikely. It could, of course, produce higher or lower prices even in stores that do not offer stamps, and would affect the price in stores that give stamps as well. We shall not consider such effects on all firms' cost curves, however, since we have no sound basis to expect them as consequences of trading stamps.

On the assumption that firm cost functions are unaffected by changes in total industry volume, consider possible effects of trading stamps on average cost at the level of the firm. Little is known about the extent to which trading stamps might substitute for other promotional expenses, but it is doubtful they would substitute completely.[6] If average cost functions of firms in retailing are either U-shaped or constant, we might expect at equilibrium some price increase at stores that offer stamps and no change in price at stores that do not offer stamps. It may be inappropriate to consider trading stamps in a situation in which all firms face U-shaped cost curves, for stamps are often regarded as devices which increase volume of business. If offering stamps had that effect, it might lead to higher prices at

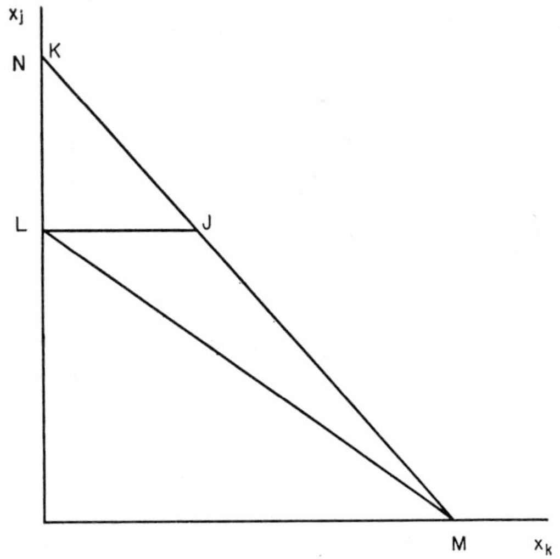

Fig. 3

stamp stores and lower prices at non-stamp stores, where volume will presumably be lower. Stores can be expected to join in offering stamps, however, until an equilibrium is reached, with all stores at minimum average cost. Non-stamp stores could then have the same prices as before, but stamp stores would have higher prices. The reduction in non-stamp store prices would have induced exit, if only into the ranks of stores offering stamps, until equilibrium was achieved, as illustrated in Figure 3. To the extent that stamps are not redeemed, of course, LJM might be slightly higher, making the slopes of LM and JM both steeper.

[6] Some substitution is indicated in [9], but little in case studies in [12].

The most frequently cited justification for the introduction of trading stamps is the existence of decreasing costs at the firm level in retailing. Decreasing cost can be consistent with equilibrium here because firms are separated spatially, and it is the cost condition claimed in empirical investigations of retailing cost[12]. Even if offering stamps can increase a store's volume it is doubtful that the store can escape a price increase,[7] and stores that do not offer stamps and lose volume may experience higher average cost and eventually have higher prices also. Such a result was represented in Figure 1. Exit of firms is not apt to alter this result. The departure of firms into the ranks of stamp-offering stores would reduce rather than enhance demand functions faced by individual non-stamp stores. Exit from the industry would affect both stamp and non-stamp stores, and is not likely to produce lower prices.

An equilibrium adjustment of price can be expected between stores that offer stamps and those that do not. Consumers might be distributed over a considerable range based on the degree to which they are attracted by premium goods. Then a larger proportion of consumers can be induced to save trading stamps only if the stamps can be made increasingly attractive. Without giving more premiums per stamp, making them more attractive requires that the price *difference* between stamp and non-stamp stores be reduced.[8] Thus, *ceteris paribus*, the difference in price that stamp-giving stores can command over stores that do not give stamps can be expected to decline as more stores offer stamps.

This effect of increasing the number of stores that offer stamps can be sketched by reference to Figure 1. Suppose that there are several firms, located close together and all at the same price level, and that there are many consumers who differ over a wide range in their marginal rates of substitution between premium and non-premium goods. For ease of illustration, assume they all have the same income, although this is not essential to conclusions. When only one firm offers stamps it can increase its price level, creating a new budget constraint LJM, and still attract all consumers who prefer point J to point N. If another firm also offers stamps, the two firms will wish to have more consumers save stamps. This can be done by

[7] The National Commission on Food Marketing [12, pp. 145–8] observed slightly decreasing average cost conditions in food retailing, but estimated that volume would have to increase 40 per cent for a firm to cover the costs of trading stamps, a sales gain that grows less likely as more firms offer stamps.

[8] If non-stamp-saving customers have further characteristics in common, they might be attracted by some means other than a price difference. For example, the non-stamp-saving customers might also prefer more service and be willing to pay for it. If non-stamp-savers are not otherwise systematically different from stamp-savers, however, we might expect higher prices in the stores that offer stamps, but we would not know how much higher.

shifting point J upward or to the right relative to N which means either lowering the level of prices relative to firms that do not give stamps or giving more premiums. Alternatively, the price level of firms that do not give stamps could rise (budget constraint NM rotates counterclockwise to KM) with the same effect, since the difference in price between firms that give stamps and those that do not determines how many consumers will shop where stamps are given and how many will shop elsewhere.

When stamps are first used in a market, the store offering them may attract consumers even with higher prices than non-stamp stores, if the price difference does not exceed the value of premium goods. And the price difference need not be that great, possibly because not all stamps are redeemed, or because other promotional expenses are reduced, or even because volume is increased and average costs decrease with store volume. As more stores offer stamps, the price difference should grow smaller. But unless cost is affected by the modest consequent change in industry volume, stores that never offer stamps cannot in the long run be expected to have lower prices than before stamps were introduced. They may continue to win some customers who do not value premium goods, yet lose some customers who do, making their scale of operations contract. This could lead either to no price change or, if costs decrease with store volume, an increase in price, but it cannot easily imply a long-run price decrease for stores that do not offer stamps.

It is important to note that the difference in price between stores that give stamps and those that do not is no measure of the effect trading stamps have had on price levels, but instead reflects the equilibrium contrast between stamp and non-stamp stores. Where cash premiums are not given for stamps and exchange of stamps among consumers is not allowed, an assessment of consumer welfare requires some knowledge of the effects stamps have had on all prices. Reckoning such absolute effects is practically impossible because analysis of entry and exit is difficult among spatially differentiated firms, but as one point of reference it seems unlikely that prices in non-stamp stores can actually fall in the long-run. If some consumers do not value premium goods, this will limit the price difference between stamp and non-stamp stores, so all firms may not find it profitable to offer stamps. Consumers who value premium goods little may then be able to shop at stores that do not offer stamps without great inconvenience, but this is not assured. Price levels may also rise in stores that do not offer stamps, which would make it impossible for a consumer to escape their effects, as Figure 1 suggests. We shall now examine possibilities for consumer harm in more detail.

III. HOW CONSUMERS MIGHT BE HARMED BY TRADING STAMPS

For trading stamps to actually harm any consumers, two requirements are clear. First, the consumers must place such a low value on premium goods that they would not have purchased them at their market price. And second, they must also be denied an opportunity to continue to purchase non-premium goods from a store on the same terms as before trading stamps were introduced (Consumer 1 is surely not harmed in Figure 1 if he can remain at N). It would seem that consumers could always escape actual harm by simply buying from a store that does not give trading stamps, but such protection cannot be assured, for three reasons: (1) The consumer's nearest store might offer stamps, so he would be inconvenienced in changing stores and must give up time which has alternative uses; (2) All stores might offer stamps, preventing any escape from them; or (3) Stores that do not offer stamps might raise their prices.

When consumers who would not prefer the premiums that stamps make available also find it inconvenient to shop at non-stamp stores where prices are lower, the stores that give stamps can use them as a price discriminating device described by Davis[6]. Such circumstances are shown in Figure 2, but could be present in any of the other figures. The consumer may still shop at the store that gives stamps, but not save and redeem stamps whenever he places a high value on his time and a relatively low value on premium goods. Of course this can benefit stamp savers, and make premium goods available to some who would otherwise not buy them. As a result, however, there will be a resource allocation bias away from goods with which the stamps are given, in favor of trading stamp premium goods.

This allocative bias, made possible by sellers being able to charge higher prices to some consumers while at the same time conferring benefits on others, can be traced to two sources. One is the monopolistic aspect due to distance among spatially differentiated firms. The other is the value of consumers' time, which can vary roughly in proportion to the wage rate of the consumer (but need not). The effect is to distort the responses of consumers, so that resources will not be applied most efficiently to the satisfaction of their preferences.

When some consumers gain from trading stamps and others lose because non-stamp store prices increase, as in Figure 1, we must ask whether any sort of agreement would enable all of them to still prefer to having trading stamps offered. We are not asking whether trade would make the two consumers in Figure 1 better off than they are with stamps at J and G′, for with assumed differences in their rates of substitution, some trade will surely benefit them. Instead, we ask whether they would together prefer J and G′ to their original positions before stamps at N and G. In Figure 1, for example, if consumer 2 gave consumer 1 *money* sufficient to purchase LN in non-premium goods in exchange for trading stamps sufficient to obtain LJ in premium goods, consumer 1 could return to his original position at N where he would at least be no worse off. And consumer 2 could move to a level of utility u_2'', at point G″, which is still better than the original no trading stamps position, G. In this case, the exchange opportunity would show that both consumers prefer to have trading stamps offered. Notice that it is just as possible for u_2'' to be below u_2, however, and in that case both would prefer no stamps.[9] Only an exchange opportunity between the parties will reveal whether, on balance, gains exceed losses.

Cash redemption of trading stamps would enable consumers to test whether those who gain benefit enough to compensate those who lose, for it would afford the equivalent of exchange and a true market test. Cash redemption is usually denied, however, beyond the few states that now require it. Even where it is permitted, cash is exchanged at only a fraction (2/3 to 3/4) of the stamps' claimed retail value. And elsewhere there remains the possibility that some consumers would not value premium goods enough to offset any rise in the price of non-premium goods. Consequently, the case may result, and persist, in which some consumers gain less from stamps than others lose, because no evaluation of new benefit is possible. The prophecy suggested by Carolyn Bell that inefficiencies will doom trading stamps could thus fail for lack of a genuine market test[3].

Cash redemption is less effective in offsetting the discrimination that arises from the value of consumers' time, which may prevent a consumer from saving stamps even to redeem them in cash. But it could reduce potential harm in this case by enlarging the consumer's choice on redemption, beyond premium goods. Its effect in Figure 2 would be to rotate indifference curves of the consumer in a clockwise direction, making it more likely that he would be satisfied to save and redeem the stamps.

There is a problem in reaching equilibrium that should also be noted. Due in part to the either-or nature of the choice, a retailer cannot be expected to have experience that would help his estimate

[9] Another way to determine net benefit is for consumer 2 to pay consumer 1 KJ in x_j goods without exchange. To do so, he must move from point G′ a distance KJ downward parallel to the x_j axis. If consumer 2 is still above indifference curve u_2, both would prefer stamps; if he is below u_2, they would prefer not to have stamps offered. Even with zero income elasticity, these two types of exchanges can give different results. An exchange of stamps for money is considered in the text because it could be carried out more easily among a large number of consumers.

sales, costs, and thus profit outcomes of the trading-stamps-or-nor trading-stamps decision. And firms may choose to adopt trading stamp plans almost simultaneously, not learning of the situation that would have been available had they not decided to do so.[10] There is also a delay in consumer response, because at any one time consumers have a marginal stamp requirement for premiums that is lower than the total requirement, due to their stamp accumulation. Thus trading stamps can mar the precision of market adjustments.

IV. CONCLUSION

Using a model of a rational, fully informed consumer, possible effects of trading stamps on the budget constraints facing the consumer have been examined. Consumers cannot usually exchange trading stamps for cash and they may not all value the premiums at their market value. Then the full market value of premiums need not appear in the difference in price levels between stores that give trading stamps and those that do not. This does not mean, however, that trading stamps have not affected price levels further. Under decreasing cost conditions for individual retailers, for example, a final market equilibrium with trading stamps could result in higher average costs for all firms. As a result, after stamps are introduced, price levels can be higher in stores that do not give stamps and stores that give them as well.

Retailers may individually be motivated to offer stamps, but as more offer them, the price difference they can enjoy over other stores diminishes. Several (not necessarily all) of the firms may to some extent be forced into offering stamps if another firm does. This force is modified when some consumers are not attracted by the premium goods for which stamps may be exchanged and would therefore prefer lower prices which a non-stamp store might be able to achieve. If the equilibrium imposes higher or lower costs on all firms, the effect of trading stamps on the prices of goods with which they are given obviously cannot be measured solely by comparison with the prices of those same goods at non-stamp-giving stores. Indeed, there is no simple way to measure their effect, but as a point of reference it is doubtful that prices in non-stamp stores will be reduced as a result of stamps, and more likely that they will remain the same or increase.

Trading stamps can produce allocative distortions even though

[10] Professor Buchanan makes the interesting point that salesmen for stamp companies visit retail stores urging them to buy stamps, while no comparable functionary exists to plead for price cuts. To the extent firms would not otherwise search out advantages from cutting price, this could increase competitiveness among firms.

price differences between stamp and non-stamp stores do not exceed the value of distributed premiums. A consumer who does not value premiums enough to buy them at their market prices can be harmed if his most convenient store offers trading stamps and raises prices, and alternative non-stamp stores maintain their prices but would require more of his time. He may shop at the store that offers stamps yet not collect and redeem premiums, thus making them available at better terms to others. The result is an allocative bias in favor of premium goods and away from non-premium goods.

Trading stamps can seldom be exchanged for cash, so there is no way to compensate for harm that can result if non-stamp store prices also rise, nor is there a means of judging whether any benefit to others would even be great enough to compensate those harmed. It is doubtful that premiums can ever be so extensive that they include goods every consumer would buy. But expanding the scope of premium goods will reduce potential harm by reducing the number of consumers who have little desire to accumulate premium goods. The ultimate is to offer cash, for cash can be converted into any good and consequently it is certain to be desired by all consumers. Allowing consumers to trade one brand of trading stamp for another would also reduce this problem, both by making available a broader range of premiums and also by enabling a consumer to by only one premium in which he might have an interest rather than one (at least) for each type of stamp he is given.[11]

This is not to say that trading stamps serve no purpose. Cost savings may warrant some incentive for consumer loyalty, particularly if retailers' average costs do decrease with greater volume. But if that is the case, alternative institutional arrangements might reward loyalty better. For the trading stamp means of rewarding loyalty has the disadvantage of constraining consumer choice so that a full market assessment of its desirability is impossible. It is possible for trading stamps to distort resource allocation and to harm some persons by more than those who benefit would be willing to pay.

UNIVERSITY OF VIRGINIA

[11] One significant effort to actually trade trading stamps was the National Stamp Exchange operated by Theodore Berkely in Utica, New York. Berkely charged 1¢ for about 10 stamps exchanged (for other stamps). Since this charge can be translated into a 20 to 50 per cent brokerage fee, it suggests that stamp savers were indeed motivated to exchange one type of stamp for another. The S & H Green Stamp Co. won a legal decision which enjoined Mr. Berkely's exchange from continuing.

ON RELATIVE FUEL EFFICIENCY AND THE OUTPUT ELASTICITY OF ENERGY CONSUMPTION IN WESTERN EUROPE*

by F. Gerard Adams and Peter Miovic

In recent years, many countries have prepared comprehensive 'energy studies' as a basis for fuel resource policy and planning.[1] The nation's aggregate energy needs are projected into the future and confronted with an analysis of prospective fuel supplies.[2] Such studies, which make it possible to establish a forward view of how future energy requirements can be met—with what fuels, from what sources, and at what costs—are also valuable for the fuel industries to establish demand and sales forecasts and for making investment, marketing, and pricing decisions.

The long term forecast of energy consumption, which is the principal building block of this research, is usually based on functional relationships between energy consumption and economic activity. Past studies in Western Europe and the United States have frequently used the 'energy elasticity', the percentage change in energy use associated with a 1 per cent change in economic activity. Recent work has tended toward increased methodological sophistication, but the implicit 'energy elasticity', overall or sector-by-sector, remains an important consideration in judging the reasonableness or consistency of the forecast. Since in advanced economies fuel use *appears* to grow more slowly than GNP; the elasticities generally have been found to be less than 1.0. Gross elasticities of energy consumption with respect to GNP have been estimated variously as between .7 and .9 and somewhat lower with respect to industrial production.[3] Figures of this range of magnitude have been widely accepted as the basis for authoritative projections of energy require-

* This is a project of the Economics Research Unit of the University of Pennsylvania. Partial support for this research was provided under a grant from the National Science Foundation.

[1] Some important recent studies are: U.S. Senate, Committee on Interior and Insular Affairs, *Report of the National Fuels and Energy Study Group*, Washington, 1962; Commissariat General du Plan, *Rapport General de la Commission de l'Energie*, Paris 1961; O.E.E.C., *Toward A New Energy Pattern in Europe* (Robinson Report), Paris, 1961; *Energy Policy: Problems and Objectives*, Paris, 1966; European Economic Community, *Etude sur les Perspectives Energetiques a Long Terme de la Communautè Europeenne*, Luxembourg 1964, and *Nouvelles Reflexions sur les Perspectives Energetiques a Long Terme de la Communautè Europeenne*, (mimeo), Luxembourg, 1966; Arbeitsgemeinschaft Deutscher Wirtschaftswissenschaftlicher Forschungsinstitute, *Untersuchung uber die Entwicklung der Gegenwärtigen und Zukunftigen Struktur von Angebot und Nachfrage in der Energiewirtschaft der Bundesrepublik*, Duncker and Humblot, Berlin, 1962.

[2] For a discussion of the problems of energy projections and the procedures which are frequently used see, United Nations, Economic Commission for Europe, *Methods and Principles for Projecting Future Energy Requirements*, New York, 1964.

[3] See Table IV on p. 54. In the developing countries, in contrast, the elasticity is frequently substantially above 1.0.

ments and as guides for public policy in Western Europe and the United States.[4]

While various arguments have been used to rationalize an energy elasticity below unity, it is surprising that energy use should be rising less than proportionately with output over a period when industrialization and capital intensity have been increasing. It is likely that the 'true' energy elasticity is being underestimated.

Some difficult technical problems arise in connection with measuring energy consumption and in connection with determining the coefficients on the basis of which future energy use can be forecast. This paper is concerned, in particular, with the problem caused by the differing efficiencies in use of various fuel sources. Since some fuels are more efficient than others, substitution of one fuel for another, oil for coal for example, affects aggregate energy consumption as measured in conventional calorific terms. In turn, estimated elasticity coefficients used to relate energy consumption to economic activity are affected and there is reason to question the validity of the energy consumption projections obtained.

In this study, we will examine the measurement of energy consumption, allowing for differences in fuel efficiency, and we will estimate efficiency coefficients by a new approach. We will, then, evaluate the implications of adjusted fuel consumption data for the elasticity of energy consumption with respect to economic activity in Western Europe.

The statistical work is based on pooled cross section data for the Common Market countries, the U.K., and the remainder of the O.E.E.C. as a group, over the period 1950–62.

MEASURING ENERGY CONSUMPTION

It is, perhaps, the *raison d'être* of energy economics that in many cases alternative fuels can serve with some degree of interchange-

[4] Some recent examples of forward estimates of energy elasticities are:

Country	*Period*	*Elasticity with respect to*		*Source*
E.E.C.	1960–70	.91	G.N.P.	E.E.C., *Etude sur les perspectives ...* pp. 36 and 248
O.E.E.C.	1955–60 1960–75	.8 .85	G.N.P.	O.E.E.C., Hartley Report, 1956, pp. 66–7
O.E.E.C.	1955–75	.87		O.E.E.C., Robinson Report, 1960, p. 26
U.S.	1955–75	.75*	G.N.P.	H. Schurr and B. Netschert, *Energy in The American Economy*, 1960
France	1959–65 1965–75	.95 .95–1.0	industrial production	Commissariat General du Plan, *Rapport General* ..., 1961, pp. 335–41

* Our calculation.

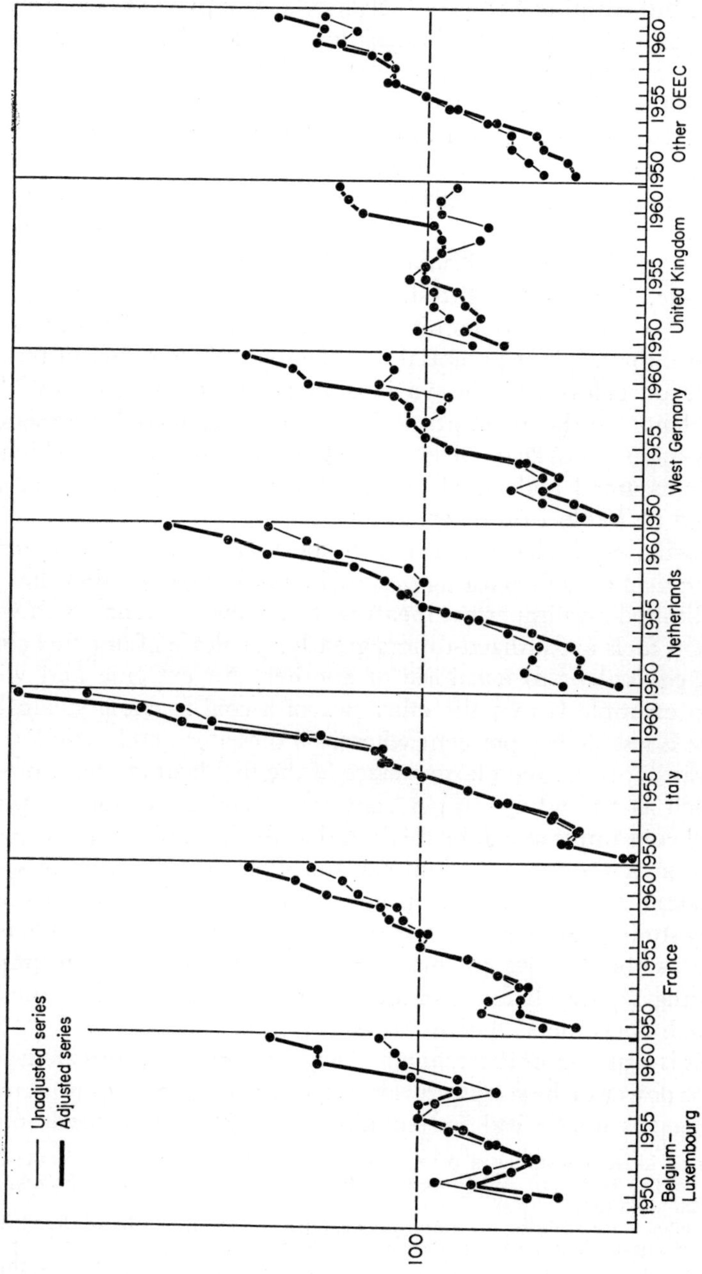
Unadjusted series
Adjusted series
100
Belgium–Luxembourg
France
Italy
Netherlands
West Germany
United Kingdom
Other OEEC
1950
1955
1960

Fig. 1

ability. Substitution between fuels has been typical of the process of industrial and technological development.[5] In Western Europe, this involves rapid change from the use of coal toward petroleum-based fuels and in the not-so-distant future to natural gas and nuclear energy. In part, this is also a shift from 'primary' energy to use in final consumption of transformed or 'secondary' fuels such as petroleum products or electricity produced in thermal power plants.

Analytical studies and projections of the fuel economy assume that it is possible to establish a meaningful measure of 'energy' as an aggregate. The usual way to sum up consumption of different fuels in terms of a common denominator is to add up a physical energy measure, the implicit potential heat content of each fuel in terms of B.T.U. or calories.[6] The various fuels are converted into 'coal equivalents' on the assumption that a kilogram of coal represents on the average 7000 kcal. of energy. The fuel equivalents which are usually assumed and which have been used in this study are summarized in Table I on p. 45.

Calorific equivalents continue to be used to measure aggregate fuel use in energy forecasting despite increasing recognition that they are a limited and imperfect measure. Since the efficiency with which different fuels are utilized differs greatly, a calorie of one fuel simply is not equivalent to a calorie of another. An extreme and widely known example is that the efficiency of a coal burning steam locomotive is less than 5 per cent whereas a diesel or an electric locomotive transforms a much larger share of the fuel heat content, perhaps as much as 30 and 65–70 per cent respectively, into motive power.

Fuel consumption can be measured at the level of 'primary' energy inputs or at the point of final consumption including, in this case, 'secondary' fuels where appropriate. While it is the usual objective of energy studies to determine 'primary' fuel requirements, fuel demand estimates should first be made at the level of final consumption (allowing separately for transformation losses) since this is the level at which consumers' choices are made.

This is a matter of thermal efficiency—the energy equivalent of the motive power or heat output relative to the calorific input. Thermal efficiency is a physical or technical concept and depends on the

[5] For an interesting survey of the role of alternative fuels in energy use in the United States see Sam H. Schurr and Bruce C. Netschert, *Energy in the American Economy 1880–1975*, Ch. 3, Baltimore, 1960.

[6] Sometimes the calorific measures are modified in the case of hydroelectricity and nuclear electricity in order not to distort the comparisons with countries which produce mainly thermal electric power. Electricity, regardless of its origin, is then measured in terms of the coal that would be required to produce it in an average thermal power plant. We have avoided this procedure since it combines two approaches, one using the implicit calorific output potential of the fuel itself, the other using the calorie input required to produce equivalent power.

technology in which the fuel is applied, its purpose, i.e. heating or motive power, and the performance characteristics of the engines used. Thermal efficiency varies greatly among fuels in motive power applications as we have noted above. In industrial or residential heat application, the efficiency of alternative fuels tends to be more equal so long as modern equipment is used. On the other hand, heating with coal fires in an open fireplace is extremely inefficient.

TABLE I

STANDARD FUEL EQUIVALENTS

Fuel	*Unit*	*Calorfic potential (000 kilocalories)*	*Hard coal equivalent (tons)*
Coal			
Hard coal (in patent fuel)	tons	7,000	1.0
Coke	tons	6,700	.96
Brown coal	tons	2,200	.31
BKB	tons	4,650	.66
Gas			
Manufactured gas and equivalent natural gas	000m³	4,200	.6
Petroleum			
Liquified gases	tons	12,000	1.71
Motor and aviation gasoline	tons	10,500	1.50
Other petroleum fuels	tons	10,000	1.43
Electricity			
Hydro and thermal electricity	000 kwh	860	.12

Sources: V. Parretti and G. Bloch, *Statistiques de l'Energie, 1950–60*, EEC, 1962, p. xiii and O.E.E.C., *Towards a New Energy Pattern in Europe*, Paris, 1960, pp. 16 and 91.

Typical thermal efficiency estimates for various uses developed from engineering sources are presented in Table II.

Thermal efficiency is not equivalent to economic efficiency which relates output of goods and services (in value terms rather than in calories of work performed) to the fuel inputs.[7] In a specific application, however, relative thermal efficiency of alternative fuels translates simply into economic efficiency since a given calorific output of work performed represents a proportional value of products regardless of the fuel source.

One approach to the problem of differential fuel efficiency has been to adjust the calorific equivalent figures by independent estimates of thermal efficiency. In this way a measure of the 'useful energy' content of the fuels is obtained but the engineering type estimates of

[7] Schurr and Netschert elaborate on the distinction between thermal and economic fuel efficiency, Schurr and Netschert, op. cit., pp. 171–4.

efficiency are, of course, fairly arbitrary and the concept of 'useful energy' is well nigh illusory. This method has recently been used in a study of U.S. energy consumption,[8] in European energy studies,[9] and in the Netherlands energy planning.[10]

An alternative approach has recently been suggested by Ralph Turvey and A. R. Nobay.[11] They argue that the proper conversion factors for different fuels are 'their marginal rates of transformation in production or their marginal rates of substitution in consumption'. Given the fact that fuel markets are not perfectly competitive and that marginal cost data are not available, they suggest the use of price or of average revenue weights. This approach has merit, despite the

TABLE II

ESTIMATED THERMAL EFFICIENCIES

	Coal	*Gas*	*Petroleum products*	*Electricity*
Motive Power				
Stationary	5–10%	35%	30%	80–90%
Moving	4–5%	—	18–25%	65–85%
Heating				
Industry	33%	39%	40%	80%
Consumer	5–60%	65–72%	60–65%	80%

Source: Approximate figures drawn from Palmer Putnan *Energy in the Future*, New York, 1953, and E.C.S.C., *Etude sur la Structure*, p. 20–1, and other sources.

problem, which the authors recognize, that average price does not generally correspond in the case of fuels, with the marginal. However, the method may not have very widespread applicability. Alternative fuels meet effectively at the margin in few uses. In many markets, one fuel is entirely dominant. Even when several fuels are used for the same purpose, the price relationship may not reflect their marginal rate of transformation because of the long time lag required until the capital equipment has been converted so that equilibrium fuel use can be achieved. For example, even when the price relationship begins to favor electricity in residential heating it will be many years before electric heating equipment is installed and, in any case, other fuels may continue to be used in special applications.

A further alternative, to be investigated here, is to estimate the

[8] See, for example, Alan M. Strout, 'Market Trends in Mineral Fuels, 1951–1960' Fuels Symposium, American Society of Mechanical Engineers, June 5–7, 1962; A.S.M.E. Paper No. 62-FUS-4.

[9] O.E.E.C., *Towards a New Energy Pattern*, op. cit., p. 102 and E.C.S.C., *Etude sur la Structure*, op. cit., pp. 20–1.

[10] United Nations Economic Commission for Europe, 'Methods ...', op. cit.

[11] 'On Measuring Energy Consumption', *Economic Journal*; December 1965, pp. 787–93.

relative productivity of the fuels directly from the production function. In the production sectors of the economy, fuel can be viewed as an input into the production function

$$O = \min(\alpha F, f(N,K)) \quad (1)$$

where O = output
F = Energy input adjusted for the differential efficiency of the component fuels
N = Labor input
K = Capital input

Proportionality between fuel input and output is assumed and there is no substitution between fuel inputs and capital and labor.[12] The remainder of the production function remains unspecified. F can then be defined as

$$F = e_c h_c C + e_e h_e E + e_p h_p P + e_g h_g G \quad (2)$$

where C = Coal in tons
E = Electricity in kilowatt hours
P = Petroleum in tons
G = Gas in cubic meters

and the h's are the respective calorific contents per unit and the e's are the efficiencies in use of the various fuels.

While the h's are known, the problem is that the e's are not known. As discussed above one may use rough and ready approximations. Alternatively, one may assume that all the e's are equal, the case of using calorific equivalents. But since in fact the e's are probably not equal, this means that the aggregate energy measure is not invariant to the composition of fuel consumption.

An empirical approach to determining the values of the e's is to estimate the function, using the known h's,

$$O = a_1 (h_c C) + a_2 (h_e E) + a_3 (h_p P) + a_4 (k_g G) \quad (3)$$

where the $a_i = \alpha e_i$, the α being common to all terms of the equation.

In order to establish an index of energy use, F, which is invariant to the proportions of the various fuels, only relative measures of the e's are necessary so that it is not vital at this point whether a more complete specification of the equation would yield a different α. This is of some assistance in view of the fact, noted earlier, that the efficiency of fuel utilization may change independently of shifts among alternative fuel sources. To the extent that these are general shifts in the

[12] The latter is an assumption which is approximately valid in the aggregate though there are important exceptions.

production function affecting all fuels the same way, they alter α but not the relative values of the a_i. To the extent that the efficiency of a particular fuel changes relative to others, the estimated relative efficiencies are affected. It is possible to deal with this problem by disentangling the relationships observed into regressions based on data 'over time' and regressions using cross section data 'between countries'.

The relative values obtained for the e's may be checked in two ways. On the one hand, limited prior information is available on the thermal efficiency of fuels in various uses as in Table II. Secondly, in those fields where more than one fuel is used, one can follow Turvey and Nobay. Making standard assumptions about the performance of the market mechanism, the marginal rate of transformation between, say, petroleum and coal in calorific equivalents

$$MRTS_{pc} = \frac{-d(h_c C)}{d(h_p P)} = \frac{f_p}{f_p} = \frac{e_p}{e_p} = \frac{Price_p}{Price} \tag{4}$$

where the f's are the respective marginal productivities and the e's the efficiency coefficients of petroleum and coal. Subject to reservations raised earlier, the price ratio would measure the relative efficiencies of the fuels at the margin of application.[13]

In those consumer uses where fuel substitution is possible, somewhat similar arguments can be presented. Consumers purchase fuels not for their direct benefit but in order to obtain heat or motive power. But in this case measurement of relative efficiencies using the production function approach would require an aggregate output measure of heat and power produced at the consumer level and such a measure is not available.

ESTIMATION OF FUEL EFFICIENCY FACTORS

Relative fuel efficiency factors have been estimated using a regression approach as in Eq. 3, above. Since only the relative efficiencies are desired, efficiency factors have been calculated relative to the efficiency of coal. Since α is common to all the fuel coefficients, the relative efficiency of fuel

$$Re_i = \frac{e_i}{e_c} = \frac{a_i}{a_c} \tag{5}$$

The data are final consumption of fuel (on a coal equivalent basis) for five Common Market countries (Luxembourg is included with

[13] No allowance is made here for the fact that different fuels may also involve different capital costs.

Belgium), the U.K. and the other O.E.E.C. countries as a group. Regressions were estimated on the pooled annual cross sections from 1950 to 1962. The analysis can only be applied to the production sectors for which production and fuel use information is available. The estimates presented apply to the overall industrial sector.

A simplified multiple regression-analysis of covariance scheme was employed which permits estimation of the equations as deviations from country means and with a time trend. Country constants were introduced as dummy variables. The linear time trend includes a set of 'time and country' interaction terms so that the effect of time can vary as between countries. This procedure yields the following types of regression estimates:

I. Without country or year terms, i.e., simply using the pooled data.
II. With separate constants for each country.
III. With time trend variables but without country constants.
IV. With time trend variables and with country constants.

The Type I regression merges cross section with time series effects. It assumes that change over time is equivalent to differences between countries at one point in time, an assumption which is probably not appropriate in this setting. Movement over time is likely to reflect shorter run factors, such as business cycle variation within established capacity, and the gradual adjustment to equilibrium through substitution between fuels. The inter-country differences are not independent of these effects but they will emphasize longer run factors and structural differences in energy use between the various countries. These effects will be mixed in the Type I regression.

In the Type II regressions, the movement over time 'within countries' is emphasized. The relative coefficients can be affected by the process of market adjustment and fuel substitution which occurs over time as output grows. For example, if the price of coal rises relative to that of petroleum, coal will tend to be phased out and petroleum will take its place. As output grows over time, the use of coal will tend to grow more slowly relative to output (or even decline) and the use of the expanding fuel, petroleum, will grow rapidly relative to output. In time series, the estimated coefficient for coal, 'a_c' will be too high (or in case of declining coal use it will be negative), whereas the estimated coefficient for petroleum 'a_p' will be too low.

In the Type III regressions the' between country' effects (which are also a part, though less clearly, of Type I equations) measure relative fuel efficiency factors from the inter-country comparisons holding constant for change over time. It is not unreasonable to assume that the same approximate level of technology is available in all the European countries at about the same time and that in general relative fuel prices are not greatly out of line among them.[14] Moreover the cross section relationship tends to avoid the problem of disequilibrium. It is not implied that in each country fuels will be consumed at their equilibrium levels, but in inter-country cross-section substitution between fuels will not be systematically related to the country's level of output.

TABLE III

PRODUCTION FUNCTION ESTIMATES OF RELATIVE FUEL EFFICIENCIES

Equation type	*Coal and gas*	*Electricity*		*Petroleum*	
	Coefficient	*Coefficient*	*Coefficient relative to coal*	*Coefficient*	*Coefficient relative to coal*
Type I (overall pooled)	.3080	.8418	(2.7)	.7637	(2.5)
Type II (within countries; with country dummy variables)	.2176	2.1608	(9.9)	.3422	(1.6)
Type III (between countries; with time and time country interaction terms)	.2396	1.0681	(4.5)	.6453	(2.7)
Type IV (Interaction; with country dummies, time and time country interaction terms)	.1168	1.6672	(14.3)	.1955	(1.7)

(all coefficients are significant at the .05 level)

Definitions of Variables and Sources of Data:

Dependent Variable—

Industrial Production-value of total industrial production in 1953 U.S. $.

Sources: Estimated on the basis of data from O.E.C.D., *Industrial Statistics 1900–1962*, Paris, 1964, O.E.C.D., *Statistics of National Accounts 1950–1961*, Paris, 1963, and percentage weights for 1954 from O.E.C.D., *Industrial Statistics 1900–1957*, Paris, 1958, p. 34.

Independent variables—

Final Consumption of Fuels by Industry-millions of tons coal equivalent.

Sources: V. Parretti and G. Bloch, *Statistiques de l'Energie, 1950–60*, E.E.C., 1962, and O.E.C.D., *Basic Statistics of Energy 1950–1963*, Paris, 1965.

The Type IV regressions derive estimates from the interaction effects of country and time. This reduces the opportunity for significant effects but on the other hand it helps to allow for inter-country differences in technology and/or fuel prices at the same time that the substitution over time phenomenon is also minimized. The problem with these estimates concerns their sensitivity to the particular time and country factors applied.

The results of the four types of regressions are summarized in

[14] There are, however, some important exceptions involving, for example, low cost hydro-electric power used in electro-metallurgical applications.

Table III. The coefficients of the fuels and their relative efficiencies with respect to coal are shown. Because of multicollinearity problems, it was necessary to merge coal and gas (largely manufactured gas) on calorific equivalent basis. The equations are linear and include constants in order to catch marginal rather than average coefficients. All four types of equations yield coefficients for coal and gas which are greatly below those for the other fuels. But the relative efficiencies obtained vary considerably with the equations. It is not appropriate to compare directly the value of the coefficients among the various types of regressions since the underlying α or average fuel coefficient is not necessarily the same 'within countries' as 'between countries'.

We turn now to the relative efficiencies of the different fuels. The cross country differences are the predominant element in the pooled regression, Type I. The coefficients obtained are different but not greatly so from those in Type III when the time factor has been allowed for. As we have indicated earlier, the cross country differences tend to be 'long run' after adjustment to the fuel cost conditions in each country and the technology prevailing. In this context, the efficiency of petroleum is approximately 2.5 times that of coal and electricity has a coefficient 2.7–4.5 times that of coal (Eq. I and III). The relatively low efficiency of electrical power reflects the fact that in the long run cross country context in those cases where electricity is relatively cheap it is used for electro-metallurgical and heating purposes which are relatively its least 'efficient' application.

The relationship over time (Eq. II) is characterized by relatively much higher efficiency for electricity (9.9 times that of coal) and a relatively lower efficiency of petroleum (1.6 times) with respect to coal. We have noted above that improvement in fuel utilization has occurred over time. This improvement is apparent for electricity whereas the figures suggest even some decline in efficiency over time for the other fuels. Trends in industrial fuel use in Western Europe which have favored electricity for highly efficient motive power uses and petroleum and coal for less efficient heating purposes can account for these results.

The interaction equation allows for linear time trends (as above the interaction terms give a separate time trend for each country) and for country levels. This means that the relationships are estimated on the interaction component; and, thus, are like 'within country estimates' after linear trend removal. The principal element of variation not already explicitly allowed for is thus the business cycle. The average of the a_i coefficients in this case is close to that obtained in the pooled (Type I) regression. The coefficients for coal (and gas) and petroleum are however relatively much lower and electricity is much higher. This means that over the cycle the efficiency of marginal electrical calorie inputs is relatively very much greater and that of coal and petroleum much smaller than over the longer term or in the cross section. Another way to see this is that industrial electricity inputs are relatively less sensitive to business cycle fluctuations than coal or petroleum. One explanation for this phenomenon is the cyclical sensitivity of heavy industry where coal and petroleum are used relatively inefficiently for industrial heating, of deoxidation of iron ore. On the other hand, outside the electro-metallurgical industry, electricity consumption is likely to be used for relatively cyclically insensitive purposes.

The empirical analysis suggests that the relative efficiency of the fuels is greatly dependent on the frame of reference, though a calorie of coal is less efficient than one of electrical power and petroleum in all cases. The 'across time' estimate or the 'interaction' estimate reflect short run elements. For long run prediction, the cross-section view allowing for time, Equation III, appears to yield the most appropriate results. These estimates of relative fuel efficiency are in line with the typical engineering type thermal efficiency calculations, averaging across various uses (Table II), but are only very approximately consistent with Turvey and Nobay's estimates based on prices.[15]

The figures developed here may be used for making aggregative projections. However, substantial refinement of the efficiency estimates should be possible if data on product output and fuel consumption by industry and/or process were used, and this is advisable if forecasts for particular fuel uses or industries are envisaged.

ADJUSTED ENERGY CONSUMPTION

A measure of energy consumption which allows for differential fuel efficiency is 'purified' of the effect of shifts between different kinds of fuels. Such a measure can be obtained by weighting calorific inputs of different fuels by their respective efficiencies as in Equation 2. If calories of various fuels are multiplied by their relative efficiency with respect to coal (Re_i as defined in Equation 5) and summed, the aggregate adjusted energy consumption measure will be in terms of calories of fuel with efficiency equivalent to that of coal. The path

[15] R. Turvey and A. P. Nobay, op. cit. Price ratios of oil and electricity relative to coal on a calorific equivalent basis calculated from their data in U.K. industrial uses are:

	1954	1959	1964
Oil	1.8	1.1	1.0
Electricity	10.3	8.1	7.8

These figures are relatively close to the Type II estimates.

over time of such an adjusted fuel consumption measure is independent of the breakdown by source of fuel.

Fuel consumption measures adjusted for differential efficiency have been prepared on the basis of the coefficients estimated above. For the estimates based on the coefficients of the Type III equation (between country estimates) a graphical comparison with unadjusted energy consumption is shown on Chart I. Two elements of this comparison are noteworthy. In all cases the rate of growth of fuel consumption after adjustment is substantially greater than in the unadjusted calorific equivalent form. Secondly, the pattern over the business cycle is closer to prior expectations in the adjusted series. The downward turns of the business cycle are greatly moderated in the adjusted data.[16] Thus the pattern is more nearly in line with that of the continued growth of industrial production, with slowdowns in growth rather than pronounced downturns, which has been characteristic of the 1950–62 period in these countries except in Belgium-Luxembourg and the U.K.

ADJUSTED ENERGY ELASTICITY

As we have seen, shifts from inefficient to efficient fuels reduce energy requirements as measured in calorific equivalents.[17] As substitution between fuels proceeds and G.N.P. grows over time, the estimated energy elasticity is downward biased. This appears to be the main reason for the unexpectedly low energy elasticities which have been obtained in past empirical studies. Even so, if substitution can be expected to continue, the projections obtained may not be far off despite the fact that the structural parameter has been underestimated. But when conversion from one fuel to another has been completed, the gains in efficiency which have been built into the projection cease and the forecaster no longer has the subterfuge of assuming that future improvement in the efficiency of fuel utilization will continue as in the past.

In line with conventional practice we have calculated energy elasticities with respect to industrial production and G.N.P.[18] Elasticities using the adjusted fuel consumption data (on the basis of efficiency coefficients obtained from all four types of regressions) are

[16] The extent to which the cyclical pattern is attenuated depends on the weighting chosen so that the cyclical movement virtually disappears (except in Belgium-Luxembourg and U.K.) when a high weight is given to electricity (as in the Type IV equation).

[17] Increased efficiency also results from technological change in the use of particular fuels, but shifts in fuel sources appear to be one of the principal ways in which improvements in fuel use take effect.

[18] Obtained from simple regressions of log energy consumption on log industrial production or log G.N.P.; pooled data, 1950–62 Common Market, U.K. and 'other O.E.E.C'.

compared with elasticities using simple calorific equivalent consumption data in Table IV.

The elasticities based on unadjusted data are smaller than 1.0. That this is to a large extent a consequence of shifting use among fuels with differential efficiency is apparent from the recalculation of the elasticity on the adjusted data. After the adjustment for fuel efficiency, the elasticities are equal to or greater than 1.0, suggesting that energy consumption increases proportionately or even more than proportionately with output. Adjustments are particularly necessary when elasticity estimates are made, as they are here, on the

TABLE IV

ALTERNATIVE ENERGY ELASTICITY ESTIMATES

Elasticity with respect to	*Unadjusted calorific equivalent basis*	*Relative efficiencies obtained from*			
		Type I	*Type II*	*Type III*	*Type IV*
		Equation			
Industrial production	.816*	1.114*	1.039	1.148*	1.071*
	(.037)	(.035)	(.024)	(.033)	(.025)
Gross domestic product	.910	1.358*	1.249*	1.405*	1.300*
	(.051)	(.042)	(.032)	(.039)	(.029)

* Different from 1.0 at the .05 significance level.

basis of fuel use at the final consumption level. In this case, the increasing use of secondary fuels, which are generally more efficient than primary fuels, tends particularly to downward bias the elasticity coefficient.[19]

ADJUSTED FUEL CONSUMPTION AND FORECASTING

It is necessary to allow for the differential efficiency of various fuel sources in forecasting for the energy economy. This can be seen in the simplest forecasting scheme, such as the 'energy balance' below, as well as in more complex models.

The 'energy balance' approach to forecasting can be summarized by the following two equation model:

$$F = \eta O \tag{6}$$

$$F = e_c h_c C + e_e h_e E + e_p h_p P + e_g h_g G. \tag{7}$$

The first equation determines total energy demand as a function of economic activity (O) where η is the energy elasticity. The second equation, which corresponds to Equation 2 above, is the energy

[19] Nevertheless, evidence from other studies suggests that elasticities derived from primary fuel consumption data tend also to be too low unless adjustments for efficiency are made.

balance, an accounting identity. In the simplest approach, total energy needs are allocated roughly among the various fuels on the basis of past fuel use patterns, relative competitiveness, available domestic production, etc. One fuel category, most often imported petroleum, is determined as a residual.[20]

The burden of the discussion above is that unless relative efficiencies of fuels are considered, such a model cannot properly be applied. In the first place, the total energy requirements estimate made in Equation 6 would not be independent of the allocation by fuel sources. On the basis of calorific (but not efficiency) equivalents, the estimated energy elasticity implies that substitution between fuels will continue as during the sample period. But this need not be consistent with the implied allocation of fuel sources and it may in fact not be possible as one or another fuel achieves market dominance. Secondly, the accounting identity does not make sense unless the summation is made in a common substitutable unit of account. And calorific equivalents for different fuels are equivalent and substitutable for one another only when they have been adjusted for relative efficiency.

Such adjustment is indispensable also for more complex approaches to energy forecasting. Once forecasts in adjusted terms have been prepared, they may, of course, readily be converted back into quantities measured in tons, barrels, K.W.H. or M.C.F. of the fuels themselves.

In recent years, energy projections have been based on increasingly sophisticated analyses, by sector and by fuel, sometimes making rough, but nevertheless appropriate, adjustments for fuel efficiency. This paper has attempted to establish the quantitative dimensions of relative efficiencies and the implications of adjustment for the energy elasticity.

There are a number of other important ways in which energy forecasting is being improved. A comprehensive model of fuel demand involves more complete specification of the relationship between energy consumption and economic activity. Changes in the relative importance of various fuels and of consuming industries and shifts in their respective fuel demand functions can be considered explicitly. The fuel demand functions should consider final fuel use,

[20] Earlier post-war studies projected availabilities of fuels from domestic sources and assumed that foreign supplies would fill the 'energy gap'. O.E.C.D., Hartley Report, op. cit. More recent calculations have emphasized relative competitiveness considering current supply curves and the long run prospects for costs of alternative fuels. See, Schurr and Netschert, op. cit. and A.D.W.F., *Untersuchung*..., op. cit. Another approach is to consider coal and fuel oil as the principal competing fuels and to treat them together as the residual category. See, A. J. Middelhoek, 'Een Sectormodel van het Energieverbruik', Reprint No. 82, Netherlands Central Planning Bureau, 1962.

as has been indicated, regardless of whether the fuel consumed is 'primary' or 'secondary'. Secondary fuels must then be traced through the transformation sector again with an allocation among the original primary fuel sources. Finally, improved models recognize the underlying long run cost/supply functions of alternative fuels which are essential for economic planning and decision making.

UNIVERSITY OF PENNSYLVANIA

REFERENCES

[1] BACON, R., 'A Note on Measuring Shopping Costs', *Journal of Industrial Economics*, Vol. XVI (1967).

[2] BECKER, GARY S., 'A Theory of the Allocation of Time', *Economic Journal*, Vol. LXXV (1965).

[3] BELL, CAROLYN S., ' "Liberty, Property, and No Stamps" ' *Journal of Business*, Vol. XL (1967).

[4] BRIEF, R. P., 'Measuring Shopping Costs', *Journal of Industrial Economics*, Vol. XV (1967).

[5] BROMLEY, J. D. and WALLACE, W. H., 'The Effect of Trading stamps on Retail Food Prices', Rhode Island Agricultural Experiment Station Contribution No. 1091, Kingston, R.I., 1965.

[6] DAVIS, O. A., 'The Economics of Trading Stamps', *Journal of Business*, Vol. XXXII (1959).

[7] HOOVER, ETHEL D. and DRAKE, MARY L., 'Trading Stamps and the Consumer Price Index', *Monthly Labor Review*, Vol. LXXIX (1956).

[8] KLASS, D., *Motivation and the Retail Food Business*, San Francisco: California Grocers Association, 1956.

[9] ROTHWELL, P., 'Impact of Trading Stamps on Food Prices', *Monthly Labor Review*, Vol. LXXXII (1959).

[10] SHERMAN, R. and WILLETT, T. D., 'The Value of Time, Consumer Behavior, and the Standardized Work Week', Harvard Institute of Economics Research Discussion Paper Number 12, February 1968.

[11] STROTZ, R. H., 'On Being Fooled by Figures; the Case of Trading Stamps', *Journal of Business*, Vol. XXXI (1958).

[12] *Organization and Competition in Food Retailing*, Technical Study No. 7, National Commission on Food Marketing, June 1966.

COST FUNCTIONS, CONCENTRATION, AND BARRIERS TO ENTRY IN TWENTY-NINE MANUFACTURING INDUSTRIES OF INDIA

by VINOD K. GUPTA

THE well-known theoretical construct of a U-shaped long-run average cost curve has been put to the test of empirical validity in quite a few studies made in some countries.[1] As the rising arm of the U has been found to be virtually flat in most of the industries studied, an L-shaped average cost curve is already becoming popular. The purpose of the present paper in this context is twofold: First, to determine the long-run cost functions in some manufacturing industries of India, and to see if their shapes tally with the findings in other countries. Second, to determine, with the help of these cost functions, the optimal plant size, and the importance of scale-economies in every industry, in order to answer a few questions regarding concentration, efficiency and barriers to entry. The first section deals with the determination of cost functions, the second with concentration and efficiency, and the third with barriers to entry.

I. COST FUNCTIONS

The annual *Census of Indian Manufactures* (brought out by the Government of India), contains cross-sectional data for twenty-nine industries (out of the sixty-three industrial classifications made by them) up to the year 1958. All the plants in an industry have been classified into nine size-groups in terms of the total number of workers employed, viz., below 20, 20–49, 50–99, 100–249, 250–499, 500–999, 1000–1999, 2000–4999, and 5000 and above. The unit of enumeration in the Census being only a 'plant', and not a 'firm', our

[1] After examining 44 sets of data on long-run cost-output relationships, Wiles concludes: 'A.C. descends like the left hand branch of a capital U, swiftly at first and then more gently. Decreasing costs with size are almost universal. But the U seldom turns up again. *Sharply increasing costs with size are practically unknown, and even slight increases are rare.* Sixty per cent of the examples . . . obey what we may call the *law of L-shaped costs.* Another 31 per cent show a slight increase of costs in the largest size-class. Most—but by no means all—of these slight increases are well within the expected margin of error that any empirical correlation should show' (see P. J. D. Wiles, *Price, Cost and Output*, Oxford, 1956, p. 205).

J. Johnston (*Statistical Cost Analysis*, Chapter 4) also makes some empirical investigations into the long-run average cost curves, and comes out with the impression of 'the preponderance of the L-shaped pattern of long-run average cost'. He also gives a list and summary of many other important inquiries in this field (ibid., Chapter 5). These empirical studies also indicate the existence of the L-shaped cost curves in most of the cases. Also see J. M. Blair, 'The Relation Between Size and Efficiency of Business', *Rev. of Eco. and Stat.*, Vol. 24, 1942.

analysis too would be relevant with 'plant' as the industrial unit. Costs, as given in the Census, include the total rupee-value of materials, fuel, electricity, lubricants, etc., consumed;[2] work done for factory by other concerns; salaries, wages and other benefits to employees; and, depreciation and maintenance charges. Output is given in terms of the ex-factory rupee-value of products and by-products. It includes the value of work done for customers on payment, and excludes the cost of transport of products and by-products from factory, and commission to selling agents, etc.

The method adopted here to determine cost functions on the basis of these data is like this: In every industry total cost and output over a period of five years[3] (1954–58) were calculated for the plants lying in each size-group. Expressing total costs as a percentage of total output gave us average cost (in terms of paisa) per rupee of output. This average cost for any given size-group is the mean of average costs of all the plants lying in that size-group. The size of plant has been measured in terms of the total number of persons employed, because the size-groups in the Census have also been taken by employment. Then, a curvilinear regression-equation was fitted to these mean cost-size observations for various size-groups in every industry.[4] The equation is:

$$Y = ax + b + \frac{c}{x}$$

[2] Materials and fuel consumed exclude any fuel, materials or electricity manufactured within the factory and consumed in it. This is a serious limitation of the data in as much as the costs of some of the larger plants would be understated, if, for example, they have their own dynamos to generate electricity.

[3] Total cost and output were calculated and averaged for a period of five years in order to avoid an important limitation of the cross-sectional data. The cost-size observation in a particular year would be influenced by the particular happenings of that year, e.g. a labour-strike, a mechanical breakdown, or a sharp curtailment of capacity-utilization due to some temporary shrinkage of demand. Such influences can, however, be greatly mitigated by taking a four- or five-year average of costs (see P. J. D. Wiles, *Price, Cost and Output*, Oxford, 1956, p. 203).

[4] The underlying assumption is that the regression fitted to the means of observations lying in various size-groups is approximately the same as the regression fitted to the entire scatter of observations, without bothering about the classification of the scatter into different size-groups.

This assumption was necessary, because, in the Census, only aggregate data are given for all the plants in each size-group. Information regarding individual plants is not at all available.

But, this assumption would be perfectly valid, if there are no extreme values of Y (average cost) in any size-group. And, extremely low values of Y should not be normally expected; because all the plants in the same size-group would be using more or less the same technique of production, and would be purchasing inputs at approximately the same prices, and managerial efficiency alone cannot account for extremely low average cost in some of the plants. Again, plants with extremely high average cost may be existing in the short run due to some reason or the other, but they cannot at all persist in the long run. Moreover, there are many plants in each of the size-groups (except the largest ones) in an industry, so that the extremely low and high values of Y, if they exist, neutralize each other in averaging. Hence, the assumption would be normally valid.

where Y is average cost and x is the size of plant.[5] It implies the equation of total cost (T) to be:

$$T = ax^2 + bx + c,$$

which gives a linear marginal cost (M) equation, namely

$$M = 2ax + b$$

In some of the industries, a linear regression was found to be a much better fit, and the equation—

$$Y = b + ax$$

was fitted. In a few others, the value of the coefficient a was found to be so negligible that the term ax became superfluous in the explanation of cost variations; so, it was dropped and the equation

$$Y = b + \frac{c}{x}$$

was fitted. These average cost equations, all of which were found to be very good fits, are given in the statement below.

STATEMENT I

LONG-RUN AVERAGE COST FUNCTIONS IN 29 MANUFACTURING INDUSTRIES OF INDIA

Serial no. (1)	*Industry* (2)	*Average cost function* (3)	*Shape** (4)
1	Sewing machines	$Y = 76.6 + \frac{139}{x} + 0.003x$	L+
2	Starch	$Y = 76.0 + \frac{413}{x} + 0.020x$	U
3	Electric lamps	$Y = 80.4 + \frac{224}{x} - 0.005x$	L−
4	Electric fans	$Y = 81.9 + \frac{302}{x}$	L
5	Soap	$Y = 92.2 + \frac{130}{x} - 0.014x$	L−
6	Iron and steel	$Y = 92.6 - 0.003x$	S−
7	Wollen textiles	$Y = 89.5 + \frac{140}{x} - 0.003x$	L−
8	Bicycles	$Y = 82.5 + \frac{65}{x} - 0.003x$	L−
9	Matches	$Y = 71.4 + \frac{876}{x} + 0.004x$	U−
10	Paints and varnishes	$Y = 82.0 - 0.011x$	S−
11	Paper and paper-board	$Y = 73.6 + \frac{963}{x}$ or $Y = 72.8 + \frac{1002}{x} + 0.001x$	L

Statement continued overleaf.

[5] This equation is based on a hypothesis about the nature of cost-output relationship put forth by H. T. Davis in his *The Theory of Econometrics*, p. 125.

STATEMENT I (*Continued*)

Serial no. (1)	*Industry* (2)	*Average cost function* (3)	*Shape** (4)
12	Fruit and vegetable processing	$Y = 82.0+\frac{46}{x}+0.004x$	L+
13	Cement	$Y = 65.6+\frac{5622}{x}+0.005x$	U−
14	Ceramics	$Y = 78.4+\frac{348}{x}$ or $Y = 77.4+\frac{370}{x}+0.001x$	L
15	Biscuit-making	$Y = 89.2+\frac{143}{x}-0.031x$	L−
16	Plywood and tea-chests	$Y = 86.1+\frac{151}{x}-0.026x$	L−
17	Vegetable oils (edible)	$Y = 93.0+\frac{207}{x}-0.009x$	L−
18	Aluminium, copper and brass	$Y = 88.6-0.001x$	S
19	Distilleries and breweries	$Y = 67.8+\frac{349}{x}+0.009x$	U−
20	Chemicals	$Y = 73.9-0.0002x$	S
21	Glass and glassware	$Y = 89.2+\frac{130}{x}$	L
22	Tanning	$Y = 95.7+\frac{83}{x}-0.009x$	L−
23	Wheat flour	$Y = 91.9+\frac{54}{x}-0.003x$	L−
24	Cotton textiles	$Y = 89.7+\frac{273}{x}$ or $Y = 89.3+\frac{269}{x}+0.0002x$	L
25	Jute textiles	$Y = 94.4-0.0003x$	S
26	General and electrical engineering	$Y = 84.4+\frac{49}{x}-0.002x$	L−
27	Sugar	$Y = 85.0+\frac{124}{x}+0.001x$	L+
28	Vegetable oils (not edible)	$Y = 100.0-0.013x$	S−
29	Rice milling	$Y = 86.4+\frac{151}{x}+0.038x$	U

* U means U-shaped
U− means U-shaped, but with the rising arm being much flatter.
L+ means L-shaped, with a slightly rising leg. (The extent of rise being dependent upon the value of *a*.)
L means L-shaped, with a virtually horizontal leg i.e. a rectangular hyperbola with $Y = b$ as the base.
L− means L-shaped, with a slightly falling leg. (The extent of fall being dependent upon the value of *a*.)
S− means a slightly falling straight line.
S means a virtually horizontal straight line.

The shape of this average cost function depends on the magnitudes and signs of coefficients a and c. The coefficient c in all the functions here, if it exists, is positive. The shape of the curve would be dominated by the magnitude of c in the earlier or smaller size-range, and by the magnitude of a in the latter or larger size-range. As the term $\frac{c}{x}$ represents a rectangular hyperbola, the smaller the value of c, the greater would be the extent of L-ness in the shape of the curve. The magnitude and sign of a in the term ax, which gives us a straight line, would determine the extent of rise or fall of the latter part of the curve. Hence, if both a and c are positive and of good magnitudes, the function would be U-shaped. This is the case in only two industries here, namely starch and rice-milling. If a is of a comparatively smaller magnitude, the function would still be U-shaped, but with the rising arm being comparatively flatter than the falling arm. Only three industries in this statement—cement, matches, and distilleries and breweries—illustrate this case. Again, if a as well as c is of a much smaller magnitude, the function would be L-shaped with a slightly rising leg (the extent of rise being directly dependent on the value of a). Such a shape is to be found again in only three industries, viz., sewing machines, fruit and vegetable processing, and sugar. The marginal cost function in all these cases is a rising straight line, the rate of rise being equal to a. If the term ax is superfluous due to an altogether negligible value of a, we have a rectangular-hyperbolic function ($Y = b + \frac{c}{x}$), which gives us an L-shaped curve with a virtually horizontal leg, asymptotic to the horizontal marginal cost function ($MC = b$). This curious type of function exists in five industries, viz., electric fans, paper and paperboard, ceramics, glass and glassware, and cotton textiles. Further, a *negative a* with a positive c would also give us an L-shaped curve, but with a falling leg (the extent of fall being directly related to the value of a). This shape occurs in as many as ten industries, viz: electric lamps, soap, woollen textiles, bicycles, biscuit-making, plywood and tea-chests, vegetable oils (edible), wheat flour, tanning, and general and electrical engineering. In the remaining six industries the function is a straight line, falling slightly in the case of iron and steel, paints and varnishes, and vegetable oils (not edible), and virtually horizontal in the case of chemicals, jute-textiles, and aluminium, copper and brass.

Thus, a U-shaped long-run average cost curve exists in only five industries out of a sample of twenty-nine manufacturing industries of India. And, we find an L-shaped curve in as many as eighteen of them, out of which only three industries reveal a slightly rising leg of the L. In three of the industries, there exists a slightly falling straight line function, whereas in the remaining three, a virtually horizontal straight line function has been observed. This majority of L-shaped and straight line functions in Indian industries corroborates the findings in other countries. But, it does not in any case rule out the possibility of a U-shaped long-run plant-average-cost curve in some of the industries in a country.

II. CONCENTRATION AND EFFICIENCY

Concentration of productive power in the hands of a few units in an industry is generally lamented on the ground of the loss of competition. The higher the concentration-ratio (defined here as the percentage of total industrial employment accounted for by the largest four units) in an industry, the higher would be the degree of monopoly and absence of competition. But, the tremendous progress made in the recent past in the fields of technology, finance and management has substantially raised the optimum size of a plant in almost every manufacturing industry, with the result that a comparatively smaller number of optimum or most efficient plants is sufficient to meet the total industry-demand. The objective of efficiency, therefore, necessitates some degree of concentration in an industry. Let us call it 'optimum concentration-ratio', defined as the percentage of total industrial employment accounted for by four optimum units. A comparison of the actual concentration-ratio with the optimum concentration-ratio would give us the extent of concentration which cannot be justified on the grounds of efficiency.

Estimation of the 'optimum concentration-ratio' in an industry involves the intricate problem of determining the optimum unit size. Engineers' estimates would be the best; but they are very difficult to come by. The next best method is to utilize the long-run average cost functions for this purpose. The function fitted by us would give the optimum plant size when it has a minimum value (i.e. at $x = \sqrt{\frac{c}{a}}$), which is possible only in those cases in which both a and c are positive. In others in which a or c is either negative or negligible, the function is constantly falling and has got no minimum value. In these industries the largest existing plant should be considered to be the optimum plant. Here, we have taken the average size of plants lying in the largest size-group to be the optimum plant size in such cases. But, in five such industries, it was found that the average cost was much smaller in the second largest size-group than in the largest one. In these industries, therefore, the average plant size in the second largest size-group was taken to be the optimum plant size.[6] The statement below gives these optimum plant sizes, optimum plant concentration-ratios, actual plant concentration-ratios, and a comparison between the two:

STATEMENT II

THE COMPARISON OF ACTUAL CONCENTRATION-RATIO WITH OPTIMUM CONCENTRATION-RATIO IN 29 MANUFACTURING INDUSTRIES OF INDIA, 1958

Serial no. (1)	*Industry* (2)	*Optimum plant size (number of workers)* (3)	*Actual concentration ratio* (4)	*Optimum concentration ratio* (5)	*Extent of unnecessary concentration (for optimum efficiency)* (6) = (4) − (5)	*Percentage of concentration not justified by optimum efficiency* (7) = (6) × 100 / (4)	*Total industry size (number of workers)* (8)
1	Sewing machines	215	88.5	16.0	72.5	81.9	5433
2	Starch	460	86.4	89.0	−2.6	−3.0	2048
3	Electric lamps	766	79.4	110.8	−31.4	−39.6	2761
4	Electric fans	1755	73.2	145.2	−72.0	−98.4	4831
5	Soap	1386	71.7	93.2	−21.5	−30.0	5959
6	Iron and steel	16222	69.6	69.6	0.0	0.0	93283
7	Woollen textiles	1076	51.5	25.2	26.3	51.1	17163
8	Bicycles	1633	47.9	54.0	−6.1	−12.7	12096
9	Matches	500	46.9	14.0	32.9	70.1	14432
10	Paints and varnishes	791	43.5	57.6	−14.1	−32.4	5495
11	Paper and paper-board	1286	36.5	14.4	22.1	60.5	35861
12	Fruit and vegetable	102	35.5	22.4	13.1	36.9	1836
13	Cement	1036	33.2	14.4	18.8	56.6	28534
14	Ceramics	616	32.7	9.6	23.1	70.7	25580
15	Biscuit-making	525	32.6	38.0	−5.4	−16.6	5543
16	Plywood and tea-chests	405	31.2	24.4	6.8	21.8	6682
17	Vegetable oils (edible)	618	29.2	29.2	0.0	0.0	8437
18	Aluminium, copper	636	27.1	9.4	17.7	65.3	24862
	and brass	636	27.1	9.4	17.7	65.3	24862
19	Distilleries and breweries	198	22.5	15.2	7.3	32.4	5204
20	Chemicals	2104	21.6	13.2	8.4	38.9	64210
21	Glass and glassware	615	17.9	9.6	8.3	46.4	25516
22	Tanning	609	17.4	29.2	−11.8	−67.8	8338
23	Wheat flour	332	16.8	16.8	0.0	0.0	7949
24	Cotton textiles	1102	9.4	0.6	8.8	93.6	712069
25	Jute textiles	5868	9.2	9.2	0.0	0.0	253880
26	General and electrical engineering	5533	8.0	10.8	−2.8	−35.0	208150
27	Sugar	370	6.8	1.0	5.8	85.3	134358
28	Vegetable oils (not edible)	785	5.1	7.6	−2.5	−49.0	40974
29	Rice-milling	63	1.3	0.5	0.8	61.5	59075

[6] In a similar study ('Economies of Scale, Concentration and Conditions of Entry in Twenty Manufacturing Industries', in *American Economic Review*, Vol. 44, March 1954, pp. 15–39), Joe S. Bain regards the average plant size in the largest size-group as an

It is evident from the statement that in four out of the six high concentration industries (that is, with a concentration-ratio above 60 per cent), *optimum* efficiency justified not only the existing extent of concentration, but also a still higher degree of concentration, as the optimum concentration-ratio in these industries is higher than the actual concentration-ratio. As a matter of fact, there should be existing only about four, or even less than four, optimum plants in all these four industries (viz., starch, electric lamps, electric fans and soap), because the optimum concentration-ratio in them is either about 100 per cent or even more than that. In the iron and steel industry, both the concentration-ratios are exactly equal, so that the existing degree of concentration is fully justified on the basis of optimum efficiency. It is in the sewing-machine industry that the optimum concentration-ratio is much smaller than the actual one, and about 82 per cent of the existing concentration-ratio is not justified by optimum efficiency.

Out of the ten medium concentration industries (that is, with a concentration-ratio above 30 per cent and below 60 per cent), existing concentration can be justified by efficiency in only three. In five out of the other seven industries, the extent of concentration not justified on the ground of optimum efficiency is above 50 per cent. Then, out of the remaining thirteen low concentration industries, optimum efficiency justifies present concentration in only six. The extent of unjustifiable concentration is more than 50 per cent in four out of the other seven of them. Thus, the objective of optimum efficiency justifies much of the existing extent of concentration in a majority of these industries.[7]

All this analysis of concentration and efficiency has been made with reference to the *optimum* plant size at the *optimum* efficiency. It may, however, be interesting as well as useful to make a study with reference to a *minimum optimal* plant size at a *reasonable level* of

[7] One important fact should, however, be noted, that in thirteen out of the fourteen industries in which the existing degree of concentration is either fully or even more than fully justified by optimum efficiency, we have a constantly falling long-run average cost curve. In fact, actual concentration should be fully justified by efficiency in all the eighteen industries with a constantly falling average cost curve. But here it is not so in the other five such industries, because we had taken the average plant size in the *second largest* (rather than the largest) size-group as the optimum plant size.

effective estimate of the optimum plant, on the ground that as soon as the average cost in a plant tends to rise, the firm would build another plant rather than expand the old one. Thus, he denies the existence of plants larger than the optimum ones. But, there is more than one reason for the existence of plants of a larger size (see P. J. D. Wiles, op. cit., pp. 209–12). Our empirical study also shows that plants in the largest size-group are comparatively less efficient in those industries in which the average cost function has some minimum value, and in these five other industries also. Hence, the method adopted by Professor Bain to estimate the optimum plant size on the basis of cross-sectional industrial data is not correct for quite a few industries.

efficiency also. Let us take only 1 per cent level of inefficiency as the reasonable level of efficiency. It is equal to the minimum average cost at the optimum plant size, plus its 1 per cent. The size of plant at this level of average cost may be called the 'minimum optimal plant' at a 'reasonable level' of efficiency (or at 1 per cent level of inefficiency). It can be easily calculated from the average cost function. At this average cost level, moreover, a 'maximum optimal plant size' would also be found, if the average cost function has a positive *a* so that it starts rising after a point. The percentage of total industry employment accounted for by four 'minimum optimal plants' has been termed as the 'minimum optimal concentration-ratio'. It indicates the minimum necessary extent of concentration for a reasonable level of efficiency. The statement below gives these minimum and maximum optimal plant sizes, actual and minimum optimal concentration-ratios, and a comparison between these two concentration-ratios (see Statement III on p. 66).

Now, the existing extent of concentration is justified by 'reasonable' efficiency in only three high concentration industries, two medium concentration industries, and three low concentration industries. Thus, 'reasonable' efficiency justifies existing concentration in only eight industries, whereas 'optimum' efficiency does so in fourteen industries. Out of the remaining twenty-one industries, the percentage of actual concentration not justified by 'reasonable' efficiency is above 80 per cent in twelve industries, and between 50 and 80 per cent in seven industries. The corresponding figures for the percentage of actual concentration not justified by 'optimum' efficiency are only three and seven again. Hence, if we are ready to tolerate just 1 per cent inefficiency, much of the existing extent of concentration in most of the industries cannot be justified on the ground of reasonable efficiency.

III. BARRIERS TO ENTRY

In his book *Barriers to New Competition*, Professor Bain has given the following three types of barriers to entry[8] due to the existence of economies of scale:

(A) 'The deterrent to entry will tend to increase as . . . the minimum optimal scale becomes a larger proportion of total industry output' (p. 55). If the minimum optimal plant size constitutes

[8] Professor Bain views the barriers to entry from the angle of the extent to which *established sellers* can raise their prices above the minimum attainable average cost without attracting newcomers into the industry. But, he does not make it explicit as to how these barriers discourage the *newcomer*. This is what we have attempted in terms of their weakening effect on the 'inducement to enter'.

a significant proportion (say 5 per cent or more) of the total industry size, entry will have the result of either a lower price for all the producers, or a higher average cost for the entrant or for all of them. The price would be lower, either because the established

STATEMENT III

THE COMPARISON OF ACTUAL CONCENTRATION-RATIO WITH MINIMUM OPTIMAL CONCENTRATION-RATIO IN 29 MANUFACTURING INDUSTRIES OF INDIA, 1958

*Industry serial no.**	*Minimum optimal plant size (at 1 per cent level of inefficiency)*	*Maximum optimal plant size (at 1 per cent level of inefficiency)*	*Actual concentration ratio*	*Minimum optimal concentration-ratio (at 1 per cent level of inefficiency)*	*Extent of unnecessary concentration (for reasonable efficiency)*	*Percentage of concentration not justified by reasonable efficiency*
(1)	(2)	(3)	(4)	(5)	(6) = (4) − (5)	$(7) = \frac{(4)-(5)}{(4)} \times 100$
1	75	610	88.5	5.6	82.9	93.7
2	42	508	86.4	8.8	77.7	89.8
3	625	—	79.4	90.4	−11.0	−13.9
4	304	—	73.2	24.8	48.4	66.1
5	1324	—	71.7	88.8	−17.1	−23.8
6	16065	—	69.6	68.8	0.8	1.1
7	751	—	51.5	17.6	33.9	65.8
8	1521	—	47.9	50.4	−2.5	−5.2
9	263	952	46.9	7.2	39.7	84.6
10	724	—	43.5	52.8	−9.3	−21.4
11	474	3333	36.5	5.2	31.3	85.7
12	29	364	35.5	6.4	29.1	82.0
13	716	1511	33.2	10.0	23.2	69.9
14	205	1808	32.7	3.2	29.5	90.2
15	195	—	32.6	14.0	18.6	57.1
16	377	—	31.2	22.4	8.8	28.2
17	525	—	29.2	24.8	4.4	15.4
18	—	—	27.1	1.0	26.1	96.3
19	106	370	22.5	8.2	14.3	63.6
20	—	—	21.6	0.6	21.0	97.2
21	118	—	17.9	1.8	16.1	90.0
22	514	—	17.4	24.8	−7.4	−42.5
23	116	—	16.8	6.6	10.8	64.3
24	203	6608	9.4	0.1	9.3	98.9
25	2151	—	9.2	3.4	5.8	63.0
26	5020	—	8.0	9.6	−1.6	−20.0
27	86	1594	6.8	0.3	6.5	95.6
28	713	—	5.1	6.8	−1.7	−33.3
29	35	116	1.3	0.3	1.0	76.9

* The serial number or order of industries is the same as in the previous statement.

firms do not want to have a new rival and they retaliate against his entry and establishment in the industry by reducing their prices, or because they do not cut down their outputs to make room for the entrant, and his additional supply lowers the price in the industry. The average cost would be higher for the newcomer, if he enters the industry at such a small and sub-optimal scale that the market-shares of the established firms are not visibly disturbed, and retaliation from their side is avoided. The average cost would rise for the established firms as well as the newcomer, even if the former are ready to cut their outputs to make a place for the latter, because the average cost curve is falling before the minimum optimal size. As a result of all or some of these factors, the post-entry profit-expectations of the newcomer would be much smaller than his pre-entry profit expectations. He knows it, when he is contemplating entry, and hence the inducement to enter is considerably weakened. This has been called the 'percentage effect' of scale economies.

(B) 'The deterrent to entry will tend to increase as . . . the rise of unit costs becomes steeper as scale is reduced below the minimum optimal scale' (p. 55). It would be so only when the minimum optimal plant constitutes a significant proportion of the total industry size. Because, if the newcomer enters the industry at this significant scale, the demand-curves of the established firms would be considerably pushed leftwards, and their outputs would be significantly cut down. Accordingly, the steeper is the average cost curve before the minimum optimal scale, the higher would become their average cost, the greater would be the cut in their profits due to entry, the more strongly they would retaliate against the entry and establishment of the newcomer, and the weaker, therefore, would be the 'inducement to enter'. Even if the entrant secures an equal share of the market without facing any retaliation, he has to start production at a scale less than the minimum optimal one, with the result that the steeper is the average cost curve, the higher would be his average cost, and the weaker would be the 'inducement to enter'. Neither of these effects would be there, if the minimum optimal scale at which the entry has got to be made constitutes only an insignificant proportion of the total industry size. Thus, the steepness of the average cost curve, or the importance of the economies of scale, as a barrier to entry is incumbent upon the 'percentage-effect' of scale-economies; the former simply accentuates the latter.

(C) The absolute capital requirements for starting a plant of the minimum optimal size in an industry 'may be so large that relatively few individuals or groups could secure the needed capital, or that the entrants could secure it only at interest rates and other terms which placed them at a net cost disadvantage to established sellers' (p. 55). This, has been termed as the 'absolute capital requirement effect' of the economies of scale.

Then he puts forth the hypothesis of a positive association of the rate of profit with the height of these barriers to entry. The rate of profit is likely to be higher in those industries in which these barriers to entry are persistently high, and particularly so if a high concentration-ratio also supports it through tacit or overt collusion. A positive association, therefore, can be expected between the profit rate, the importance of these barriers to entry, and the concentration-ratio. But, 'the profit-rates of smaller firms, with inefficiently small plants or firm scales, . . . might be expected to show a less certain or distinct relationship to a condition of entry calculated primarily with reference to the positions of the dominant firms. Thus the profit rates of the dominant firms alone provide the most acceptable data for testing the hypothesis in question' (pp. 190–1). We have attempted below to estimate the extent of these barriers to entry, and to test this hypothesis on Indian data.

With the help of the average cost functions, we have already estimated the minimum optimal plant sizes at a 'reasonable' efficiency level (i.e. at 1 per cent inefficiency level). Expressing this as a percentage of the total industry size would give us the relative market size of the minimum optimal plant in an industry. It is an estimate of the 'percentage effect' of scale-economies as a barrier to entry. Then, multiplying this minimum optimal plant size (which is in terms of employment) by the capital-labour ratio of that size-group in which it falls, we get an estimate of the 'absolute capital requirement effect' of scale-economies as a barrier to entry in an industry. And, a simple measure has been devised in order to estimate the steepness of the average cost curve as a barrier to entry. The steeper is the average cost curve, the smaller would be the relative difference between the *optimum* plant size and the *minimum optimal* plant size (at 1 per cent level of inefficiency). Hence, we get a rough measure (suitable for our purpose) of the degree of steepness of the average cost curve by dividing the latter by the former plant size. It has been termed as the 'coefficient of steepness' of the average cost curve. The statement below gives these estimates of the barriers to entry due to scale-economies, the profit-rates of the four largest or dominant plants, and the actual concentration-ratios in the same manufacturing industries of India (see Statement IV).

Let us make the following attributive classification of these three barriers to entry, and of the profit-rate and concentration-ratio also:

(a) Relative industry-size of the minimum optimal plant as a barrier to entry: high if above 20 per cent, medium if 10–20 per cent, and low if 5–10 per cent. (b) Coefficient of steepness of the average cost curve as a barrier to entry: very high if above 0.9, high if 0.8–0.9, and medium if 0.7–0.8. (c) Absolute capital requirements for a minimum optimal plant as a barrier to entry: extremely high if above Rs 1000 lakhs, very high if 250–1000 lakhs, high if 100–250 lakhs, medium if 50–100 lakhs, and low if 30–50 lakhs. (d) The rate

STATEMENT IV

ESTIMATION OF BARRIERS TO ENTRY DUE TO ECONOMIES OF SCALE IN 29 MANUFACTURING INDUSTRES OF INDIA, 1958

Serial no. (1)	*Industry* (2)	*Relative market-size of the minimum optimal plant* (3)	*Coefficient of steepness of the AC curve* (4)	*Capital-requirements for the minimum optimal plant size* (Rs Lakhs) (5)	*Rate of profit in four largest plants* (6)	*Actual concentration-ratio* (7)
1	Sewing machines	1.4	0.35	3.4	15.8	88.5
2	Starch	2.2	0.09	0.9	11.7	86.4
3	Electric lamps	22.6	0.82	39.5	16.3	79.4
4	Electric fans	6.2	0.17	37.9	13.6	73.2
5	Soap	22.2	0.96	252.2	27.0	71.7
6	Iron and steel	17.2	0.99	4051.9	31.7	69.6
7	Woollen textiles	4.4	0.70	60.2	22.6	51.5
8	Bicycles	12.6	0.93	182.5	21.6	47.9
9	Matches	1.8	0.53	12.1	17.0	46.9
10	Paints and varnishes	13.2	0.92	85.2	34.1	43.5
11	Paper and paper-board	1.3	0.37	27.2	24.4	36.5
12	Fruit and vegetable processing	1.6	0.28	1.8	19.8	35.5
13	Cement	2.5	0.69	172.6	14.2	33.2
14	Ceramics	0.8	0.33	6.5	22.9	32.7
15	Biscuit-making	3.5	3.7	20.6	26.5	32.6
16	Plywood and tea-chests	5.6	0.93	31.3	24.4	31.2
17	Vegetable oils (edible)	6.2	0.85	100.5	10.5	29.2
18	Aluminium, copper and brass	0.1	0.00	2.5	17.1	27.1
19	Distilleries and breweries	2.1	0.54	9.1	27.8	22.5
20	Chemicals	0.1	0.00	0.2	15.9	21.6
21	Glass and glassware	0.5	0.19	2.6	15.4	17.9
22	Tanning	6.2	0.84	30.9	10.0	17.4
23	Wheat flour	1.5	0.35	10.1	7.0	16.8
24	Cotton textiles	0.03	0.18	17.6	10.0	9.4
25	Jute textiles	0.9	0.37	67.4	7.0	9.2
26	General and electrical engineering	2.4	0.91	435.9	15.0	8.0
27	Sugar	0.1	0.23	1.2	11.0	6.8
28	Vegetable oils (not edible)	1.7	0.91	10.1	5.6	5.1
29	Rice-milling	0.1	0.56	1.2	3.0	1.3

of profit in the four largest plants: very high if above 30 per cent, high if 20–30 per cent, medium if 10–20 per cent, and low if below 10 per cent. (e) Concentration-ratio: high if above 60 per cent, medium if 30–60 per cent, and low if below 30 per cent. On the basis of these arbitrary classifications, the statement below presents a summary of the barriers to entry along with the profit-rate and concentration-ratio in those industries in which such barriers exist.

STATEMENT V

SUMMARY OF THE BARRIERS TO ENTRY DUE TO SCALE-ECONOMIES AS THEY EXIST IN 13 (OUT OF 29) MANUFACTURING INDUSTRIES OF INDIA, 1958

Serial no.	*Industry*	*Relative industry size of the minimum optimal plant*	*Coefficient of steepness of the AC curve*	*Absolute capital requirements for the minimum optimal plant*	*Rate of profit in the largest four plants*	*Actual concentration ratio*
(1)	(2)	(A)	(B)	(C)	(3)	(4)
1	Electric lamps	High	High	Low	Medium	High
2	Electric fans	Low	—	Low	Medium	High
3	Soap	High	Very high	Very high	High	High
4	Iron and steel	Medium	Very high	Extremely high	Very high	High
5	Woollen textiles	—	—	Medium	High	Medium
6	Bicycles	Medium	Very high	High	High	Medium
7	Paints and varnishes	Medium	Very high	Medium	Very high	Medium
8	Cement	—	—	High	Medium	Medium
9	Plywood and tea-chests	Low	Very high	Low	High	Medium
10	Vegetable oils (edible)	Low	High	High	Medium	Low
11	Tanning	Low	High	Low	Medium	Low
12	Jute textiles	—	—	Medium	Low	Low
13	General and electrical engineering	—	—	Very high	Medium	Low

Type A barrier exists in nine industries, out of which it is highly supported by type B barrier in as many as eight industries, and type C barrier is faced in thirteen industries. These barriers are very high and strong in the iron and steel and the soap industries, in which the concentration-ratio as well as the rate of profit is also high. Then, these barriers are fairly high in the electric lamps, bicycles, and edible vegetable oils industries, out of which the rate of profit is high in one and medium in two, but the concentration-ratio is high in the first, medium in the second and low in the third industry. In the paints and varnishes industry, these barriers are not so high, but the rate of profit is very high. Out of the four industries in which A and B type barriers do not exist, type C barrier is high and strong in the cement and general and electrical engineering industries, and medium in the woollen and jute textile industries. In the remaining three industries, viz: electric fans, plywood and tea-chests, and tanning, these barriers are low in general.

Finally, we come to the test of the above-mentioned hypothesis regarding a positive and significant association of each one of these three barriers to entry with the profit-rate of the dominant firms or plants, and also with the concentration-ratio. These six coefficients of correlation (and also of attributive association) were calculated on the basis of the information contained in statement IV above. All of them came out to be positive, but small and insignificant. But, the hypothesis relating to the association between any one of these barriers to entry and the profit-rate of the dominant units seems to be perfectly tenable on *a priori* grounds. A high barrier to entry does provide the leading established firms in an industry with a power to fix the price at a comparatively higher level. The fact may, however, be that the accounting profit-rate data as given in the Census do not give us an estimate of the true 'theoretical' rate of profit,[9] on the basis of which this hypothesis should be checked. Hence, the hypothesis cannot be rejected on the basis of these insignificant correlation-coefficients. A very rigorous and sensitive method of calculating the 'theoretical' rate of profit has got to be developed and used, in order to test this hypothesis. As to the hypothesis regarding the association between any one of these barriers to entry and the concentration-ratio, it can be easily rejected on the basis of these insignificant correlation-coefficients; because, the height of a barrier to entry at present should be expected to be negatively associated with the *changes* in concentration-ratio in near future, rather than with the present concentration-ratio which is a result of the circumstances operating in the past.

CONCLUSIONS

The main conclusions emerging from this investigation may be summarized as below:

(a) The long-run average cost curve is U-shaped in only five out of twenty-nine manufacturing industries of India. It is L-shaped in as many as eighteen of them, out of which only three industries possess a slightly rising leg of the L. In six of them, it is linear—slightly falling in three, and virtually horizontal in the other three. Thus, economies of scale exist, and diseconomies of scale do not exist, in a majority of them. This corroborates the findings in many industries in other countries also.

(b) The requirements of optimum efficiency fully justify the existing extent of concentration in about half of these industries, particularly so in (five out of six) high concentration industries. But, the requirements of a 'reasonable' level of efficiency (i.e. 1 per cent level of inefficiency) justify the existing extent of concentration in about

[9] It may be so due to many reasons. See Joe S. Bain, *Industrial Organization*.

only one-third of all these industries, and in half of the high concentration industries. Hence, if we want efficiency in production and distribution, the present degree of concentration and monopoly power cannot be avoided in most of the industries in which it exists significantly.

(c) The three types of barriers to entry due to the presence of scale-economies exist in thirteen out of these twenty-nine industries. The 'percentage effect' of scale-economies as a barrier to entry is high in two, medium in three, and low in four industries. It is supported by a very high 'coefficient of steepness' of the average cost curve as a barrier to entry in all these nine industries. The 'absolute capital requirement effect' of scale-economies as a barrier to entry is very high in three, high in three, medium in three, and low in four of these industries. On the whole, these barriers to entry are not very strong in more than six or seven industries.

(d) The height of none of these barriers to entry was found to be significantly correlated or associated either with the 'accounting' rate of profit in the largest four plants, or with the actual concentration-ratio. This does not, however, enable us to reject or accept the hypothesis of a strong positive association between the rate of profit and the height of these barriers to entry.

PANJAB UNIVERSITY, CHANDIGARH

SALES REVENUE MAXIMIZATION—A NOTE*

by LEONARD WAVERMAN

I

IN the April 1967 *Journal of Industrial Economics*, Marshall Hall tests the hypothesis that a firm maximizes sales revenue subject to its profit rate being above some critical level.[1]

The hypothesis can be interpreted as saying that when profits are above (below) this minimal acceptable level, the firm will consciously attempt to increase (decrease) sales revenue.

The test that Hall runs is elegant in its simplicity. If the effects on output decisions of all the factors other than profits are netted out, and if the change in profits is measured from a minimal profit constraint, then the hypothesis is verified by a positive relation between sales and the change in profits ($\alpha_{ijt} > 0$).[2]

The results of the test would appear to disprove the sales revenue maximization hypothesis. The α_{ijt} coefficients are not consistently positive. In fact, the coefficients alternate in sign as the lag increases.

It is this author's contention that the test results are ambiguous for three reasons. Hall's procedure does not remove the effects on sales revenue of exogenous variables other than profits. It therefore

* The author wishes to thank Professor R. W. Crandall for helpful criticism. Errors belong solely to the author.

[1] M. Hall, 'Sales Revenue Maximization: An Empirical Explanation', *Journal of Industrial Economics*, April 1967, pp. 143–6.

[2] The model represented here reproduces that of Professor Hall, except for a slight change in notation.

$$\Delta S_{ijt} = \sum_{T=t}^{t-3} \alpha_{ijt}\, \Delta\overline{P}_{ijT} + \sum_{T=t}^{t-2} \beta_{JT} \frac{Q_J(T)}{Q_J(T-1)} + \sum_{T=t}^{t-1} \gamma_{ijT}\, \Delta A_{ijT} + V61 + V62 + C \qquad (1)$$

$$\Delta\overline{P}_{ijt} = \frac{P_{ijt}}{A_{ijt}} - \overline{P}_j \qquad (2)$$

ΔS_{ijt} = The change in sales of the ith firm in the jth industry between periods t and t−1.

P_{ijt} = Accounting profits of the ith firm in the jth industry in the tth year.

A_{ijt} = Assets of the ith firm in the jth industry in the tth year.

ΔA_{ijt} = A_{ijt} minus $A_{ij(t-1)}$.

$\overline{P}_j$ = The industry mean profit to asset rate for those firms in the sample, 1958–62 (the minimal acceptable profit rate).

$\frac{Q_{JT}}{Q_J(T-1)}$ = The Federal Reserve Index of industrial production for the jth industry in the tth year divided by the index of the previous year. This was the proxy for variations in industry demand.

V61 = Dummy variable that has the value 1 for all observations in 1961, zero elsewhere.

V62 = Dummy variable that has the value 1 for all observations in 1962, zero elsewhere.

The variations in V61, V62 and the constant account for variations in sales peculiar to each year.

cannot differentiate between alternative maximization hypotheses. The minimal profit constraint is not well formulated. Therefore, deviations from it as measured do not necessarily show disequilibrium conditions which will induce a change in long-run sales revenue. The use of accounting profits instead of real profits in a single stage least squares format may result in a regression bias of unknown direction and magnitude. Finally, an heuristic attempt is made to explain the test results.

II

Consider a firm which is in disequilibrium in period t, meaning that its profit rate is above the equilibrium profit rate. Hall correctly suggests that if sales revenue increases in period $t+\eta$, to conclude that the firm is of the Baumol type, one must first remove the effects on sales revenue of all variables other than profits. For example, if an increase in demand accounts for all the revenue increase, then we cannot conclude that the firm is a sales revenue maximizer, for a profit maximizer may also increase sales revenue when demand rises. To the extent then that Hall's independent variables do not absorb these effects, his test cannot distinguish between alternative maximization hypotheses.

The problem unfortunately is even more complex. The model must also specify the exogenous variables which induce the change in profits. To understand this point, visualize a case where the increase in profits above the equilibrium level is caused by a decrease in the price of labor. One would then expect a profit maximizing firm, as well as a sales revenue maximizer, to expand output. However, both the initial profit increase and subsequent sales changes are themselves caused by the change in a third exogenous variable. These exogenous effects must be eliminated in order to discriminate between maximization hypotheses in a cause and effect model.

Hall explicitly removes the influence on sales revenue of variations in industry demand[3] by including as an independent variable the changes in the Federal Reserve index of production for that industry. Dummy variables are introduced (one for each industry for each of three years), to absorb the effects of all other exogenous variables. This procedure is grossly inadequate. One single industry dummy cannot remove the effects of changes in factor prices, factor productivity, tariffs and advertising. The exclusion of exogenous variables which are correlated with the change in profits biases the parameter

[3] Since the firms examined are the major firms in highly concentrated industries, they tend to dominate the production indexes, and positive parameters β_{JT} may show correlation without causation.

estimates (the α_{ijt}). '... it often happens that omission of an important exogenous variable entails serious error. It leads us wrongfully to attribute to the variables which have been included some of the influence due to the omitted variable.'[4]

The parameter bias greatly impairs the ability of the test to distinguish between alternative hypotheses.

III

In the model, all the firms in an industry are pictured as operating with the same profit constraint. This constraint rate is computed as the 5-year mean of past actual profit rates for firms in the industry sample.

Hall places firms into an industry according to the 3 digit Standard Industrial Classification. This gross grouping includes in the petroleum products industry for 1962, Standard Oil of New Jersey and Ashland Refining, one-fiftieth its size. Included in the motor vehicles and parts industry are giant General Motors (1962 sales of $14,640,241,000) and Kelsey Hayes Wheel (1962 sales of $189,792,000). In the electrical machinery industry, diversified General Electric is combined with specialist I-T-E. In non-ferrous metals, the Aluminum Company of America is included with Phelps Dodge (copper).

It is far fetched to suggest that companies which differ vastly in all aspects of their operation—size, products, processes, and resource ownership—operate under the same profit constraint merely because their principle products fall under the same broad generic title.

Even where the firms in the grouping ostensibly produce the same line of products with the same production techniques, it is improbable that the mean of all their past profit rates represents a meaningful constraint for an individual firm. Take the case of the automotive industry. Will a series of unprofitable years for American Motors *decrease* General Motors' minimal acceptable profit level? It is more likely that General Motors would feel free to raise its minimal profit constraint under these conditions, for the chances of A.M.C. retaliation are less. In the computing industry, does I.B.M. lower its profit rate constraint if its competitors are unsuccessful? It may be that the other firms in the computing industry view I.B.M.'s profit rate as their target rate because this represents the point at which they will all be equal.

If the profit constraint used by Hall is not the true constraint, then deviations from it do not represent conditions which will cause

[4] E. Malinvaud, *Statistical Methods of Econometrics* (Chicago, 1966), p. 264.

output changes. No systematic correlation would then be expected between these measured deviations and the change in sales.

IV

In a recent article, Marshall Hall and Leonard Weiss assert that the published profit figures of large corporations understate their true economic profit.[5]

If so, Hall should not utilize single stage least squares as his regression procedure, for such a procedure yields biased parameter estimates.[6]

The understatement in the profit figures does not result in a systematic bias in the parameter estimates.[7] The direction and magnitude of the bias cannot be established on theoretical grounds. Moreover, the estimates are inconsistent, i.e., the bias does not disappear as the sample size becomes infinitely large.

Unbiased estimates of the parameters requires the use of two stage least squares utilizing the method of instrumental variables.[8] The instrument must be a variable which is highly correlated with real profits and uncorrelated with the error in reported profits. Finding such an instrument is generally difficult, but until it is used the results are unacceptable.

V

The use of one parameter, the industry mean as the profit constraint assumes that *any* variance around this mean induces changes

[5] M. Hall, and L. Weiss, 'Firm Size and Profitability', *Review of Economics and Statistics*, August 1967, pp. 319–31.

[6] This footnote follows J. Johnston, *Econometric Methods* (1962) Chapter 6, pp. 148–76. Suppose that the true theoretical relation is

$$X = aY + e \qquad (1)$$

The error term e has zero expected value, a constant variance and is independent of Y and X. If Y were known, an application of single stage least squares on (1) would yield unbiased estimates of a.

Assume, however, that when we attempt to measure Y we get Z instead where

$$Z = Y + u \qquad (2)$$

Substituting (2) in (1)

$$X = aZ + v \qquad (3)$$

$$v = e - au \qquad (4)$$

Even if the errors u and e are independent, and u is independent of X and Y, the application of single stage least squares on (3) will yield biased estimates of a since v is not independent of Z.

$$E\{v[Z - E(Z)]\} = E[(e - au)u] = -a[\text{variance }(u)]$$

[7] If all firms consistently report x per cent of their true profit, no bias results from using single stage least squares. However, the observed regression parameter a always overstates the true parameter by the factor of 1/x.

[8] Since the instrument is constructed to be independent of the errors e and u, it essentially eliminates the covariance between the combined error term v and the independent variable Z.

in output. Firms in the real world probably desire a more permanent indicator on which to base policy decisions.

If a firm operates so as to maximize the present value of its assets, it may not operate so as to decrease output if profit temporarily falls. This is especially true of large firms in highly concentrated industries.

Consider, once again, the automotive industry. If General Motors suffers a decline in profits in period t, it will not, therefore, decrease sales in periods $t+1$ and $t+2$. Cars on the road are in effect advertising for the firm. If General Motors decreases output and some competitor increases his output, then General Motors has lost an advertising advantage.

Firms then may not decrease output when profits decrease within some accepted range.

TABLE I
PROFIT CHANGES, FORTUNE'S TOP 500

	Change in total net profits	
Year	*Direction*	*Amount**
1957–58	–	6.1%
1958–59	+	25.1%
1959–60	–	3.0%
1960–61	0	0%
1961–62	+	16.1%

$$* \frac{\text{Change in Profits Between Years t, t+1}}{\text{Total Profits, Year t}}$$

Source: *Fortune* magazine, relevant years.

If we analyze the changes in net reported profits of Fortune's 500 companies (Table I) for 1957–62 under the above assumption of continual sales expansion in the face of temporary profit declines, a regression of the change in sales on the change in profits (lagged) would yield parameters which change in sign.

MASSACHUSETTS INSTITUTE OF TECHNOLOGY

SALES REVENUE MAXIMIZATION—REPLY

by MARSHALL HALL

MR. WAVERMAN has raised some interesting points about the validity of my analysis of the Baumol S.R.M. thesis. He finds my analysis deficient due to specification error and to measurement error and while I would welcome empirical research which seeks to take account of his comments I do not find the arguments he presents damaging to my analysis and conclusions. These two kinds of errors are valid reasons for condemning any econometric work and are also errors that it is impossible for any econometric researcher not to commit in some degree. A case for the relevance of these criticisms must, therefore, depend on proof that these errors are important and that they lead to 'known' (at least in direction) biases in the coefficients actually estimated [3, p. 265].

The specification error of which I am accused is the omission of important exogenous variables. Factor prices, factor productivity, tariff and advertising are the variables explicitly cited. My technique was to introduce either the industry variable, relative changes in the Federal Reserve Board index of industrial production, or industry and year dummy variables, to isolate the industry effects that are common across firms in a given industry. I would regard changes in factor prices as being roughly identical for firms in a given industry because the firms I analyzed are large firms from oligopolistic industries which means they face industry-wide wage bargaining in essence if not in fact. Moreover, given the laws against price discrimination and the absolute size of the firms studied it is unlikely that important differences in prices for the same factor could go undetected for very long.

Variations in factor productivity and advertising expenditures do not in any way affect my analysis. Greater factor productivity should mean higher factor prices and to the extent that this occurs it presents, of course, no problem to my method of analysis. If some firms succeed in earning a rent from underpaying their more productive factors this is reflected in profits which, if the firms are operating under the S.R.M. principle, would indicate *ceteris paribus* a desire for more sales. Baumol has explicitly discussed the role of advertising in his model and as he points out advertising expenditures are varied in response to departure from the constraint to either achieve the constraint or increase sales revenue [1, pp. 58–60]. Changes in advertising are in my study assumed to achieve their goal, hence, it is unnecessary to include advertising expenditures in the equations estimated [2, p. 144].

Tariff changes were not considered in my analysis as tariff changes were not particularly important in the period analyzed. The trade expansion act for example was enacted in October of 1962.

The measurement errors stressed by Mr. Waverman are my use of accounting rather than economic profits, and a bad measure of the profit constraint due to improper classification of firms into 3 digit S.I.C. industry groups, the use of a common profit constraint for all firms in a given industry, and my specification of the profit constraint in terms of only one parameter—the mean.

I plead guilty to the charge of using accounting rather than economic profits. I am, however, testing a model which explicitly seeks to relate firm behaviour and performance to a known and readily identifiable profit constraint. Since firms do not know and do not seek to know their economic profits its use in this paper would indeed be a measurement error. All of Mr. Waverman's comments in section IV are, therefore, irrelevant.

A stronger criticism, however, is my use of the same profit constraint for all firms in a given industry. I agree that this formulation has deficiences. My profit constraint, however, is based on Baumol's loose development of the constraint and I further tried to select firms and industries where it was most likely that my formulation would not be at variance with Baumol's concept of the profit constraint [2, p. 144]. I do not, therefore, think my formulation of the Baumol thesis does violence to Baumol's concept of the profit constraint although I would welcome other tests of the S.R.M. thesis based on alternative measures of the profit constraint.

Any grouping of large firms into industries, has serious limitations due to the high degree of product diversification that is now typical of large firms. If, however, it is necessary, to combine industry data with firm data or more fundamentally, to use the concept of an industry as a collection of firms then the S.I.C. three digit level is the best level at which to combine firms [4]. The central notion of an industry is high substitutability between its products, and the criticism that the firms I grouped together into an industry differ in size, resource ownership and type of process is largely irrelevant. Differences among firms in these variables are quite compatible with the firms being classed in the same industry. Even in the few specific examples mentioned by Mr. Waverman the products produced by the respective firms have a high cross elasticity of demand.

To the comment that I used the mean of the industry profit constraint and not a more sophisticated formulation I can only say that I was testing Baumol's thesis and his profit constraint is formulated as a constant and not as a constant $\pm$ some measure of the variance.

I do not, however, think the results would change if a range rather than a fixed constraint was introduced.

In the final section of his critique, Mr. Waverman presents a table which shows changes in profits increasing and decreasing while sales increased for the aggregate of Fortune's top 500 firms. He then states that a regression of the 'change in sales on the change in profits (lagged) would yield parameters which change in sign'. This it seems to me is consistent with my findings although given the level of aggregation I would not want to use these findings as evidence against the S.R.M. thesis.

WASHINGTON UNIVERSITY, ST. LOUIS

REFERENCES

[1] Baumol, W. J., *Business Behaviour, Value & Growth*, Harcourt, Brace and World, 1967.

[2] Hall, Marshall, 'Sales Revenue Maximization: An Empirical Examination', *The Journal of Industrial Economics*, April 1967.

[3] Malinvaud, E., *Statistical Methods of Econometrics*, Rand McNally, 1966.

[4] Stigler, George, *Capital and Rates of Return in Manufacturing Industries*, Princeton University, 1963.

[5] Waverman, Leonard, 'Sales Revenue Maximization—A Note', *Journal of Industrial Economics*.

PROFESSOR M. A. ADELMAN

THE editors wish to express their warm thanks to Professor Adelman, who for many years has carried out the arduous duties of doyen of our American editors, arranging for the reading of all manuscripts arising in North America.

The Journal, since its foundation in 1952, and indeed before in the planning stages, has always been a co-operative Anglo-American venture. Professor E. S. Mason was the American co-founding-father, if he will forgive that expression, and he assembled the first American board consisting of himself, Professor Joel Dean and Professor Richard Heflebower, all of whom we are proud still to have as members of our Board. The detailed American editorial work, once we were founded, was in the capable hands of Professor Heflebower, until he handed over to Professor Adelman in October 1958.

During the last decade the Journal has shown a steady growth year by year. We have been greatly indebted to Professor Adelman's care and interest, backed by the continuing work of Professor Heflebower, and indeed by all Professor Adelman's unnamed colleagues, notably at M.I.T., who have so willingly acted as unpaid readers for the Journal. We thank them all. The Journal has been enabled to retain its genuine Anglo-American flavour and interest, and the tradition that it is open to authors of any shade of opinion or orthodoxy, subject only to quality standards.

Professor Adelman has happily agreed to stay on our Board. He has handed over his role as doyen to Professor J. A. Menge. We are glad to welcome Professor Menge to the Board and ask that all manuscripts arising in North America should now in the first instance be sent to him at the Department of Economics, Dartmouth College, Hanover, New Hampshire 03755.

THE GENERAL EDITOR

OPTIMAL PLANT UNDER CONDITIONS OF RISK

by T. M. WHITIN[1]

G. STIGLER[2] has pointed out various problems of selecting an optimal plant when there is some uncertainty with respect to the level of competitive price. A different set of problems exist when there is uncertainty with respect to the amount that can be sold at a given price. It will be shown that the entrepreneur cannot select his optimal plant without explicit consideration of price, the probability distribution of demand, inventory level, and the discount rate. Indeed, an optimal dynamic *production policy* must be determined, indicating the optimal level of production for each level of initial inventory, before the optimal plant selection can be accomplished. The necessity of such a calculation points out the futility as well as the impossibility of separating the cost and demand components of economic analysis. Such a separation is futile if an optimization of profits that involves both aspects must be carried out before the cost component can be defined. Its impossibility is illustrated by numerical examples showing how the optimal plant varies in response to changes in the values of price, inventory, and the discount rate. It is incorrect to average costs over the probability distribution of demand as suggested by various authors.

The model constructed is a stationary dynamic model with an infinite time horizon, a specified price, a specified discount rate, and two different plants, represented by two extremely simple, discrete cost functions. Demand is represented by a simple discrete probability distribution. The optimal production policy for each cost function as well as the discounted value of expected profits corresponding to each cost function was calculated by the use of R. A. Howard's dynamic programming technique.[3] The entrepreneur is faced with a choice of two types of plant, one having a U-shaped average cost curve whose minimum contains the lowest possible average cost, while the other plant has a flatter cost curve with a higher minimum. The following example is a simple numerical illustration with the above properties. Although it is extremely oversimplified, the

[1] The initial draft of this article was written while the author was on a U.S. National Science Foundation Fellowship at the Netherlands School of Economics, Econometric Institute. Charles P. Whitin assisted with the computations.

[2] 'Production and Distribution in the Short Run', *Journal of Political Economy*, June 1939, pp. 305–27.

[3] *Dynamic Programming and Markov Processes*, Wiley, 1960. The use of Howard's policy improvement routine in a production-inventory context is explained in T. M. Whitin's 'Dynamic Programming Extensions to the Theory of the Firm', *Journal of Industrial Economics*, April 1968, pp. 81–98.

principles which it illustrates are valid for more complicated and realistic cases. The entrepreneur has two possible choices of 'plant', the relevant aspects of which are summarized in two average cost functions. One plant can produce any number of units at a constant average (and marginal) cost of \$1.90 per unit. The alternative plant can produce one, two, or three units at an average cost of \$2.60, \$1.50, or \$2.60 respectively. These plants are selected to give a somewhat exaggerated picture of Stigler's flexible plant and plant with a steeper U-shaped average cost curve with a lower minimum. The discount rate,[4] β, is 0.9; the price per unit sold is \$9; and the probability distribution of demand is that one unit is demanded with probability 1/4, two units with probability 1/2, and three units with probability 1/4. Four units was selected as the maximum ending inventory. The optimal policy for the first plant is to produce enough so that initial inventory plus production is three units. For the

TABLE I

(i, x)	*Ending inventory*						*Expected single-period payoff*
	0		*1*		*2*		
0, 3	21.3	1/4	12.3	1/2	3.3	1/4	12.3
1, 2	23.2	1/4	14.2	1/2	5.2	1/4	14.2
2, 1	25.1	1/4	16.1	1/2	7.1	1/4	16.1

alternative plant the optimal production policy is slightly more complicated, namely if initial inventory is zero, produce three units; if initial inventory is one, two or three units, produce two units; and if initial inventory is four, produce nothing. Tables I and II correspond to the constant cost plant and the U-shaped cost plant, respectively.

The left-hand border of each table, (i, x), represents the inventory and production policy. For example (1, 2) represents the policy, 'if initial inventory is 1 unit, produce 2 units'. The row bordering the top indicates the levels of ending inventory. The numbers in the right-hand side of each cell contain the probabilities for each possible level of ending inventory. For example, in Table I, the value of 1/4 found in the cell in the first ending inventory of 0 when initial inventory was 1 unit and production 2 units is 1/4. This is the probability that 3 units are demanded. The other numbers in the cells are the profits associated with the initial and ending inventories. For the cell

[4] $\beta = 1/1+r$ where r is the appropriate one-period interest rate.

just discussed the value of 23.2 indicates that a profit of $23.20 is incurred. The figure is the $27 revenue from selling 3 units minus the $3.80 cost of producing 2 units. The column on the far right is the expected pay-off in the current period. For the row labeled (1, 2) in Table I, the number 14.2 is obtained by multiplying the profits in each cell in the row by the associated probability in the cell and adding, i.e., 1/4 (23.2) + 1/2 (14.2) + 1/4 (5.2) = 14.2. The expected single-period profits corresponding to initial inventory i will be indicated by the symbol q_i. In the infinite-horizon, stationary model assumed, the discounted value of expected profits can be described as the immediate profits, q_i, plus the discounted value of profits in subsequent periods. Let V(i, x) represent the discounted value of expected profits when initial inventory is i and production x. Then for the constant cost case, one obtains:

$$\begin{aligned} V(0, 3) &= q_0 + \beta[\tfrac{1}{4}V(0, 3) + \tfrac{1}{2}V(1, 2) + \tfrac{1}{4}V(2, 1)] \\ (1)\quad V(1, 2) &= q_1 + \beta[\tfrac{1}{4}V(0, 3) + \tfrac{1}{2}V(1, 2) + \tfrac{1}{4}V(2, 1)] \\ V(2, 1) &= q_2 + \beta[\tfrac{1}{4}V(0, 3) + \tfrac{1}{2}V(1, 2) + \tfrac{1}{4}V(2, 1)] \end{aligned}$$

TABLE II

(i, x)	*Ending inventory*										*Expected single-period payoff*
	0		*1*		*2*		*3*		*4*		
0, 3	19.2	1/4	10.2	1/2	1.2	1/4					10.2
1, 2	24	1/4	15	1/2	6	1/4					15
2, 22			24	1/4	15	1/2	6	1/4			15
3, 2					24	1/4	15	1/2	6	1/4	15
4, 0			27	1/4	18	1/2	9	1/4			18

Substituting 12.3, 14.2, and 16.1 for q_0, q_1, and q_2 respectively and 0.9 for β gives the solution V(0, 3) = 140.10; V(1, 2) = 142.00, and V(2, 1) = 143.90.[5]

Note that V(1, 2) = V(0, 3) + 4.8 and V(4, 0) = V(2, 2) + 3.

For the U-shaped cost case, one obtains:

$$\begin{aligned} V(0, 3) &= 10.2 + 0.9[\tfrac{1}{4}V(0, 3) + \tfrac{1}{2}V(1, 2) + \tfrac{1}{4}V(2, 2)] \\ V(1, 2) &= 15 + 0.9[\tfrac{1}{4}V(0, 3) + \tfrac{1}{2}V(1, 2) + \tfrac{1}{4}V(2, 2)] \\ (2)\quad V(2, 2) &= 15 + 0.9[\tfrac{1}{4}V(1, 2) + \tfrac{1}{2}V(2, 2) + \tfrac{1}{4}V(3, 2)] \\ V(3, 2) &= 15 + 0.9[\tfrac{1}{4}V(2, 2) + \tfrac{1}{2}V(3, 2) + \tfrac{1}{4}V(4, 0)] \\ V(4, 0) &= 18 + 0.9[\tfrac{1}{4}V(1, 2) + \tfrac{1}{2}V(2, 2) + \tfrac{1}{4}V(3, 2)] \end{aligned}$$

[5] Here V(1, 2) = V(0, 3) + 1.9 and V(2, 1) = V(0, 3) + 3.8. On substituting these in the first equation the solution for V(0, 3) is easily obtained.

Making these substitutions and solving gives the solution: V(0, 3) = 140.36; V(1, 2) = 145.16; V(2, 2) = 147.78; V(3, 2) = 149.40; and V(4, 0) = 150.78. One can conclude from this that the optimal plant is the plant with the U-shaped cost curve since V(0, 3) for this plant exceeds V(0, 3) for the constant cost plant by $0.26.

To illustrate the influence of the discount factor, suppose the discount rate is raised, i.e. β is lowered, say, to 0.8. Then the resulting discounted expected values for the constant cost case are V(0, 3) = 69.10; V(1, 2) = 71.00; and V(2, 1) = 72.90. For the U-shaped case the production policy used above for $\beta = 0.9$ results in V(0, 3) = 67.42. However, profits can be increased by changing production policy to produce 2 units (instead of 3) when initial inventory is zero. On solving for the new production policy, one obtains V(0, 2) = 68.12, still $0.98 short of V(0, 3) for the constant cost plant.[6] Note, however, that the possession of a single unit of inventory could reverse this conclusion since V(1, 2) for the U-shaped plant exceeds V(1, 2) for the constant cost plant by $1.49. The intuitive explanation of this phenomenon is that initial inventory of 1 unit reduces the expected number of stockouts in the early periods. We shall henceforth focus on the comparisons for the zero stock starting conditions, although non-zero stocks could be highly relevant when considering plant changes at a later date. The reduction of the discount factor from 0.9 to 0.8 reversed the choice of plant from the U-shaped alternative to the constant cost alternative. Further reduction in the discount factor can change the optimal choice back again to the plant with the U-shaped curve. For example, if $\beta = 0$, the U-shaped alternative gives V(0, 2) = 12.75 while for the constant-cost plant V(0, 3) = 12.30, the expected single-period payoff. In summary, $\beta = 0.8$ leads to the choice of the constant-cost plant,[7] while $\beta = 0.9$ and $\beta = 0$ give more profits with the U-shaped cost curve.

Several authors have suggested averaging costs at various levels of output although they are not explicit concerning how the average is to be calculated.[8] If the average cost is calculated by averaging over the probability distribution of demand, the U-shaped plant gives an average cost of $2.05 and hence would never be preferred to the $1.90 constant cost plant. It is the contention of this paper that the relevant weights are obtainable *only after* optimal production policy has been determined.

[6] The remaining values in the solution for the U-shaped alternative were V(1, 2) = 72.49; V(2, 2) = 74.35; V(3, 2) = 75.57; and V(4, 0) = 77.35.

[7] Values of β between 0.4 and 0.8 also result in selection of the constant cost plant, while values below 0.4 result in the selection of the U-shaped plant.

[8] J. M. Clark, *The Economics of Overhead Cost*, Chicago 1923, p. 189 mentions striking a 'fair weighted average'. See also S. Weintraub, *Intermediate Price Theory*, Philadelphia, 1964, pp. 61–63.

The above example assumed a price of \$9.00. To show the effect of price on the choice of plant, consider a price of \$2.00 with the same probability distribution as in the above example, (i.e. probability 1/4, demand = 1, probability 1/2, demand = 2; and probability 1/4, demand = 3). Calculation shows the plant with the U-shaped cost curve to be preferable for all values of the discount rate. Indeed this plant would be preferable even if the constant cost plant produced at as low as \$1.52 per unit.[9] Thus, the advantage of the flexibility associated with constant costs is almost worthless at the \$2.00 price.

At the lower (\$2.00) price optimal policy differs considerably from optimal policy at the \$9.00 price. For example, for $\beta = 0.8$, the optimal production policy is to produce 2 units if initial inventory is either zero or one; otherwise produce nothing. Average production in this case is 11/6 unit per period,[10] one-sixth unit less than the average quantity demanded. The difference is accounted for by lost sales averaging one-sixth unit.[11]

It is a straightforward matter to include inventory carrying charges in the above model. The inclusion of such charges would increase the advantage of the constant cost plant over the U-shaped plant, since production at the minimum point of the average cost curve can be achieved only at the expense of holding inventory. The relevant inventory cost is subtracted from the profit value in each cell of the payoff tables. The model can also be extended to include any known interaction between inventory and sales, by appropriate adjustment of the payoff table.

In summary the above illustration shows that the selection of optimal plant depends on the price level, the probability distribution of demand, the discount rate, and the optimal production policy in addition to the cost aspects of various production alternatives considered in conventional economic analysis. Note that the determination of the optimal production policy involves a thorough consideration of both demand and supply side of the problem. In the presence of risk the optimal plant cannot in general be determined without such an optimizing procedure.

WESLEYAN UNIVERSITY

[9] An accurate recalculation indicates that at $\beta = 0.7$ the constant cost case results in a 1 cent higher discounted present value. Rather than changing the constant cost to \$1.53 this odd result is left as a curiosity.

[10] The steady state probabilities for initial inventory 0, 1, and 2 are 7/12, 1/3, and 1/12 respectively. Weighting these by the optimal production levels (2, 2, 0) gives 11/6.

[11] The expected value of lost sales is $(P_0 + P_2)\ 1/4 = 1/6$ where P_0 and P_2 are the steady state probabilities of initial inventory 0 and 2 respectively.

MEASURING THE PROFITABILITY OF ADVERTISING: AN EMPIRICAL STUDY

by JEAN-JACQUES LAMBIN*

ABSTRACT

Statistical analysis of internal data available to a firm can reduce substantially the area of uncertainty which characterizes advertising decisions. The econometric model presented here has been successfully utilized by the firm for predicting sales and for deciding on the level of the total advertising appropriation. The model is periodically updated and revised in the light of new information.

INTRODUCTION

EACH YEAR corporations spend ever larger sums on advertising, yet little progress in the last 10 years has been made in the study of the profitability of advertising. While it is current practice to study all facts relevant to the cost of a product, and while every capital investment project is subjected to a detailed study of its profitability, the determination of an advertising budget still depends largely on an empirical approach and is often based on poor knowledge of economic analysis.

The purpose of this article is to show, with the help of a concrete example, that by analysing internal data available to a company, the area of uncertainty which characterizes advertising decisions can be considerably reduced. The study presented here is based on a distributed lags model fitted by multiple regression analysis based on time series data. The limits and pitfalls of the econometric approach to the study of advertising have frequently been pointed out.[1] From a purely statistical point of view, a regression model can only be descriptive since it deals with association, rather than with causal relationships. In that sense, it has no predictive power, unless one postulates that the relationships within the universe from which the sample was taken remain unchanged. This paper tends to support the view that this limitation is less severe than it might appear at first sight, if the model is periodically updated with fresh market information and data.

The conditions and circumstances described in this study are

* The author wishes to thank Kristian S. Palda for his helpful comments and Miss Leboutte from the Computer Center of Louvain University, for her programming assistance.

[1] Richard R. Quandt, 'Estimating Advertising Effectiveness: Some Pitfalls in Econometric Methods', *Journal of Marketing Research*, I (May 1964).

real, and are based on Belgian market data. However, at the request of the company concerned, certain figures have been modified but without significantly affecting the general conclusions reached. The analysis is based on data available within the company over a period of 20 years. The article is divided into three sections. In the first, an attempt is made to define the demand function of the product studied, and to describe the different variables. In the second section, an evaluation of the statistical results of the regression analysis is made, and the most promising model is chosen. Lastly, an economic interpretation of the results and an evaluation of advertising investment profitability is presented.

THE DEMAND FUNCTION

The case examined is that of a frequently purchased food product for which the total demand has increased at an average annual rate of 7 per cent during the last 10 years. This spectacular growth in consumption is attributable to several causes, of which one is the increased purchasing power of the population and, in particular, of the lower income groups. Another stimulus was provided by a changing standard of living and especially improvements in housing and the introduction of television. It would also seem that the increased car ownership and more time for leisure activity and sports had a positive influence on sales.

In this product market, our brand enjoyed a dominant quasi-monopolistic position in the Chamberlinian sense.[2] The characteristics and quality of the product on the one hand, and the high level and continuity of advertising on the other, contributed directly to the development of a strong brand loyalty. The product is sold in four packaging sizes and has a very dense distribution network. The management of the company acknowledges the decisive influence of advertising on the expansion of sales.

The Variables

On the basis of these considerations, and also on the basis of information gained from periodic studies of the market, it appears on a *a priori* basis that the demand for the product depends principally on three environmental variables and four decision variables. These variables are shown in the demand function represented below. They will be commented upon briefly, explaining the choice of the units of measurement.

$$q = F(n, y, w, \ldots, s, d, v, p, \ldots) \qquad (1)$$

[2] E. H. Chamberlin, *The Theory of Monopolistic Competition* (Cambridge, Mass.: Harvard University Press, 1956, 7th edition).

where

q = dependent variables: sales in physical units
n = number of potential consumers: best consuming age-group
y = private disposable income
w = weather conditions: rainfalls adjusted for seasonal variation
s = advertising: total advertising outlays
d = distribution: number of sales outlets
v = visit-frequency: number of weekly visits to sales outlets
p = average retail price

Two factors usually considered do not figure in the basic model. They are 'competition' and 'quality' or communication value and creativity of advertising. Reasons for the absence of these variables from the demand function are discussed below.

While there is a net expansion in industry demand, competition is lively in the sector, mainly due to the introduction of a large number of minor brands on a regional basis. Unit prices are low and have not been greatly modified during the period under consideration. In general, price is the same, whatever the brand, as the companies tend to compete chiefly by advertising and through the distribution network. While strong brands compete in the national market, they are sufficiently differentiated so that they are not good substitutes for each other. As far as the brand studied is concerned, this differentiation is especially pronounced with regard to taste. Imitations exist, but their market share is small. We are considering, therefore, a market of monopolistic structure with each producer maintaining a relative independence in the development of his marketing activity. This competitive structure not having altered during the period studied, it was not considered useful to introduce an index of competitive activity as a variable or to express the dependent variable in terms of 'market share' rather than in terms of absolute sales. Another possibility would have been to express the company's advertising expenditure in relative terms.[3]

The company had no objective criteria for comparing the quality of its advertising in one period with the quality in another period. Furthermore, during the last few years, there has been no major change in the policy followed by the company which has maintained the same overall advertising style and copy appeals. Moreover, during the whole of the period studied, the same agency was employed and disposed of the entire advertising appropriations. As far

[3] See my *Optimal Allocation of Competitive Marketing Efforts: An Empirical Study*, Center of Socio-Economic Studies in Advertising and Marketing (CESAM)—Louvain University Belgium—Working Paper no. 1 (September 1968), p. 62.

as the allocation of total advertising expenditures between different media is concerned, the trend has been to concentrate increasingly on mass media to the detriment of 'reminder' type of advertising vehicles. Since this change has been more of a gradual evolution than a rapid shift in the media mix, it is assumed that 'quality' of the advertising effort has remained unchanged during the period in question. Thus, no 'quality of advertising' variable is introduced into the model.

The Model

In order to limit the number of independent variables, and thereby to increase the reliability of the statistical estimates, the original demand function was simplified in the following manner. First, the variables 'quantity sold', 'advertising' and 'income' were expressed in 'per 1,000 potential consumers'. Second, the 'sales outlets' and 'visit-frequency' variables were merged by multiplying one by the other, the frequency of visit being used to weight in this way the number of sales outlets. The new distribution variable which was thus obtained, and also retail price, were put into the form of first difference, to reduce suspected collinearity. These variables thus measure the *change* in retail price and in the total number of visits to retailers during each time period. Finally, the variables advertising, income and price were divided by the general retail price index. The demand function which then emerges is written as:

$$q_t = F(y_t, w_t, q_{t-1}, s_t, \Delta d_t, \Delta p_t, u_t) \qquad (2)$$

where

q_t = unit sales per 1,000 potential consumers
y_t = real private disposable income per 1,000 potential consumers
w_t = weather: rainfalls adjusted for seasonal variations
q_{t-1} = goodwill: lagged dependent variable
s_t = real advertising expenditures per 1,000 potential consumers
Δd_t = change in visit-frequency to sales outlets
Δp_t = change in real retail price
u_t = residual, or unexplained variation

The mathematical model is a distributed lag model of the semi-logarithmic type:

$$q_t = k + b_1 \log y_t + b_2 q_{t-1} + b_3 \log s_t + b_4 \log \Delta d_t + \ldots$$
$$\ldots + b_5 w_t + b_6 \Delta p_t + u_t \qquad (3)$$

The choice of this semi-logarithmic form is based on the assumption that there are diminishing returns to advertising and distribution and that income elasticity tapers off at higher income levels. This assumption has been verified by earlier work during which various functional forms were compared.[4] We expect a negative sign for the price and the weather variables.

With this model, and more particularly with the help of regression coefficients of the advertising variable (b_3), it is possible to give a numerical expression to the advertising–sales response function and to calculate the elasticity of demand with respect to advertising expenditures. Using logarithms in the base 10, the elasticity may be calculated in the following way:

$$\eta_s = (0.4343 . b_3/\bar{s}) . (\bar{s}/\bar{q}) \qquad (4)$$

where ($\bar{s}$) represents the average sample advertising expenditures and ($\bar{q}$) the average sample unit sales.

The introduction into the model of the lagged dependent variable q_{t-1} here called 'goodwill', makes it possible to evaluate the cumulative effects of advertising. As it has been shown, the regression coefficient of this variable (b_2) constitutes an estimate of the advertising retention rate (λ) or, inversely, the decay rate ($1-\lambda$), in a given period, provided the estimate of λ is included between zero and one. This model was first introduced by Koyck,[5] and used by Telser,[6] Palda,[7] Frank and Massy.[8] Knowledge of the retention rate permits us to calculate the cumulative effect of the advertising and to estimate the elasticity in the long term, in the following manner,

$$\eta_s^* = (0.4343 . b_3/\bar{s})/(1-\lambda) . (\bar{s}/\bar{q}) \qquad (5)$$

With the help of these different estimates, methods employed in studying the profitability of capital investments projects can be used in the calculation of the return on advertising investment.

THE REGRESSION RESULTS

The above demand function takes into account all factors considered *a priori* as possibly exerting a specific influence on sales. The calculations below are intended to verify this hypothesis.

[4] J. J. Lambin, 'Investissement publicitaire et étude de rentabilité', *Annales de Sciences Economiques Appliquées*, no. 2 (Mai 1967) pp. 141–229.

[5] L. M. Koyck, *Distributed Lags and Investment Analysis*, Amsterdam: North Holland Publishing Co., 1954, chap. 2.

[6] Lester F. Telser, 'Advertising and Cigarettes', *Journal of Political Economy*, 70 (October 1962), pp. 471–99.

[7] Kristian S. Palda, *The Measurement of Cumulative Advertising Effects*, Englewood Cliffs, N.J.: Prentice-Hall, 1964.

[8] Ronald E. Frank and William F. Massy, 'Short Term Price and Dealing Effects in Selected Market Segments', *Journal of Marketing Research*, II (May 1965), pp. 171–85.

Statistical Evaluation of the Results

The basic model was fitted with the help of an IBM 360-40 computer stepwise program which ranks the variables by their explanatory power, i.e. by the reduction in total variance attributed successively to each factor. Usually, the program eliminates variables which do not attain a degree of significance specified in advance. In the present case, however, it was decided not to specify any such level. Rather, appeal was made to a variety of statistical criteria and information available within the company in judging the real influence of each separate variable. The results of this first phase are presented as follows:

$$q_t = -32{,}733 + \underset{(3.7)}{12.423} \log y_t + \underset{(2.8)}{0.443}\, q_{t-1} + \ldots$$

$$\ldots + \underset{(2.5)}{1.704} \log s_t - \underset{(2.1)}{2.2}\, w_t + \underset{(2.6)}{823} \log \Delta d_t + \underset{(0.3)}{48}\, \Delta p_t$$

$$R = 0.983 \qquad F = 127 \qquad S_e = 233 \qquad N = 20$$

The variables are in order of their relative importance. Below each regression coefficient is shown its t-value, i.e. the ratio of its coefficient to its estimated standard deviation. On the last line are shown the principal statistical criteria with which to evaluate the model. They are the unadjusted coefficient of multiple correlation (R), the F-test and the standard error of estimate (S_e); N represents the number of observations.

A first examination of these results shows that the most significant variables are (in order): income, goodwill, and advertising. These are the same variables that were considered *a priori* as the most important. Furthermore, all coefficients have the expected signs with the exception of the coefficient of price. Its positive sign and the fact that it is statistically insignificant tends to confirm the opinion that price was not a determining influence on sales. The elimination of this variable is therefore likely to improve the quality of the model.

In order to check the stability of these results over time, the model was recalculated for each of the last three periods of observation dropping off, successively, the last period, the last two and three periods. The results are presented in Table I in the same order as before, with the exception of the statistical criteria which have been regrouped in the lower section of the table (dw represents the Durbin-Watson statistic). The very high value of the coefficient of multiple correlation and of the F-test, both of which are highly significant, are noteworthy. The standard error of estimate (expressed in terms of the dependent variable) is moreover very small representing only

5.3 per cent of the average sales calculated over the 20 years of observation, and only 3.4 per cent of average sales for the last 4 years. All the regression coefficients are significant at the 5 per cent level and most of them at the 1 per cent level; they also show good stability over the last 3 years. The last point is important because the purpose of the study is to predict the influence of advertising. A comparison of actual sales and calculated sales with the help of the model is represented graphically in Fig. 1. Predicted sales are very close to actual sales and there appears to be no systematic trend in residuals. These too are reproduced graphically at the bottom of Fig. 1, so that a judgment may be made of their independence.[9]

TABLE I
THE REGRESSION RESULTS

Coefficients	*Models code number*				
	(A-18)	*(A-19)*	*(A-20)*	*(B-20)*	*(C-20)*
Constant (k)	−31,583	−31,882	−32,733	−5,372	−53,721
Income	12,178	12,186	12,423	—	20,632
(log I_t)	(3.8)	(3.4)	(3.7)		(12.2)
Goodwill	0.473	0.491	0.507	0.979	—
(q_{t-1})	(3.3)	(3.4)	(3.7)	(11.4)	
Advertising	1,723	1,668	1,777	1,478	2,432
(log s_t)	(2.7)	(2.4)	(2.6)	(1.6)	(3.6)
Weather	−2.0	−1.9	−2.2	−1.4	−2.3
(W_t)	(3.7)	(3.6)	(2.1)	(1.9)	(3.2)
Distribution	864	813	843	325	1.232
(log d_t)	(3.1)	(2.8)	(2.7)	(0.9)	(3.6)
R	0.982	0.978	0.987	0.962	0.964
F-test	163	201	203	98	104
Se	202	208	212	294	282
dw	1.67	1.76	1.72	1.43	1.19
N	18	19	20	20	20
Chi-square	N.A.*	N.A.	71	45	37

* N.A. = Not Available.

Test for Multicollinearity

The results have been tested for collinearity. Difficulties associated with a multicollinear set of data depend on the severity of the problem. As interdependence among explanatory variables grows, the correlation matrix approaches singularity. In the limit, perfect linear dependence leads to perfect singularity on the part of the correlation matrix and to a complete indeterminate set of parameter estimates. D. E. Farrar and R. R. Glauber[10] have proposed a

[9] E. Malinvaud, *Methodes statistiques de l'économétrie*, Paris: Dunod, 1964, chap. 6.
[10] D. Farrar and Robert R. Glauber, 'Multicollinearity in Regression Analysis—The Problem Revisited', *Review of Economics and Statistics*, February 1967.

systematic procedure for detecting the existence, measuring the extent and pinpointing the locations and causes of multicollinearity within a set of independent variables. In order, the tests are:

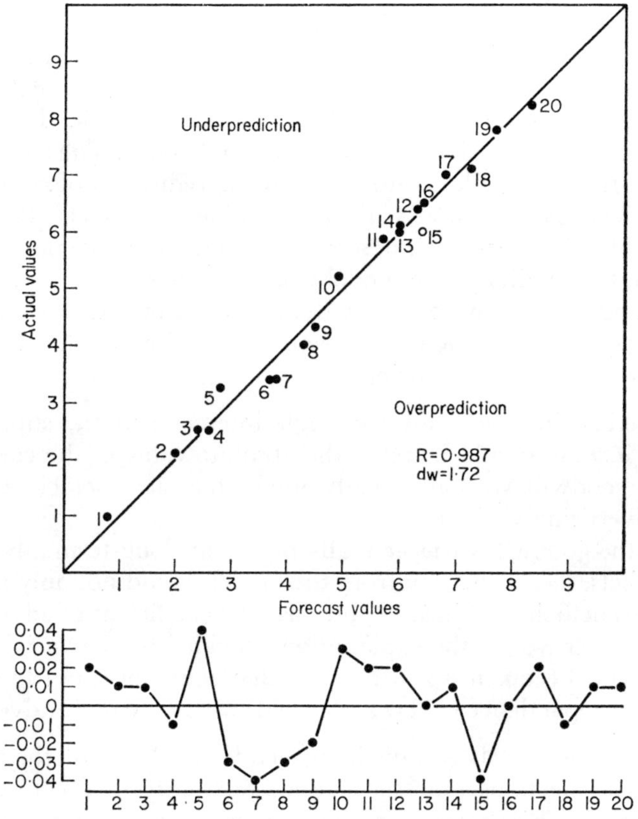

Fig. 1 Forecast values versus actual values (model A 20)

(*a*) an approximate *Chi square* transformation of the determinant of the correlation coefficients matrix to assess the presence and the severity of multicollinearity between the independent variables;

(*b*) *F-tests* to indicate the dependence of a particular variable on other independent variables;

(*c*) *t-tests* and *partial correlation* coefficients to indicate the pattern of interdependence within the set of explanatory variables.

Applying these tests to our data, we found a Chi-square value of 71, superior to its critical value at the 95 per cent level for 10 degrees of freedom. The F-tests show the variables to be relatively stable, only the lagged dependent variable (goodwill) and the income variable are affected by collinearity ($F = 78$ and 54). Partial correlation coefficients and associated t-ratios confirm the dependence of these two explanatory variables.

To evaluate the implications of this dependence on the various coefficients, two supplementary regressions have been calculated, one without income and the other without goodwill. The results of this two new regressions are presented in Table I. The elimination of one of these variables contributes to the reduction of collinearity as evidenced by the lower Chi-square values of models (B-20) and (C-20). Should there be no separate influence of income and of goodwill, the quality of the model would be, no doubt, improved by eliminating one or the other of these two variables. Therefore, in comparing these two new regressions to the initial model (A-20), we should expect the following:

(*a*) Taking into account the high intercorrelation, suppression of income should increase the absolute value of the coefficient of goodwill without greatly modifying the coefficient of the advertising variables.

(*b*) If the goodwill variable really represents long-term advertising effects, its elimination from the model should not only increase the coefficient of income, but also the coefficient of advertising. In other words, the explanation provided by the variable q_{t-1} should be taken up in part by the factor income (due to the interdependence effect) and in part by the variable advertising.

Considering first (B-20), distinguished from (A-20) by the absence of income, one finds that the overall reliability of the results has diminished. This is shown by an increase of 39 per cent in the standard error of residuals and by a significant decrease in the coefficient of multiple correlation and of the F-test. However, on checking the regression coefficients it is seen that the income effect is entirely accounted for by the goodwill variable whose coefficient has doubled in absolute value. Furthermore, this modification has had no serious effect on the coefficient of the advertising variable which maintains practically the same relative importance as in model (A-20). When we compare models (A-20) and (C-20), the latter without the goodwill variable, we find a decrease in overall reliability and an increase of 33 per cent in the standard error. Thus the second opinion formulated above is confirmed by these results since, despite a net increase of the income effect, a very large increase of the advertising effect can be observed which thus provides a much larger contribution to the total explanation. It is interesting to note that a part of the goodwill effect is also accounted for by the variable distribution which measures the activity of salesmen in terms of visit frequency to sales outlets. This implies that the goodwill variable does not only embrace the long-term advertising effect but also takes into account the cumulative effect of the total selling effort, or more simply of the whole marketing pressure exerted by the company on its market.

Summing up, it therefore seems reasonable to accept that the goodwill and income variables make a distinct contribution to the reduction of the total variance. Despite the presence of multicollinearity caused by these two factors, it is advisable to maintain them in the model. This decision is further justified as it improves the overall reliability of the model and of each coefficient in particular.

ECONOMIC INTERPRETATION OF THE RESULTS

Having shown that model (A-20) is statistically acceptable we can use its results to calculate the effect of advertising on demand and thus evaluate the profitability in the short and in the long term of the advertising investment.

The Short- and Long-term Elasticities.

The advertising elasticity coefficient measures the sensitivity of unit sales to variation in advertising pressure. It is defined as

$$\eta_s = \frac{\delta q}{\delta s} \cdot \frac{s}{q} \qquad (6)$$

where it is useful to remind ourselves $\delta q/\delta s$ measures the slope of the net advertising unit sales relationship, and where 'q' is the physical unit sales. These elasticities are reproduced in Table II. For the last time period, model (A-20) yields the following estimate:

$$\eta_s = 0.190$$

This means that, all other things remaining constant, an increase of 1 per cent in advertising pressure will cause an increase of 0.190 per cent in the quantities sold. Thus taking into account only the short-term effects, it appears that the company is close to saturation level, that is to say, the stage when any increase in advertising expenses would have practically no influence on sales. If, however, in addition to the immediate advertising effects, one takes into account the lagged effects, a very different conclusion is arrived at because the cumulative elasticity is practically twice as great, and has in the corresponding period the following value:

$$\eta_s^* = 0.385$$

Thus by looking at the question in a long-term perspective, it is seen that an increase of 1 per cent in advertising expenditures will cause an increase of 0.385 per cent in the quantities sold, although this total effect will be spread over several years. The difference observed between these two elasticities is due to the level of the retention rate (λ) which appears in the denominator for the calculation of marginal product in the long term and which gives expression to the cumulative influence exerted by advertising on demand. The estimated values of the retention rate are reproduced in Table II. Model (A-20) yields the following estimate:

$$\lambda = 0.507$$

The higher this value (or inversely the smaller the decay rate), the more pronounced will be the difference between the long- and short-term elasticities. If the advertising effect declines at a relatively moderate rate, a progressively larger part of current sales will be attributable to past advertising. This means that the goodwill 'capital' of the product will be growing. Indeed, Table II shows that the long-term marginal product is quite different from the short-term one. As about 50 per cent of the total advertising effect is maintained from one period to another, this fact tends to demonstrate the accumulation of brand reputation of the product.

It is interesting to note that the advertising policy undertaken for this particular product cannot be justified on rational grounds, without accepting this notion of long-term effect. As suggested by Palda,[11] it can be shown, indeed, that the breakeven advertising elasticity, i.e. the lowest advertising elasticity which still ensures a profit for the company, must be greater than 0.304. It is only at this level indeed that, for a 1 per cent increase in advertising, the following relationship is verified:

(Elast.) . (Sales rev.) > (Elast.) . (Sales rev.) . (Percent of profit) + Adv. Exp.

$$(\eta_s') \cdot (\bar{p} \cdot \bar{q}) > (\eta_s') \cdot (\bar{p} \cdot \bar{q}) \cdot (m) + \bar{s} \qquad (7)$$

[11] Kristian S. Palda, *op. cit.*, p. 81.

TABLE II

COMPARING SHORT- AND LONG-TERM ADVERTISING ELASTICITIES

	Short term				Long term	
Model: code number	*Marginal product of advertising* (1)	*Elasticity* (2)	*Retention rate* (3)	*Decay rate* (4)	*Marginal product of advertising* (5)	*Elasticity* (6)
(A-18)	0.249	0.232	0.473	0.527	0.472	0.440
(A-19)	0.221	0.248	0.494	0.506	0.437	0.490
(A-20)	0.224	0.190	0.507	0.493	0.454	0.385

In a semi-log model, (base 10): $\delta q/\delta s = (\delta q/\delta \log s) \cdot (0.4343/\bar{s})$

(5) The long term marginal product of advertising is given by: $(\delta q/\delta s)/(1-\lambda)$

where

η'_s = critical advertising elasticity
$\bar{q}$ = average sales volume (physical)
$\bar{p}$ = average sales price
$\bar{s}$ = average advertising expenditures
m = gross profit margin expressed as a percentage of price

Thus, lagged effects of advertising must have been taken into account in the development of the company's advertising policy.

The Short- and Long-term Profitability

While the notion of elasticity permits an evaluation of the sensitivity of demand to advertising it does not help determine the real profitability of advertising expenditures. Even if the company is very close to saturation point, an increase in advertising expenditures may very

TABLE III

THE SHORT- AND LONG-TERM PROFITABILITY OF THE ADVERTISING INVESTMENT

	Short term			*Long term*		
Models: code number	(1) *Marginal revenue product* (μ)	(2) *Gross margin* $GM = (m) \cdot (\mu)$	(3) *Gross profit* (1-GM)	(4) *Marginal revenue product* (μ')	(5) *Gross margin* $GM = (m) \cdot (\mu')$	(6) *Gross profit* (1-GM)
(A-18)	1.494	0.821	−0.179	2.466	1.356	0.356
(A-19)	1.326	0.729	−0.271	2.254	1.240	0.240
(A-20)	1.344	0.739	−0.261	2.328	1.280	0.280

well be profitable if resulting revenue exceeds corresponding cost. To measure the profitability of past advertising, it is therefore necessary to take the analysis a step further.

This problem is first studied in the short term by assuming that the sales price remains constant at 6 francs (BF). On the basis of the regression results (model A-20), it appears that the last franc invested in advertising yields the following marginal revenue product

$$p\delta q/\delta s = (6).(0.224) = 1.344 \text{ FB}$$

Let us define the marginal revenue product of advertising, $p\delta q/\delta s$ as μ. The various estimated values of μ are presented in Table III, column 1.

Dorfman and Steiner[12] have shown that, at the optimal advertising

[12] Robert Dorfman and Peter O. Steiner, 'Optimal Advertising and Optimal Quality', *The American Economic Review*, 64 (no. 5, 1954).

expenditures level, the following relationship holds

$$MC = p\left(1-\frac{1}{\mu}\right) \tag{8}$$

where MC is marginal cost (approximated by variable cost). From this equation, we obtain

$$\mu = \frac{p}{p-MC} \tag{9}$$

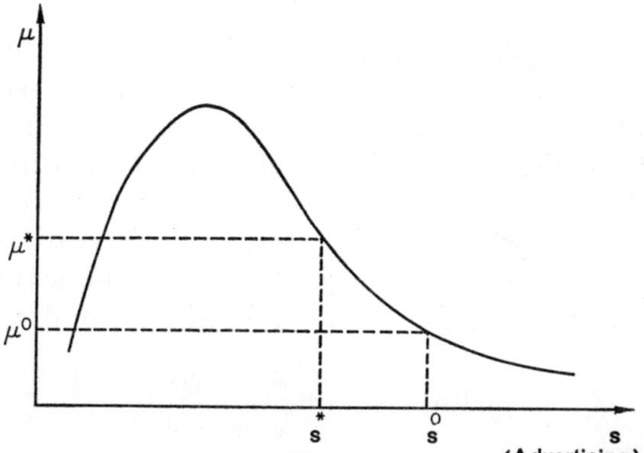

Fig. 2

μ^* = the value of 'μ' corresponding to the optimum situation;
μ^0 = the average observed value of μ

Equation (9) states that, at optimum, the marginal revenue product of advertising equals the reciprocal of the markup on the cost of the marginal unit produced. Equation (9) can be rewritten as:

$$\mu^* = \frac{1}{m} \tag{10}$$

where m is gross margin expressed as a percentage of price. Knowing that in the present case m is 55 per cent, the value of μ in the optimum situation should be:

$$\mu^* = \frac{1}{0.55} = 1.818 \text{ francs}$$

But the observed value of μ in this case is:

$$\mu = 1.344 \text{ francs}$$

This shows that equation (10) is not satisfied. If we postulate a relationship between s and μ as expressed in Fig. 2, one might speculate that the optimal level of advertising expenditure has been exceeded by this firm.

In order to reach optimum and thereby improve profitability, the company should reduce its advertising expenses.

In Table III, it is possible to see that for each model considered, once the costs of production (advertising not included) are deducted, the gross margin so obtained (column 2), being inferior to the franc invested, the gross profit (advertising deducted) will be negative (column 3). In other words, the last franc spent on advertising costs more than the return it yields. Thus if only the short-term effects of advertising are taken into account, the firm does not seem to have operated near an optimal level of advertising expenditures.

In this latter conclusion, however, no account is taken of the lagged advertising effect already considered when we calculated short- and long-term elasticities. Thus, it is obvious that in order to measure the real economic worth of advertising, it is necessary to consider in the calculation, the *long-term marginal product*. It is possible to show[13] that the present value of the marginal revenue product of advertising can be directly calculated using the following formula:

$$1 \text{ franc} = (\mu) \cdot \left(\frac{1+r}{1+r-\lambda} \right) \qquad (11)$$

where

$\mu = p\delta q/\delta s$
r = cost of capital (in per cent)
λ = retention rate

By discounting at a cost of capital rate $r = 0.20$, and by using the estimates of Table III, we obtain the following results:

$$1 \text{ franc} = (1.344) \cdot \left(\frac{1+0.20}{1+0.20-0.57} \right) = 2.328 \text{ francs.}$$

The other present values estimated, as well as the corresponding profit margins, are reproduced in columns 4 and 5 of Table III. It can be seen that by taking into account long-term effects, the gross profit margins (col. 6) have turned positive. It is clear that advertising is profitable to the firm, only when its cumulative effects are considered.

A confirmation of the plausibility of our results is given by a further appeal to Dorfman and Steiner (same reference). These authors have shown that, under optimum conditions, price elasticity in

[13] See Kristian S. Palda, op. cit., p. 17.

absolute value (η_p) and marginal revenue product of advertising (μ) are equal. We do not have a direct estimate of the price elasticity of the demand curve upon which the firm operates. Thus μ is our best estimate of it. Recalling that the short-term estimate of μ is 1.3 and the long-term one 2.8, and given that our firm is in a strong monopolistic position, a value of 1.3 appears quite likely. Our knowledge of the cost conditions which are here very low confirm this view. We know, however, that a monopolist must fear entry by potential rivals in the long run; therefore, the price elasticity of the demand in the long term which he faces must be much higher.[14] Thus, here again, a value of 2.3 does not seem out of line. This would confirm our previous conclusion on the long-term perspective of the firm's marketing policy. Should our speculation on the price elasticity not be on as safe a ground as we assume, the company ought perhaps to increase its advertising expenditures. Since the firm operates already in the region of rapidly decreasing returns, this would bring the long-term value of μ down and close to the expected price elasticity.

USES OF THE RESULTS

The purpose of our econometric model is to present in quantified form all the relationships and constraints which describe past sales behaviour, in order to give management a starting point for defining its future marketing strategy. In practice, the model has two main uses: that of predicting sales, and that of determining the advertising appropriation.

In so far as an econometric model clarifies the past with precision, it becomes a tool for forecasting sales, since it reproduces the underlying structure of the phenomenon studied. As such it thus allows calculation of future sales on the basis of assumption concerning the environmental and decision variables which are present in the demand function. In this particular case, the predictive value of the model has been tested by forecasting backward (here we refer to the description of regressions underlying Table I) with equations fitted to sample data that left out the last three periods. The sales for each of these three successive periods were forecast. Only information available previous to that of the forecast period was utilized; normal weather conditions were assumed. Then a comparison was made between predictions generated by the model and those actually prepared by the company. The model emerges as a better forecasting instrument.

[14] George J. Stigler, *The Theory of Price* (New York: The Macmillan Co., 1966, 3rd edition), pp. 227 and 236.

Besides the interest which the model has in forecasting sales, it is also useful in the decision on the level of the total advertising appropriation. As an example, we take model (A-20). If we estimate the future level of private disposable income, the frequency of visit to sales outlets and if we assume normal weather conditions for the rainfall variable, we can predict the particular influence of these variables upon sales and add this influence to the constant term k. We then get the following relationship

$$q_t = k + \lambda q_{t-1} + b \log s_t \qquad (12)$$

On subtracting q_{t-1} from both sides

$$q_t - q_{t-1} = k + b \log s_t - (1-\lambda) q_{t-1} \qquad (13)$$

This last expression means that the increase in sales (Δq_t) expected for period t depends on three parameters:

—k, the constant term which summarizes the influence of the other environmental and decision variables
—b, the marginal (physical) product per franc spent on advertising multiplied by log s, the chosen amount of the advertising appropriation
—$(1-\lambda)$, the decay rate of the goodwill capital.

Since we know the sales of the preceding period and the decay rate, and if we plug in the firm's sales objective, we can solve directly this equation for log s. We thus get the amount of advertising appropriation upon which management can base its final decision on the overall allocation of marketing budget.[15]

In conclusion, it might interest the reader to know that the firm discussed, utilized the model not, of course, as a tool designed to yield precise recommendations, but rather to give indications of the direction and magnitude of changes that will increase sales and profit. (Naturally, the model is periodically updated and revised in the light of new information.) In this sense, the model has passed the most difficult test of all.

LOUVAIN

BIBLIOGRAPHY

CHAMBERLIN, E. H., *The Theory of Monopolistic Competition*, Cambridge, Mass.: Harvard University Press, 1956 (7th edition).

[15] Equation (13) is in fact very similar to the model presented by Vidale and Wolfe, 'An Operations-Research Study of Sales Response to Advertising', *Operations Research*, 5 (June 1957, no. 3), pp. 370–81.

DORFMAN, ROBERT and STEINER, PETER O., 'Optimal Advertising and Optimal Quality', *The American Economic Review*, 64 (no. 5), 1954.

KOYCK, L. M., *Distributed Lags and Investment Analysis*, Amsterdam: North Holland Publishing Co, 1954, chap. 2.

PALDA, KRISTIAN S., *The Measurement of Cumulative Advertising Effects*, Englewood Cliffs, N.J.: Prentice-Hall, 1964.

FARRAR, D. and GLAUBER, ROBERT R., 'Multicollinearity in Regression Analysis—The Problem Revisited', *Review of Economics and Statistics*, February 1967.

STIGLER, GEORGE J., *The Theory of Price*, New York: The Macmillan Co., 1966 (3rd edition), pp. 227 and 236.

TELSER, LESTER G., 'Advertising and Cigarettes', *Journal of Political Economy*, 70 (October 1962), pp. 471–99.

VIDALE, M. L. and WOLFE, H. B., 'An Operations-Research Study of Sales Response to Advertising', *Operations Research*, 5 (June 1957, no. 3), pp. 370–81.

MARKET STRUCTURE AND INDUSTRIAL PERFORMANCE: RELATION OF PROFIT RATES TO CONCENTRATION, ADVERTISING INTENSITY, AND DIVERSITY

by RICHARD A. MILLER*

INTRODUCTION

MARKET structure has long been considered as a prime determinant of industrial performance. Firms in the search for profit restrict output, raise price, and earn supernormal profit if the market structure in which they find themselves permits. This article reports an empirical attempt to relate industrial performance with market structure in the U.S. manufacturing sector: measures of profit rates are regressed on measures of market structure.

The primary performance variable is a profit rate, computed in two ways: income after taxes plus interest paid on borrowed capital as a percentage of total assets, and income after taxes as a percentage of net worth. The independent variables reflecting market structure are (1) the four-firm concentration ratio; (2) the marginal eight-firm concentration ratio (the share of industry output produced by firms ranked 5 through 8, thus the difference between the eight-firm and the four-firm CR); (3) advertising intensity (advertising expenditures as a percentage of sales); and (4) the degree to which firms classified in the industry specialize in the product of that industry or are diversified into other industries. The industry observations are Internal Revenue Service minor industries, roughly the three-digit Standard Industrial Classification level of aggregation. The multiple regression equations are based on all 106 minor industries in manufacturing and on two divisions of these industries, one based on producer goods–consumer goods classification and the other based upon national–non-national and homogeneous–non-homogeneous market classification.

MARKET STRUCTURE AND PERFORMANCE VARIABLES

The four market structure variables—concentration, marginal concentration, advertising intensity, and industrial diversity—as well as the performance variables require brief explanations of their

* The study was greatly facilitated by National Science Foundation Grants (GS 709 and GS 1274). I am grateful to Stephen Kidd and James McFarlane for programming assistance and to Jon Joyce, Stanley Lebergott, and Robert Blake for comments on a previous draft of this paper.

relevance and the expected results. The data, discussed more fully in the appendix, are derived from publications of the Bureau of the Census and the Internal Revenue Service.

1. *Seller Concentration*

Price and output behavior in oligopolized industries, described by 'mutual dependence recognized' theories, derives from a small number of sellers. The four-firm concentration ratio is one measure of this fewness: the larger is the share of industry output supplied by a few firms, the greater is the probability that these firms will evolve some implicit or tacit collusion to raise price and restrict output.[1] Profitability and four-firm concentration should be positively related.

2. *Marginal Seller Concentration*

The marginal concentration ratio, the difference between the eight-firm concentration ratio and the four-firm concentration ratio, measures the share of industry output supplied by the second largest four firms. If implicit collusion is viable among eight firms, then the larger is MCR_8 the greater is the probability of a monopoly-like industry performance; MCR_8 would be similar to CR_4, and the signs of their regression coefficients would both be positive. On the other hand, if collusion is not viable among eight (although it may be among four, given the requisite share of output), the second group of four firms may show evidence of competitive activity in price; rivalry in price may result from their actions independent of any implicit cartel, and the sign of the coefficient of this marginal concentration ratio would be negative. Results reported elsewhere[2] suggest that these second four firms tend not to participate in tacit collusion.

[1] The problems of using a concentration ratio as an index of monopoly are well known; they are discussed, for example, in Gideon Rosenbluth, 'Measures of Concentration', *Business Concentration and Price Policy* (Princeton University Press; National Bureau of Economic Research, 1955), pp. 57–95; and Marshall Hall and Nicolaus Tideman, 'Measures of Concentration', *Journal of the American Statistical Association*, vol. 62, no. 317 (March 1967), pp. 162–8. A standard reference elaborating the concentration ratio–profit rate relationship is Joe S. Bain, 'Relation of Profit Rate to Industry Concentration: American Manufacturing, 1936–1940', *Quarterly Journal of Economics*, vol. 65 (August 1951), pp. 293–324.

[2] My 'Marginal Concentration Ratios and Industrial Profit Rates: Some Empirical Results of Oligopoly Behavior', *The Southern Economic Journal*, vol. 34, no. 2 (October 1967), pp. 259–67. The other marginal concentration ratios (shares of industry output accounted for by firms ranked 9–20 and 21–50) are not statistically different from zero. The remaining marginal concentration ratio (100 minus CR_{50}) is highly negatively correlated ($r = -0.834$ for $n = 106$) with CR_4. Statistically its use adds nothing (beyond the other four concentration ratios) to the explanation of the variance in the profit rate, since all these concentration ratios sum to a constant. Economically its use cannot be distinguished from CR_4, since a large value of $100-CR_{50}$, implying competitive structure, is closely associated with a small value of CR_4, implying an absence of monopoly (oligopoly) structure.

3. *Advertising Intensity*

Another dimension to market structure involves 'barriers to new competition', impediments to increased supply by firms new to the industry, in response to profit opportunities. The higher are such barriers, the greater is the freedom of established sellers to pursue implicitly (or explicitly) collusive price and output policies without fear of the intrusion of alternative suppliers.

Bain has classified entry barriers as: (1) economies of large scale; (2) 'absolute cost advantages of established firms'; and (3) 'product differentiation advantages of established firms'.[3] Scale economies are significant (*a*) if the plant (or firm) with lowest unit cost possesses a capacity equal to a substantial fraction of industry sales and (*b*) if the rate of decline of unit costs as scale increases (how fast the envelop of AC curves falls) is marked. As a result, if scale economies truly are 'significant', so that industry sales could support (say) only four or five or six plants (or firms) of optimum size, then the concentration ratio would provide a proxy for the scale economies barrier to entry. Firms of suboptimal size would wither.

Absolute cost advantages are a barrier, according to Bain, if the unit costs of established firms are lower than the prospective unit costs of potential firms. 'Established firms may control superior production techniques', purchase factors at lower prices, control the supplies of essential factors, or obtain funds at lower interest rates, than prospective entrants. However, the differential in unit costs between established and prospective sellers would be reflected directly in industry profit rates: if two industries differed only in the height of the absolute cost barrier to entry, the profit rate would be higher in the industry with the higher barrier. Thus a profit rate has built into it the effects of absolute cost differentials among industries without explicit measurement of those cost differences.

Bain's third entry barrier, product differentiation, can be measured roughly by the intensity of advertising:

> [T]here should generally tend to be a positive association between the height of the product-differentiation barrier to entry to an industry and the size (measured probably as a percentage of sales) of its costs of sales promotion. This association would presumably rest on the suppositions (1) that stronger product differentiation is ordinarily accompanied by or rests upon larger selling costs; and (2) that higher product-differentia-

[3] Joe S. Bain, *Barriers to New Competition* (Cambridge: Harvard University Press, 1956), pp. 33, 201.

> tion barriers to entry are generally erected and maintained by higher selling costs.[4]

This variable, the ratio of advertising expenses to total revenue ($\times 100$), is used, as Bain suggests, as a measure of product differentiation barriers to new competition; a positive relationship between this variable and profit rate should emerge. Comanor and Wilson have used this variable as a major variable of interest.[5] Their analysis suggests and their regressions produce a positive coefficient.

4. *Corporate Diversity*

Another possible barrier to entry involves the diversity of output mix produced by individual manufacturing firms. Fuchs argues that industries composed of multi-plant firms have higher entry barriers than industries composed of single-plant firms: prospective entrants, to be successful, possibly require multi-unit operations also, with the requisite larger capital and greater managerial skills. He finds industry concentration to be positively and strongly related to industry diversity, measured by percentage of industry value added accounted for by multi-unit establishments.[6] In addition, the analysis supporting antitrust policy links conglomerate and vertical *mergers* to the creation of monopoly power in violation of the revised Section 7 of the Clayton Act.[7] If the underlying eco-legal analysis is correct, then firms which are *integrated* in conglomerate and vertical dimensions should possess monopoly power.

On the other hand, firms may be diversified in a conglomerate sense for reasons other than the erection of entry barriers: cost saving; joint production; decreasing risk by selling in several markets simultaneously, when shifts in demand in the various markets are unpredictable and not perfectly correlated; and an increased probability that the somewhat unpredictable results of research and development activity might be profitably utilized. And firms may be vertically integrated to effect price discrimination, to reduce cost, to evade rate regulation, or to avoid monopoly pricing at another

[4] Bain, op. cit., p. 201. See also pp. 41, 125.

[5] William S. Comanor and Thomas A. Wilson, 'Advertising Market Structure and Performance', *The Review of Economics and Statistics*, vol. 49, no. 4 (November 1967), pp. 423–40.

[6] Victor R. Fuchs, 'Integration, Concentration, and Profits in Manufacturing Industries', *Quarterly Journal of Economics*, vol. 75 (May 1961), pp. 278–91, especially pp. 285–9.

[7] The particular diversity measure used here does not distinguish between conglomerate diversity and vertical integration. Antitrust policy, in determining competitive effects of conglomerate and vertical mergers, views both as potentially monopoly creating. *Brown Shoe Company v. United States*, 370 U.S. 294 (1962), especially 323–34 ('The Vertical Aspects of the Merger'), *Federal Trade Commission v. The Proctor and Gamble Company*, 386 U.S. 568 (1967), and 'Merger Guidelines', Department of Justice, May 30th, 1968 (mimeo), especially sections 11–13, 17–20.

level. These reasons for diversity (both conglomerate and vertical) have no necessary relation to the erection of entry barriers and to monopoly creation, but they provide additional reasons for suspecting that industrial diversity and industrial profits are positively related. In any case, diversity in both vertical and conglomerate directions is an important corporate fact in the manufacturing sector; many of the largest firms in the manufacturing sector are diversified into several or many markets.

The measure of diversity, the Industry Specialization Ratio for 1958, is provided by the industrial classifications of firms (both single- and multi-unit) and of the individual plants or units operated by these firms. Single-unit (or plant) firms are obviously single-industry firms, since any particular plant can be classified in but a single industry.[8] Multi-unit firms are either single-industry firms or multi-industry firms, depending on whether all the units of a firm are classified in the same industry as or in a different industry from the firm. If all the firms in an industry are single-unit firms, then the industry is not diversified. To the extent that plants of multi-plant firms of the industry are classified in *other* industries, the industry is diversified. The diversity measure used here is simply a ratio (× 100) of (labor) employment: (*a*) the employment in plants classified in the *same* industry as the controlling firm divided by (*b*) the employment in *all* plants of firms classified in the industry. To the extent that an industry's firms control plants classified in *other* industries, this ratio falls below unity; greater diversity is measured by a smaller ratio.

5. *Profit Rates*

The performance variable is a profit rate, a rate of return on capital used in an industry. Under competitive conditions rates of return tend to equality among industries. Variations in rates of return among industries should reflect variations in the market structure variables. Since both a return on total capital and a return to common stockholders have been used in similar studies, both profit rate concepts are used here; the high correlation between these variables indicates that the regression results will be quite similar.

THE 'INDUSTRY' OBSERVATIONS

The Internal Revenue Service minor industries in manufacturing provide the 106 observations used in this study. The profit variables

[8] Despite the diversity of *output* from a single plant or firm, the measure developed here catches only interplant, intrafirm diversity. If a single plant produces several products (intraplant diversity), then this element escapes the measure.

are constructed directly from the *Sourcebooks* of the *Statistics of Income Corporation Income Tax Returns* for the four years 1958–59 through 1961–62. The advertising intensity variable is an average for the first two of these years of the ratios of advertising expenditures to sales (× 100). The concentration variables were constructed from

TABLE I

REGRESSION RESULTS: PROFIT RATES REGRESSED ON CONCENTRATION (CR_4), MARGINAL CONCENTRATION (MCR_8), ADVERTISING INTENSITY, AND CORPORATE DIVERSITY; ALL OBSERVATIONS (n = 106)

		Independent variables					
Dependent variable	*Intercept*	CR_4	MCR_8	*Advertising intensity*	*Diversity**	R^2	$\bar{R}^2$
PR_1	4.74	0.0432 [3.91]	−0.113 [2.68]			0.136	0.120
PR_2	6.24	0.0674 [3.92]	−0.186 [2.84]			0.140	0.123
PR_1	4.27	0.0421 [4.75]	−0.141 [4.14]	0.511 [7.60]		0.449	0.432
PR_2	5.49	0.0657 [4.82]	−0.230 [4.42]	0.813 [7.88]		0.465	0.449
PR_1	5.34	0.0411 [3.51]	−0.117 [2.72]		0.00589 [0.539]	0.139	0.113
PR_2	7.55	0.0629 [3.45]	−0.195 [2.92]		−0.0129 [0.759]	0.145	0.119
PR_1	6.68	0.0336 [3.68]	−0.160 [4.76]	0.557 [8.29]	−0.0241 [2.76]	0.487	0.467
PR_2	9.70	0.0508 [3.67]	−0.265 [5.17]	0.894 [8.76]	−0.0421 [3.17]	0.513	0.494

Observations: 106 Internal Revenue Service minor manufacturing industries.
[ ]: *t*-ratios.
R^2 is coefficient of multiple determination unadjusted for degrees of freedom; $\bar{R}^2$ is corrected.
* See footnote 12.
Variables:
PR_1: (Retained Earnings plus interest paid) ÷ total assets, average of four annual rates 1958–59 to 1961–62.
PR_2: Retained Earnings ÷ net worth, average of four annual rates 1958–59 to 1961–62.
CR_4: Four-firm concentration ratio 1958 (weighted average of four-digit concentration ratios).
MCR_8: Marginal eight-firm concentration ratio 1958.
Advertising intensity: advertising expenditures ÷ business receipts, average of two annual ratios 1958–59 and 1959–60. (× 100).
Diversity: Industry Specialization Ratio 1958 (labor).

the four-digit concentration ratios for 1958 by weighted averages (weights = value of shipments). The link between the minor industries (n = 106) and the four-digit industries (n = 443), as well as the Industry Specialization Ratio, were provided by the Census–IRS link project (*Enterprise Statistics 1958*, part 3).

STATISTICAL RESULTS

Table I presents the results for the least squares regression equations using concentration, marginal concentration, advertising intensity, and diversity in turn, for all observations. All the variables are statistically significant, and together they account for about half of the variance in the profit rates. As expected, the four-firm concentration ratio (CR_4) is positively related to profit rates: the larger the share of industry output produced by the largest four firms, the higher the profit rate.

The marginal eight-firm concentration ratio is significant and the sign is negative: the larger the share of industry output produced by the second largest four firms, the lower the industry profit rate. Evidently implicit collusion or monopoly-like performance in oligopolies is effective if the number of firms producing *substantial shares* of industry output is four (or perhaps three or five; the concentration variables cannot discriminate this 'division' so precisely). But if the number of firms exceeds five, six, or seven, substantial shares in this second rank of four firms produce independent competitive action on price.

The advertising/sales ratio likewise is statistically significant. If this variable reflects barriers to entry, as Bain and Comanor and Wilson suggest, then product differentiation affects profit rates; profit rates are higher *ceteris paribus* in those industries in which advertising expenditures are a higher relative share of business receipts.

Each equation in Table I can be read in two directions; the preceding interpretation (and the specification of the equation) imply the causality running from the independent variables to the dependent variables. The generally accepted interpretation of the correlation between the profit rate and the four-firm concentration ratio is the one presented here: firms are better able to collude tacitly in highly concentrated industries than in less concentrated industries, hence concentration leads to relatively high profit rates. In an analogous fashion, marginal concentration presumably affects profit rates rather than vice versa. However, might the reverse be plausible, too? High profit rates encourage entry, which is undertaken (by new firms or the expansion of old firms) by firms which rank 5 through 8, rather than by larger or smaller firms. The negative coefficient thus may appear because firms are entering at intermediate (rank 5 through 8) size in response to profit opportunities. The former argument is somewhat more intuitively appealing as well as plausible, on two grounds. First, it is symmetrical with the accepted argument regarding the effects of four-firm concentration on industry performance. Second, the latter argument seems inconsistent with the observation that over time eight-firm concentration appears not to be increasing, given that the four-firm concentration ratio seems stable over time. One implication of the latter argument is necessarily an increase through time of the eight-firm concentration ratio, an increase which has not appeared in the data.

The causality of the profit rate–advertising/sales ratio is somewhat more suspect, also on two grounds. First, the use of ratios raises statistical problems. Relatively large industries are large regardless of the measure used to measure size; industry sales and assets and net worth and employment are highly correlated. These measures of size appear in the denominators of the advertising/sales ratio and the two profit rates (as well as in the concentration ratio), hence a regression of either profit rate on the advertising/sales ratio may be the equivalent of regressing the inverse of one measure of industry size on the inverse of another measure.[9] On the other hand if the ratios themselves are the variables of interest, as they are in this study, then one should not be concerned about spurious correlation.[10]

The second suspicion of the advertising/sales ratio–profit rate causality rests on the argument that high profits may permit high advertising expenditures; since advertising expenditures are tax deductible, the federal government shares the cost. Thus viewed, decisions on advertising expenditures are made with an eye on realized profit, not on the expected profit which advertising presumably generates.[11] If this interpretation is generally valid, then one would expect aggregate manufacturing profits to be positively correlated year by year to aggregate manufacturing advertising expenditures. A rank correlation coefficient (Spearman's) was computed for the 16 years 1947–48 to 1962–63 between advertising expenditures and retained earnings (IRS categories 'Total compiled net profit less income tax' less 'distributions to stockholders'); the correlation was negative (−0.68). Using profit after taxes and

[9] For examples and discussion of spurious correlation arising from the use of ratios see W. Allen Wallis and Harry V. Roberts, *Statistics: A New Approach* (The Free Press of Glencoe Inc., 1956), pp. 546–9, and G. U. Yule and M. G. Kendall, *An Introduction to the Theory of Statistics* (14th ed.; New York: Hafner Publishing Co., 1950), pp. 330–31.

[10] Edwin Kuh and John R. Meyer, 'Correlation and Regression Estimates when the Data are Ratios', *Econometrica*, vol. 23 (October 1955), pp. 400–16, at pp. 401–2.

[11] See Professor Comanor's testimony in *Competitive Problems in the Drug Industry Hearings* before the Subcommittee on Monopoly, Select Committee on Small Business, U.S. Senate, 90th Cong., 1st and 2nd Sessions, Part 5, 1968, pp. 2041–63, especially pp. 2052–3. The causality discussed here, from profit availability to advertising expenditures, is contrary to other views on advertising expenditures, e.g. E. H. Chamberlin, *The Theory of Monopolistic Competition*, chapters on Selling Costs (any edition), and Norman S. Buchanan, 'Advertising Expenditures: A Suggested Treatment', *The Journal of Political Economy*, vol. 50 (August 1942), pp. 537–57.

before payments to stockholders, the rank correlation between profit and advertising was positive (+0.34). Lagging advertising expenditures by one year (n = 15), the rank correlation coefficients are −0.71 and −0.09. These correlation coefficients seem to provide little general support for this direction of causality; the initial hypothesis, as formulated by Bain, thus seems more plausible.

Corporate diversity, as measured by the Industry Specialization Ratio, and profit rates are positively[12] related when the diversity measure appears in the same regression equation with the advertising intensity variable (and the two concentration variables); the diversity variable (without the advertising variable) contributes nothing to the explanation of the profit rate variance beyond that contributed by the two concentration measures. The general theoretical argument for corporate diversity has yet to be developed, hence no inferences are attempted regarding the monopolistic or competitive aspects of diversity.

CONSUMER GOODS–PRODUCER GOODS INDUSTRIES

Bain's interpretation of advertising intensity as a barrier to entry applies only to consumer goods industries. For producer goods industries, product differentiation among firms, by advertising expenditures, is considerably more difficult. And if differentiation is possible, advertising probably is not the vehicle. If this argument is sound, then the statistical significance of the advertising intensity variable, when all 106 minor industries are used in the regression, should rest largely on those industries which may be classed as consumer goods industries. A division of the 106 observations into producer goods and consumer goods should retain the significance of this advertising variable only for the latter group; producer goods industries should exhibit reduced (or no) significance for this variable.

The 106 minor industries were divided into two groups on the basis of whether the greater value of shipments was made to manufacturers for further processing or to distributors for sale to consumers. In practice the choice generally turned on whether the major (by value) product(s) of each industry reached the final consumers in physically altered or unaltered form. The regressions of Table II reflect this division into 35 consumer goods industries and 71 other (generally producer goods) industries.[13]

[12] The industry specialization ratio, reflecting diversity, is an inverse measure: the greater the diversity the greater the measure falls below unity. Hence the negative sign in the regressions of Table I reflects a positive correlation between diversity and profitability.

[13] These 35 industries are quite similar to those used by Comanor and Wilson.

The advertising intensity variable is statistically significant for both groups, despite the difference in means (3.041 for consumer goods industries, 0.935 for producer goods industries), a difference clearly expected by Bain and by Comanor and Wilson. In addition the size of the coefficients is larger for producer goods industries than for consumer goods industries. Several possibilities exist for this result. (1) The aggregation of economic industries into IRS minor industries may yield a number of minor industries which produce both consumer goods and producer goods. The significance of the advertising variable may result in these actual consumer goods industries showing through the producer goods industries in which they are lumped. (2) Advertising may serve several purposes, one

TABLE II

REGRESSION RESULTS: PROFIT RATES REGRESSED ON CR_4, MCR_8, ADVERTISING INTENSITY, AND DIVERSITY; CONSUMER GOODS (n = 35) AND PRODUCER GOODS (n = 71) INDUSTRIES*

		Independent variables					
Dependent variable	*Intercept*	CR_4	MCR_8	*Advertising intensity*	*Diversity*	R^2	$\bar{R}^2$
Consumer goods (*n* = 35)							
PR_1	5.86	0.0482	−0.202	0.597	−0.0189	0.742	0.708
		[3.98]	[4.39]	[7.91]	[1.25]		
PR_2	9.86	0.0655	−0.345	0.936	−0.0424	0.759	0.727
		[3.67]	[5.10]	[8.42]	[1.90]		
Producer goods (*n* = 71)							
PR_1	6.45	0.0187	−0.104	0.756	−0.0240	0.267	0.223
		[1.40]	[2.14]	[3.27]	[2.16]		
PR_2	8.96	0.0325	−0.174	1.16	−0.0400	0.284	0.240
		[1.57]	[2.30]	[3.25]	[2.35]		

* See footnotes in Table I.

of which is product differentiation and the erection of entry barriers. This purpose might be more important for consumer goods industries, and other purposes, perhaps institutional or informational or company (vice product) advertising, might be more important for producer goods industries. The IRS data would not differentiate those purposes in their data. (3) Advertising expenditures may not reflect the erection of entry barriers by product differentiation but instead may reflect other purposes and functions common to producer and consumer goods industries alike.

The coefficients of multiple determination suggest that the four independent variables are much stronger joint influences on profit rates for the consumer goods industries than for the producer goods industries. The R^2 indicates that close to 3/4ths of the variance in the dependent variables is explained for the former industries, while about 1/4th of the variance is explained for the latter group. Correspondingly the *t*-ratios of the concentration variables are smaller in the producer goods equations than in the consumer goods equations. The relative size of the coefficients of the concentration variables—smaller for the producer goods industries than for the consumer goods industries—suggests that the effects of concentration on profit rates are attenuated in producer goods industries, possibly because the buyers of their output have more alternatives than the buyers of consumer goods industries. However, the Chow test for equality of sets of coefficients does not permit the rejection of the null hypothesis, that the sets of coefficients are the same.[14] Perhaps these buyers of the output from producer goods industries can integrate backwards[15] or perhaps they possess 'buying power' (as in a bilateral monopoly)—at least to a greater extent than the wholesalers and retailers who purchase the output of consumer goods industries. If so, then concentration in selling, as measured by CR_4 and MCR_8, would be less effective *either* in raising profit (as a high CR_4 apparently does) or in lowering profit (as a higher MCR apparently does).

NATIONAL–NON-NATIONAL AND HOMOGENEOUS–NON-HOMOGENEOUS MARKETS

A second problem inherent in using all 106 IRS minor industries involves the assumption that the market dimensions—product and geographic—are adequately reflected in the concentration variables. Some economic markets may be considerably smaller (or larger) than the entire country, which results in a deceptively smaller (or larger) concentration ratio based on national boundaries. Similarly some four-digit concentration ratios may include non-substitutable products and others may exclude substitutes. A division of the 106 minor industries, on the basis of homogeneity of the four-digit concentration ratios and national boundaries, produced the regression results of

[14] Gregory C. Chow, 'Tests of Equality Between Sets of Coefficients in Two Linear Regressions', *Econometrica*, vol. 28, no. 3 (July 1960), pp. 591–605. For PR_1, $F = 1.14$ and for PR_2, $F = 0.91$; the 5 percent significance level ($n_1 = 5$, $n_2 = 96$) is $F = 2.30$.

[15] As perhaps they have, since the diversity variable (which includes some vertical integration) displays a somewhat greater *t*-ratio in the producer goods equations. To the extent that the industry specialization ratio reflects vertical integration (see discussion in footnote 7, supra), the integration is downstream by the *sellers* in the producer goods industries. This suggests that these sellers (by such integration), may be bypassing some concentration on the buying side. Similarly, *buyers* may integrate upstream to bypass seller concentration. On the other hand, the extreme values of the diversity measure appear to be generally producer goods industries. Even so, the diversity coefficients are remarkably similar in Table II.

Table III. The Chow test again does not permit the rejection of the null hypothesis.[16]

CONSUMER GOODS INDUSTRIES AND NATIONAL, HOMOGENEOUS MARKETS

Using the criteria both for consumer goods industries and for national, homogeneous markets, 24 of the 106 minor industries can be selected for estimating the same regression equations. Table IV presents the results using all four as well as three independent variables (diversity dropped because of its low *t*-ratios). Again about

TABLE III

REGRESSION RESULTS: PROFIT RATES REGRESSED ON CR_4, MCR_8, ADVERTISING INTENSITY, AND DIVERSITY; NATIONAL AND HOMOGENEOUS (n = 62) INDUSTRIES AND NON-NATIONAL AND NON-HOMOGENEOUS (n = 44) INDUSTRIES*

		Independent variables					
Dependent variable	*Intercept*	CR_4	MCR_8	*Advertising intensity*	*Diversity*	R^2	$\bar{R}^2$
National and homogeneous industries (n = 62)							
PR_1	6.80	0.0333 [3.17]	−0.154 [3.78]	0.548 [7.45]	−0.0269 [2.70]	0.560	0.529
PR_2	9.63	0.0535 [3.26]	−0.251 [3.95]	0.870 [7.58]	−0.0441 [2.84]	0.571	0.541
Non-national and non-homogeneous industries (n = 44)							
PR_1	6.08	0.0353 [1.76]	−0.157 [2.31]	0.627 [3.52]	−0.0184 [0.925]	0.358	0.292
PR_2	9.22	0.0427 [1.46]	−0.264 [2.65]	1.01 [3.87]	−0.0359 [1.23]	0.391	0.328

* See footnotes in Table I.

70 percent of the variance in the profit rates is explained by the independent variables; the diversity coefficient, however, no longer is statistically different from zero.

SUMMARY

The statistical results reported in Tables I–IV tend to conform with the expectations of basic microeconomics: the profit rates for

[16] For both PR_1 and PR_2, $F < 1$. An initial attempt at this division, reported in my 'Marginal Concentration Ratios . . .' (p. 262), used 77 of the minor industries as 'acceptable' in both product and geographic dimensions. Professor Frank Kottke criticized this division ('The Profitability of Industry Leaders and Measurable Characteristics of Industry Structure and Experience', mimeo, April 1967, at p. 7). The division reported here (n = 62 and 44) reflects his evaluation of the IRS minor industries. I gratefully acknowledge with thanks his expertise and counsel. A listing of the industries indicating both this division and the consumer goods–producer goods division is available on request.

the IRS industries are positively related to the four-firm concentration ratio, the percentage of sales revenue devoted to advertising, and (to some extent) the degree to which companies are diversified into industries other than their own. The negative relation between the share of output produced by the second largest four firms and the industry profit rates tends to support the observation that cartels are fragile, particularly implicit cartels without the (illegal) mechanisms of agreements on price or output or market sharing. Jointly these four variables account for about half the profit rate variance for all observations and for about 70 per cent of the profit rate variance in consumer goods industries.

On the other hand, the relationships shown by the diversity variable appear to be comparatively weak. Its statistical significance

TABLE IV

REGRESSION RESULTS: PROFIT RATES REGRESSED ON CR_4, MCR_8, ADVERTISING INTENSITY, AND DIVERSITY: CONSUMER GOODS INDUSTRIES AND NATIONAL, HOMOGENEOUS MARKETS COMBINED (n = 24)*

Dependent variable	Intercept	Independent variables				R^2	$\bar{R}^2$
		CR_4	MCR_8	Advertising intensity	Diversity		
PR_1	4.97	0.0520 [3.54]	−0.204 [3.49]	0.594 [6.74]	−0.0109 [0.551]	0.751	0.699
PR_2	8.71	0.0693 [3.08]	−0.341 [3.82]	0.924 [6.85]	−0.0314 [1.04]	0.751	0.699
PR_1	3.92	0.0552 [4.16]	−0.203 [3.54]	0.585 [6.87]		0.747	0.710
PR_2	5.69	0.0785 [3.79]	−0.339 [3.78]	0.899 [6.76]		0.737	0.698

* See footnotes in Table I.

appears in regressions using the producer goods industries and the national, homogeneous industries. The advertising intensity variable retains its statistical significance throughout the tables, although in weakened form for producer goods industries and for non-national, non-homogeneous industries. Its interpretation as a proxy for the height of entry barriers is somewhat questionable, since the rationale for this interpretation has been developed only for consumer goods industries.

APPENDIX

DATA

The minor industries in the manufacturing sector as defined by the Internal Revenue Service provide the sample of industries for this study.

From the IRS *Sourcebooks* of the *Statistics of Income* series, two profit rates were computed for the 106 manufacturing industries (omitting twelve minor industries composed of miscellaneous four-digit industries): profit as a return on total assets (PR_1), and profit as a return on net worth (PR_2). PR_1 for each minor industry is the mean of the four annual profit rates 1958–59 through 1961–62, where each annual rate for each industry is 'compiled net profit less income tax' plus 'interest paid' divided by total assets. PR_2 is the mean of the four annual profit rates, 'compiled net profit less income tax' divided by net worth, where net worth is the sum of capital stock (common and preferred), 'paid-in or capital surplus', 'suplus reserves', and 'earned surplus and undivided profits'.

The IRS minor industries are somewhat broader than Census four-digit industries. The appropriate four-digit industries were combined by taking a weighted (by value of shipments) mean of the 1958 concentration ratios to produce an average four-firm concentration ratio for each of the 106 industries. A similar procedure produced an average eight-firm concentration ratio for each industry. The marginal eight-firm concentration ratio is the difference between these two CRs (i.e., $MCR_8 = CR_8 - CR_4$). Basic concentration data came from *Concentration Ratios in Manufacturing Industry 1958*, Report prepared by the Bureau of the Census for the Subcommittee on Antitrust and Monopoly of the Committee on the Judiciary, U.S. Senate (Washington: U.S. Government Printing Office, 1962) Table IV. These data are based on the 'commodity approach'. The link between the four-digit industries as used by the Census Bureau and the minor industries in the IRS is found in U.S. Department of Commerce, Bureau of the Census, *Enterprise Statistics: 1958*, Part 3 (Washington: U.S. Government Printing Office, 1964), pp. 28–30.

Advertising intensity was measured by the ratio of advertising expenditure to sales revenue ($\times 100$); for the two years 1958–59 and 1959–60 for each industry this ratio was constructed, and a simple (equally weighted) mean for each industry produced this variable. The IRS categories are 'Advertising [expenditure]' and 'Business Receipts' (*Sourcebooks* of the *Statistics of Income* 1958–59 and 1959–60). These advertising expenditures, moreover, are those made by the manufacturing corporations classified in each IRS industry. Excluded are advertising expenditures made by wholesalers and retailers not classified in these industries, and naturally expenditures by the distributors on advertising are undertaken at least in part to influence consumer choice of brands. Also excluded are advertising expenditures which manufacturing corporations report to the IRS as other kinds of expenditure.

The industry specialization ratio is derived from *Enterprise Statistics: 1958*, Part 3 ('Link of Census Establishment and IRS Corporation Data'), Table 2, Column 3. Plants are 'census establishments' not including 'central administrative offices, auxiliaries, sales branches, and sales offices'. The data of this table are derived from a sample of companies used for the Census–IRS link. If some companies in an industry own plants classified in a different industry, the ratio for the industry drops below 1. Diversification thus is reflected by the extent to which the measure falls below unity: the greater is the diversity of firms in the industry, the lower is the industry specialization ratio.

WESLEYAN UNIVERSITY,
MIDDLETOWN, CONNECTICUT

THE BEHAVIOR OF THE FIRM WITH A FINANCIAL RESTRICTION

by Guido di Tella

I. The process of growth has generally been analyzed at the macroeconomic level, to the detriment of its implication at the level of the firm.

In this article we want to analyze the behavior of the firm under conditions prevalent in some underdeveloped economies. We will assume that the firm does not have access to the financial market, either because it is nonexistent, or because there are institutional factors which preclude transactions between the firm under analysis and the financial market. We will also assume that the consumer cannot obtain financing from the financial market for his purchases of the firm's products. This may seem an extremely limiting assumption, but it is probably more relevant for countries in the process of growth than the usual alternative hypothesis which assumes an infinite supply of finance at a certain rate.

The more normal hypothesis is to assume the existence of two different markets, for goods and for finance, where consumers and producers try so maximize separately. In our case, the two markets have become one and the consumer and producer have to maximize. They both have a problem of joint maximization.

Our work has been inspired by the observation of certain situations and behavior in the real world which, unfortunately, is likely to mitigate the level of sophistication and abstraction in which our profession takes so much pride. We therefore have to apologize for having kept some real-world expressions.

Our work will try to analyze the way in which a firm with a limited supply of finance, tries to maximize its profits using its scarce resources to shift the demand (through the granting of installment finance), and/or expand the size of the firm.

Each one of these alternatives has different profitability and requires different financial inputs, which should not exceed the available finance.

Obviously, we are facing a problem which lends itself beautifully to linear programming techniques. However, in this work we will try to analyze the way in which the problem is posed, rather than the particular solutions.

II. We will first show a simplified model of a firm, making a comparative static analysis of its behavior throughout the period. Further on, we will try to see the changes in its behavior as a consequence of the elimination of some of the restrictive hypotheses.

Our initial assumptions are the following:

(1) The firm is analyzed in the short run; therefore, we will only consider variations in the volume of production, maintaining the plant fixed.
(2) The fixed capital is not used up during the period, which is the same thing as saying that the cost includes amortization and maintenance, and that these are done.
(3) All that is produced is sold, therefore there are no problems connected with variations in stocks.
(4) No profits are derived from the financing of sales.
(5) There is only one way of financing sales: the rate of interest is fixed, a certain proportion of the value is paid in cash and the balance at the end of the period under analysis. The only variation that can be introduced is the change in the cash proportion.
(6) The firm is in a monopolistically competitive market.
(7) Demand is a function of prices and of financial conditions, that is, it shifts to the right as the firm gives better financial conditions to the purchasers.
(8) Increases in output at the given level of the plant do not require a greater financial amount.[1]
(9) There are no financial resources external to the firm.
(10) At the beginning of the period the firm is selling in cash and is producing at the optimum level, maximizing profits. The firm has enough financial resources to take care of its requirements at its level of activity, being therefore in an initial financial equilibrium situation. At the end of the period this equilibrium situation will change as a consequence of the profits obtained during the period, that may allow a change in the volume of production, attaining a new financial equilibrium at a higher level.

Our basic idea concerns the maximizing behavior of the firm, subject to the financial constraint implied by the assumption we have made of the lack of financial sources, external to the firm.

Taking into account the hypotheses mentioned above, we will

[1] We can assume that the period of production diminishes, therefore offsetting the greater financial requirements.

start our analysis assuming that the firm is selling exclusively in cash, and that the available resources are sufficient to finance only the initial volume of production and sales. However, the firm may be in a position to start financing its sales.

According to our assumption number (5), we will only consider changes in the percentage received in cash, without introducing variations on the time required to receive the balance (which coincides with the period under analysis) and we will not change the rate of interest on the outstanding. We will assume that for certain financial conditions F_1 (vg., 50 percent in cash and 50 percent in terms), the demand curve will shift to the right, as this will be the normal expectation in the case of any improvement in the financial conditions. We will obtain a new optimum corresponding to the new level of production at which the firm will now maximize its profits. As each financial condition yields a different demand curve, we will have to determine, for each one of these curves, the optimum level of production, and the corresponding cash inflow in each case. We can now determine the functional relationship (Fig. 1) between the various financial conditions and the corresponding cash inflows. In the horizontal axis we will measure the amounts received in cash. In the other axis we will measure the financial condition expressed as the percentage not received in cash. Point 1 represents the initial situation, with only cash sales. This functional relationship will have a shape determined by the degree in which the financing of the sales influences the demand curve.

This curve allows us to define a new concept, which we could call 'financial elasticity', which relates the relative variations in the cash inflow to the relative variations in the financial conditions. The analytical expression of the financial elasticity is derived in the Appendix at the end of the article.

It is important to mention that the curve is defined for a given level of the plant, because if it varies, the marginal cost curve also changes and the equilibrium situation for a given demand curve will change. The level of output and the price will vary as well as the total revenue and the cash revenue. If the financial elasticity of the cash revenue curve of the firm is of the type shown in Fig. 1, the initial situation in which all sales are made in cash will not be the best. Despite the financial constraint, the firm can move from Point 1 to Point 2. This is due to the fact that although in the initial situation there is no financial surplus that allows the financing of the sales at that level of output, the improvement in the financial conditions will increase demand to such an extent as to increase the cash revenue, enabling therefore the financing of the process.

In that case the firm can choose from the array of possible situations (from 1 to 2), that in which profits will be highest, which will coincide with the situation where sales are the largest, that is to say, point 2. If however, some situation above Point 2 were better for the firm, it would not be able to reach it, as the financial constraint does not allow financial conditions exceeding F_2.[2]

Fig. 1

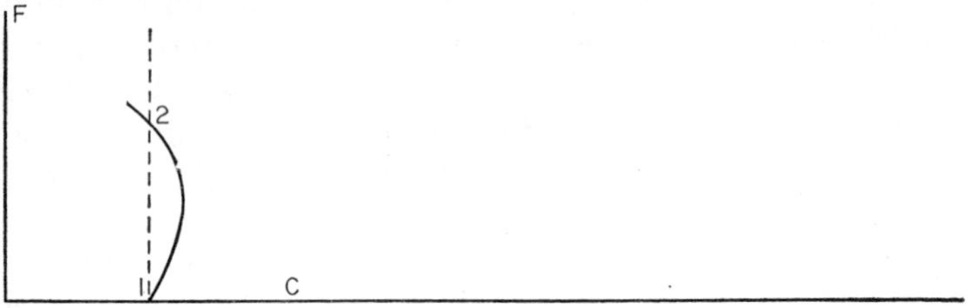

Fig. 2

III. We think we now have to go back and re-examine some of the restrictive hypotheses that we made in the initial part of this paper. We will try to see to what extent it is possible to extend the degree of generalization of this work, through the elimination of some of those restrictions.

[2] The function defined in Fig. 1 is only one of many possible ones, and we do not say it is the most interesting, nor the most realistic. The most interesting and relevant case might be a law of variable proportions. In a first phase, an improvement in the financing conditions may expand demand to a very small degree, decreasing the cash revenue. In a second phase, an improvement in the financial conditions may substantially increase demand. At the final phase, further increases in financial conditions may not increase demand substantially. In this case we will have a curve like the one presented in Fig. 2. The firm can either choose the initial situation described by Point 1, or the range of solutions comprised between Points 2 and 3, maximizing profits at Point 3. The financial constraint will not allow any financial condition exceeding F_3, nor those comprised between F_1 and F_2. The firm now has a much greater constraint, not only because it has a similar range of possible solutions, but because it has to approach the solution through a discontinuous decision, having to vary from F_1 to a point at least above F_2, incurring therefore in a much greater risk. In the previous case it could approach the optimum solution through marginal decisions.

(a) *Financing required by variations in the volume of production.* Up to now we have assumed that an increase in output does not increase the financial requirements, namely, a greater volume of output was taken care of with the same amount of financial resources. Then, if we assume that an availability of greater resources in relation to the increase in production is necessary, we will have to establish some functional relation between output and the minimum financial resources necessary to obtain this output.

Figure 1 must be corrected according to this new criterion, so therefore, a greater minimum volume of cash necessary for production will correspond to each financial condition.

The curve which expresses the financial restriction, as can be seen

Fig. 3

Fig. 4

in Fig. 3, is now rising (the form depending on the type of relation between financial conditions with respect to the quantity of output optimally produced, and between the latter and the minimum cash corresponding to each level of output), and the new opportunities of choice open to the firm are spread between points 1 and 3, with a tendency toward Point 3, a point which implies profit maximization.

As can be observed in the diagram, the level of F (and of the corresponding output) reached at Point 3, is lower than the corresponding level in Point 2, in which the restriction was constant. The same happens to the profit earned, which is less in Point 3. When financial restriction increases, there is a narrowing of the range within which profits can be maximized.

(b) *Initial Financial Availability*. We can now assume that at the beginning of the period of analysis, the conditions were such that the sales made in cash were sufficient to support that volume of production, leaving a certain cash surplus.

In that case there is an obvious decrease in the financial constraint, increasing the range in which the firm can maximize its profits. In this case, a situation like the one described in Fig. 4 may be relevant.

If the distance 2–1 represents the initial financial availability, it will allow financial conditions ranging from F_1 to F_3, which would have otherwise been impossible.

(c) *Multiple-period Analysis*. The conclusions drawn from the simplified model which we have been analyzing up to now, are not changed if we consider more than one period.

Fig. 5

At the end of the first period, we will have a greater financial availability, as the firm will receive the deferred revenue of the sales financed at the beginning of the period. Further, the profits made during the period plus the initial resources, will allow the firm a greater range of optimizing solutions in period two.

(d) *Profits from Financing*. Up to this point we have not taken into consideration the profits made by the firm on the finance given to purchasers. It is necessary to take this very important aspect into account since, according to our hypothesis, we do not have an organized financial market available to the firm. Therefore, the financial resources that can be used to finance sales will not have, as an alternative use, one which will allow similar profits through loans made to other parties.

It is important to note that part of the interest earned is obtained, as in Fig. 5, not as a result of the initial financial resources, but as a consequence of the expansionary process of sales.

A simple way to analyze the profits made on sales financing, would consist in the incorporation of said profits into the price, which implies that the firm faces a new demand curve with higher prices for each quantity. Then the firm maximizes profits, taking into account this new curve, which includes interest earnings.

In Fig. 5 we have a given demand curve, which corresponds to certain financial conditions. Each point of the curve defines a certain quantity and a certain price, and a certain total revenue. We can determine, for a given interest rate, the total interest earnings corresponding to a certain quantity, and a certain price, and a certain financial condition. Therefore, it is possible to obtain a curve like D′D, where each one of its points, such as Point 1, is at a certain distance from the original curve (1 1′) measured vertically, which is the result of dividing the financial earnings corresponding to that level of production, by its volume. This distance will therefore be equal to:

$$p.F.i$$

where q is the volume, p the price, F the percentage of the price deferred, i the rate of interest. This value will, therefore, be proportional to the price for given values of F and i.

The market demand curve is therefore D D, but the firm maximizes with respect to D″D, that is, the firm tries to maximize the total revenue originated from its productive activity, and from its financial activity.

IV. As we have seen, it is possible to eliminate some of the initial restrictive hypotheses. We can take into consideration a certain initial financial availability, we can take into consideration profits originating from the interest on the credit given to the purchasers, we can take into consideration the financial requirements necessary to vary the volume of production, and we can also extend our analysis to more than a single period. But in order to obtain a sufficiently general model, it is necessary to modify our assumption number 1, that is, the possibility of varying the size of the plant. Only then will we be able to analyze the three principal alternatives open to firms subject to a financial constraint: investment in fixed plant, financing of sales, financing of the volume of production. In this case it is possible to consider the various situations arising from the degree of divisibility of the investments in the plant and according to the increasing or decreasing cost (to scale) situation.

As an example, we may analyze a case in which we assume two possible sizes of plant, the initial situation and a possible addition, of an indivisible character. We will combine these two-plant possibilities with three alternative financial conditions, which will give rise to three different demands. We will assume that the firm has increasing returns to scale, so that the larger plant has a lower minimum cost, at a higher volume of output. If we assume that the three demand curves, D_1, D_2 and D_3, of Fig. 6, already include profits originated in financing of sales, the points where marginal costs are equal to marginal revenues will be with Plant No. 1 A, B, and C. With the larger plant, No. 2, the equilibrium points will be D, E, F. The combination of Plant No. 1 with demand D_1, resulting from financial condition F_1, will give place to production OG at the price OI, which thus includes interest on sales. Total revenue, originated by sales and by profits on financing, is represented by the area OIJG, the profit by HIJK. The cash revenue can be obtained by multiplying total revenue from sales, at the price OI, by the percentage received in cash corresponding to the financial condition F_1.

Fig. 6

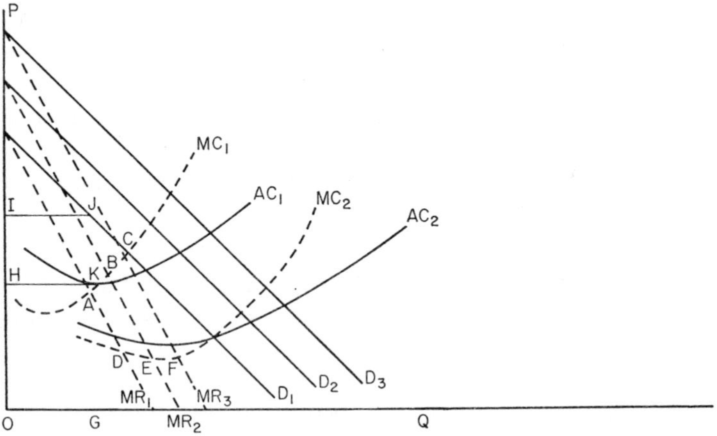

In the same way, curves similar to the one drawn in Fig. 1 can be made, making also the same corrections as those indicated in Fig. 2 and 3.

We can now determine the additional investment necessary to move from the level of plant No. 1, to the level of plant No. 2. We are now in a position to determine in which of the two situations we can make a larger profit, subject always to the financial constraint implied in our initial financial availability. In order to maximize profits, the firm will have to allocate its scarce resources among the three competing strategies: increasing the size of the plant, increasing financial conditions, or financing a greater volume of production. We cannot make any conclusion *a priori*, since it would depend on the particular shapes and elasticities of the various curves.

As an example, we can mention a case which could correspond to Fig. 6.

Size of Plant	*Demand*	*Profits*
1	1	7
1	2	12
1	3	18
2	1	9
2	2	16
2	3	24

If there were no financial constraint, the firm would maximize its profits investing in the increase of the size of the plant, granting financial condition F_3, and allowing the firm to be faced by demand D_3. But under conditions of financial constraint, we have to take into consideration:

(a) our initial financial availability, in excess of the normal requirements, when all are cash sales;
(b) the investment necessary for the variation in the size of the plant and consequently, in the cost curves;
(c) the financial elasticity, which corresponds to each size of plant and to each possible financial condition.

It is quite obvious that in the above example, if the firm—after investing in the increase in plant size—does not have sufficient financial resources to enable it to reach demand curve D_3; and on the other hand, if by not making the investment, it can reach that demand curve, the latter case will then be preferred. Saving the cash required to enlarge the size of the plant, and using all its resources in the financing of the sales, will allow the firm to reach D_3, therefore maximizing its profits (18 units instead of 16 units).

If we take into consideration various periods, instead of only one, the maximizing behavior will require that the firm maximize in each period, as the financial constraint is, in turn, a function of the profits made in each period. In other words, we will not be presented with a possible conflict between maximizing in the short run, or maximizing in the long run, under the assumptions we have made up to now. The firm will have a unique solution for its optimum growth path. The problem could only be posed if we allowed the existence of a financial market, external to the firm, in which the firm could place its surplus funds, or request transitory finance.

Up to now we have not considered the shareholders of the firm. If we do so, we introduce a further restriction in the growth of the firm. The shareholders will prefer to receive a certain proportion of the cash that the firm would generate as a dividend. This preference would exist even if it means—and it will certainly mean—a reduction in the process of expansion, and would imply a certain willingness to forsake future earnings, future cash availability, and therefore, future cash dividends. The preference of the shareholders for present or future dividends, will obviously depend on their time preference.

V. The consideration of demand as a function of financial conditions is an approach similar to the one used by Chamberlin in the analysis of monopolistic competition, because we could say that variations in financial conditions are a kind of product differentiation.

The model has, as its only virtue, the fact that it combines in a unique solution, profits obtained from three different activities; the firm as producer, as financier, and as investor; and that solution is subject to a constraint of a financial character. It would be possible to present a similar treatment with continuous functions, for variations in the size of the plant, and for variations in the financial conditions. It seems, however, more realistic to utilize an approach based on discontinuities, such as the one put forward in this paper, since business decisions are probably made on the basis of a limited number of possible alternatives. It would be relatively easy to make this extension, if necessary.

We have also introduced the concept of financial elasticity because, due to the conditions under which the firm operates, certain market conditions may allow a process of expansion where finance is, to some extent, the consequence of the very process of expansion of the firm.

In our model the financial constraint means that the firm will not always try to be on the long-run minimum-average cost curve. Due to this financial constraint, it would be more convenient for the firm to remain at the curve with greater average cost, devoting the resources to expand the demand through the granting of better financial conditions.

The basic hypothesis that has given origin to this model is the non-existence of a financial market. This may seem a rather extreme and unrealistic hypothesis. However, if there is a financial market, and it is less than fully developed, we will have problems similar to those put forward here, although to a lesser degree. Also, even where more mature financial markets exist, firms do not have access to unlimited amounts of financing and they depend, to a great extent, on their own financial structures. As soon as we go beyond a certain amount of finance used, the financial ratios of the firm will worsen in such a way as to, in a first stage, increase the cost of the financing, and at a latter stage, make internal financing impossible.

In those cases the firm may try to improve its financial ratios, even at the expense of its present earnings, for the sake of future profit maximization.

We would have a conflict between maximizing earnings in the short run, which does not require us to take into consideration the financial ratios; versus the maximization of profits in the long run, which certainly requires us to take the financial ratios into consideration. In order to give more relevance to the model, we should consider the existence of various degrees of imperfection of financial intermediaries, as it is probably more realistic to assume neither one of the two extremes: that is, perfect financial markets, or nonexistent financial markets. We have to add that we question the fact that even in a perfect financial market, the firm would have unlimited finance, as this would imply a very original definition of perfection, which would not take into consideration the financial structure of the firm.

It is true that in a more general analysis we should take into consideration the possibility of changing the financial conditions in the sense of deferring payment for more than one period. We should also have to consider the financing of the investment and the financing of the inputs, which we have not considered here because they introduce considerable analytical complications while adding very little to the general model.

We should be very careful to generalize our conclusions to the economy as a whole, as we should take into consideration the behavior of other entrepreneurs and the possibility of reprisals. The reprisals can take the form of price policies as well as financial policies.

The basic conclusion, in our view, is that in the absence of a perfect financial market, the behavior of the firm is sub-optimum. The firm will react to the non-existence of a financial market by beginning to operate in such a market directly. Its maximizing behavior will be similar to that of a multiple product firm and will be subject to all the problems inherent to that situation.

This lack of specialization, and the sub-optimal behavior implied in it, may become so evident, that at a later stage we can see the emergence of some firms that may specialize in the new product, financial funds, rather than in the old product, and may therefore solve one of the basic problems that may lie in the path of optimum behavior. This rise of financial intermediaries may allow firms to revert to the initial position as specialists in the production of goods.

UNIVERSITY OF BUENOS AIRES

APPENDIX

FINANCIAL ELASTICITY

As was expressed before on page 121 there exists a relation between the cash received by the firm when output is sold, and the percentage of deferred revenue. Let us define financial elasticity as the ratio between the percentage change of cash and the percentage variation of the financial condition.

We will continue by expressing the financial elasticity as a function of the partial elasticities of demand.

To begin, let C represent the cash received, q (p, F) represent the demand as a function depending on the price of the product and the financial condition (F is the percent of deferred revenue). We also assume (according to hypotheses 1 and 6) that the marginal costs are defined for a given plant and the firm is in a monopolistically competitive market.

The cash received by the firm will be:

$$C = (1-F).p.q(p, F) \tag{1}$$

with the additional condition that for each F, marginal revenue equals marginal cost.

Differentiating the expression (1) with respect to F we obtain:

$$\frac{dC}{dF} = \left[(1-F)\frac{dp}{dF} - p\right]q + \left(\frac{\partial q}{\partial p}\frac{dp}{dF} + \frac{\partial q}{\partial F}\right)(1-F)p$$

$$= \left[\frac{(1-F)}{F}\frac{dp}{dF}\frac{F}{p} - 1\right]pq + \left(\frac{\partial q}{\partial p}\frac{p}{q}\cdot\frac{dp}{dF}\frac{F}{p} + \frac{\partial q}{\partial F}\frac{F}{q}\right)\frac{(1-F)}{F}pq \tag{2}$$

taking account of:

$\bar{\eta}_{p,F} = \frac{F}{p}\frac{dp}{dF} =$ total elasticity of price with respect to the financing percentage

$\bar{\eta}_{q,p} = \frac{p}{q}\frac{\delta q}{\delta p} =$ partial elasticity of demand with respect to the price

$\eta_{q,F} = \frac{q}{F}\frac{\delta q}{\delta F} =$ partial elasticity of demand with respect to the financing percentage

the equation (2) may be rewritten in the following way:

$$\frac{dC}{dF} = \left[\frac{(1-F)}{F}\bar{\eta}_{p,F} - 1\right]pq + \left(\eta_{q,p}.\bar{\eta}_{p,F} + \eta_{q,F}\right)\frac{(1-F)}{F}p.q \tag{3}$$

Finally, dividing the derivative obtained (3) by C, and multiplying by F, we get the financial elasticity:

$$\varepsilon = \frac{F}{C}\frac{dC}{dF} = \bar{\eta}_{p,\,F}\left(1+\eta_{q,\,p}\right) - \frac{F}{(1-F)} + \eta_{q,\,F} \qquad (4)$$

After this, we must analyze the sign of the expression obtained.

First, $\bar{\eta}_{p,\,F}$ is positive because an increase would shift the demand to the right, and as the marginal cost must rise with a greater production, the quantity of output at which marginal cost equals marginal revenue will correspond to a higher price.[3] With respect to the expression between brackets, the results are negative when marginal cost is positive and zero when marginal cost is zero. In the first case, marginal revenue must be positive and the firm must operate in the elastic range of demand ($\eta_{q,\,p} < -1$). If marginal cost was zero for every volume of production, the equilibrium point for each F will be attained when the price elasticity of demand equals (-1). In this case $[1+\eta_{q,\,p}] = 0$, but this would not affect the conclusions.

From above, it follows that the product $\bar{\eta}_{p,\,F}(1+\eta_{q,\,p})$ is negative (or zero for $\eta_{q,\,p} = -1$), and so the term $F/1-F$ which is preceded by a sign minus. Therefore, the only element greater than zero is the partial derivative of demand with respect to financing. From the formula (4) is obtained that the sign of the financial elasticity will depend mainly on the influence that financing has on demand, and on the price-elasticity of demand.

It must be remarked that this formula makes no sense in the case of pure competition, for it would not be justifiable to use financing as a device for increasing sales.

[3] Even in the case in which marginal cost was constant, $\bar{\eta}_{p,F}$ would be positive, because a demand shift would bid the price up, although it would reach a lower equilibrium in comparison with the case in which the marginal cost curve is rising. If marginal cost decreases with more output, the situation is not so clear, provided that it may invalidate the first order condition for profit maximizing, depending upon the way in which the marginal revenue curve cuts the marginal cost curve. However, this case is irrelevant for the analysis and may be neglected.

Note. The author wants to thank Mr. Héctor Diégnez and Mr. Osvaldo Baccino for their assistance, particularly for their suggestions on the treatment of interest and for the appendix.

STOCK MARKET VALUATION AND ACQUISITIONS: AN EMPIRICAL TEST OF ONE COMPONENT OF MANAGERIAL UTILITY*

by D. A. Kuehn

I. INTRODUCTION

Between 1948 and 1961, 735 public companies quoted on the London Stock Exchange were taken over by other quoted companies, or one-quarter of the original population. There also appears to have been two or three hundred unsuccessful bids during this period. It is the object of this paper to examine the effects the threat of take-over may exert on a firm's behaviour within the theoretical constructs of the managerial theories of the firm.

The behavioural revisions to the theory of the firm, recognizing the importance of the separation of ownership and control in modern corporations, have attempted an examination of managerial motivations in order to explain the firm's behaviour. There is, however, little agreement to be found in the literature as to the nature of the ingredients in the objective function which are to replace the profit maximization assumption. For example, Baumol[1] believed managers sought to maximize dollar sales; Marris[2] saw the primary motivation in terms of an attempt to maximize the growth rate of the firm; while Williamson[3] included a variable for pecuniary and non-pecuniary emoluments and staff size in the objective function. In all approaches, however, managers are seen as constrained from making decisions which could lead to loss of employment or bankruptcy because of a competing desire for security. Baumol and Williamson impose this security constraint by requiring that profits do not fall below some minimum level which satisfies the owners in terms of dividends and provides for financial safety. Marris, on the other hand, views the constraint as being imposed directly by the firm's valuation on the stock market which reflects not only shareholder approval of the firm's financial policies (by way of both satisfactory dividends and capital gains), but also affects the likelihood that the firm will receive a take-over bid. Since it is usual for all or part of the existing manage-

* This paper was submitted as partial fulfilment of the requirements for an M.A. at the University of Warwick. I am grateful to Dr. K. G. Cowling who made numerous helpful comments during the writing and revision of this paper and to Robin Marris, John Williamson and Professor F. G. Pyatt who offered suggestions on an earlier draft of this paper.

[1] Baumol, W. J., *Business Behaviour, Value and Growth*, New York, Macmillan Co. 1959.

[2] R. L. Marris, *The Economic Theory of 'Managerial' Capitalism*, Macmillan & Co. Ltd., London, 1964.

[3] O. E. Williamson, *The Economics of Discretionary Behaviour: Managerial Objectives in a Theory of the Firm*, Prentice Hall, Inc., N.J., 1964.

ment to be displaced when a firm is taken over,[4] the effect the probability of take-over exerts on managerial security is obvious. The security constraint competes with the maximization of the objective function in so far as the attainment of adequate levels of security either by maintaining satisfactory profits and dividends or more generally by keeping the firm's share prices at a 'safe' level, tends to reduce the ability of the firm to stimulate demand to raise its sales, or reduces the level of retained earnings with which to provide emoluments or stimulate the growth rate of the firm.

Formulated within the American context where shareholding is diffuse and take-over rare, Baumol's and Williamson's minimum profits constraint is likely to be the appropriate constraint on managerial behaviour. Within the U.K. setting, however, where shareholdings are less diffuse and take-over common, the security constraint is more likely to be imposed as in the Marris model via the stock market valuation ratio (defined as the ratio of the market value of the ordinary shares to the book value of the net assets).

For there to be an externally imposed security constraint of this form, it must be true that there exists a statistically significant inverse relationship between the firm's valuation ratio and the probability that it will be taken over (assuming, of course, manager's reactions are rationally based on the objective probability of take-over). The body of this paper is devoted to an empirical examination of the nature of this security constraint, in which the existence of a causal relationship between the firm's valuation ratio and the probability of take-over, will be tested.

II. THE MODEL

The inclusion of the valuation ratio as a constraint on the managerial utility function may be justified on the basis of three considerations. First, it is likely that the market valuation of a company in itself may directly affect managerial utility. Because policies must affect the price of the company's shares, managers may feel prestige as the result of healthy share prices, as it may be taken as a sign of confidence from the shareholders, or they may feel loyalty to their shareholders. Secondly, share prices may also affect the supplies of finance, not only from new issues but also through their effect on the strength of the company's borrowing power in the bond market. Thus if managers desire growth of the firm, their utility may be directly affected by unhealthy stock prices. In the longer run, if the limitations on the supplies of external finance prove inimical to

[4] See 'How Managements get Tipped Over', *Fortune*, May 1959; 'Pirates by Proxy', *Management Review*, December 1957; 'How Well-Bred Investors Overthrow a Management', *Fortune*, May 1959.

expansion, other firms will tend to surpass it in the market. Hence, financial policies not favouring growth do not have survival value. Thirdly, the prices of the ordinary shares may affect the probability of the firms being taken over.

While one may believe in the first two justifications for the inclusion of share prices in the utility function, it is difficult, if not impossible, to demonstrate this empirically. First of all, only by the somewhat dubious technique of questionnaire would it be possible to shed some light on the presence of a managerial super-ego with respect to the price of their firm's ordinary shares. Any inferences from such an investigation would be subject to the usual methodological criticisms. Secondly, while one might be able to employ valid statistical techniques to examine the relationship between share prices and growth, there would be difficulties involved in the functional identification[5] and therefore in the interpretation of the results. Specifically, when regressing share prices on growth, one could not be sure the line of causation was only one way. In fact, it is likely that the rate of growth of the firm's assets would have an important effect on the price of its shares. A simultaneous equation model is suggested as a solution but it is difficult to think of any quantifiable exogenous variables which could serve to identify the direction of causation.

It is possible, however, to examine the proposition that the valuation ratio directly enters the managerial utility function through its causal relationship with the probability of being taken over, and hence with security. The primary difficulty with the formulation of a model to test this theory is that the probability of a firm being taken over is a non-observable parameter. All that is observable in a sample of companies is whether they were taken over or not taken over within a given time period. The dichotomous nature of the data, however, suggests the use of a dummy variable taking on values of unity when a take-over is observed and zero elsewhere.

Because the employment of a dummy as the dependent variable is somewhat uncommon, it might be useful to offer some comments on its interpretation. This technique has been extensively explored by Guy H. Orcutt and his associates at the Social Systems Research Institute of the University of Wisconsin.[6] When the dependent variable takes a bi-valued form, unity may be used to indicate the

[5] An equation in a system is said to be identified if it is not possible to derive from linear combinations of the variables an equation in terms of the same variables.

[6] G. H. Orcutt, M. Greenberger, J. Korbel and A. M. Rivlin, *Microanalysis of Socio-economic Systems: A Simulation Study*, Harper & Row, New York, 1961. An account of this technique can also be found in J. Johnston, *Econometric Methods*, McGraw-Hill, 1960, pp. 224–8.

occurrence of an event and zero its non-occurrence. By running a multiple regression of such values of the dependent variable Y on several explanatory variables X, the calculated values of Y for any given value of X may be interpreted as an estimate of the conditional probability of Y, given X. Thus in the present context, Y compute is interpreted as the probability of being taken over for any given valuation ratio. The intercept term is then the expected probability of take-over when the valuation ratio is zero. This technique is very similar to the analysis of the mean and variance of cells of data with the use of the chi-square test when the cell probabilities are functions of some unknown parameters. For our purposes, however, regression analysis has several advantages. First of all, it yields parameter estimates and standard errors, thus making a more intensive use of the data and allowing the model to be predictive. Secondly, it avoids the difficulties which arise out of the use of the chi-square test when there are unequal cell frequencies. Furthermore, experience with the use of the chi-square test has shown it to yield poor approximations when the number of observations in a cell is small. When formulating the model it was anticipated that this situation would in fact occur. As a result, this estimating technique was rejected in favour of multiple regression analysis.

Another difficulty in the formulation of a testable hypothesis is the calculation of the valuation ratio. Because there exists a different valuation ratio for every market price that prevailed during the sample period, the choice become somewhat arbitrary. The problem is less dramatic although it still exists for those firms which have been taken over. It was decided in this case to employ the lowest valuation ratio over the twelve months previous to the first mention of a bid. The purpose of this lag is to avoid picking up any stock market reaction to the bid and to allow for the time that would be required to prepare the bid. Thus the valuation ratio would approximate that which faces the bidder and upon which he is assumed to act. Using the lowest valuation ratio over the year previous to the bid may, however, be unrealistic in some instances if for some reason the share price dipped temporarily and artificially to a low level. In order partially to avoid this possibility, a second measure of the valuation ratio was employed; the mean value of the valuation ratio for the twelve months previous to the bid.

For those firms not taken over, we were faced with the same problem, though of a greater magnitude. If the inverse relationship between the valuation ratio and the probability of take-over existed, then it seemed reasonable to suppose that the measure of the valuation ratio employed for firms taken over would be somewhere near the lowest that had existed in the recent history of the firm. In order to be consistent with the data, the valuation ratio for firms not taken over was calculated at the lowest level it had reached during the sample period. Again a second measure was employed—the lowest annual mean value of the valuation ratio during the sample period—to avoid the possibility that the first measure represented a temporary and artificial low.

In formulating the model it was soon realized that a third category existed in addition to the occurrence or non-occurrence of a take-over. There seemed to have been a significant number of unsuccessful take-over bids made during various periods since the war. On the Marris data, the proportion of unsuccessful to successful take-overs was approximately one-third. From the discussion above, it would be a mistake to ignore these for several reasons. First, any bid, whether ultimately successful or not, is likely to significantly affect managerial utility if it involves managers in taking some sort of defensive action;[7] or in terms of the theoretical utility function, if it forces management to alter the policies designed to maximize the rate of growth. Secondly, since our prime concern is the relationship between the valuation ratio and the probability of take-over, it would be a mistake to allow whatever influences the likelihood of the bid being successful once it is made (such as the ability of firms to fight a take-over bid), to be included in a disguised form in the relationship. In any case, the argument for the effect of take-over bids as opposed to actual take-overs on managerial utility is only slightly less convincing.

[7] See S. C. Hayes, III and R. A. Taussig, 'Tactics of Cash Take-Over Bids', in *Harvard Business Review*, March–April 1967. The authors describe seven methods which have been successfully employed in the opposition of take-over bids:

1. Split the stock—which has the effect of not only increasing the price of the stock for psychological reasons (people regard a split as an extra dividend) thereby reducing the premium over the pre-bid market price, but also makes the premium look smaller.
2. Raise the dividend—one-third of the companies in their sample used this tactic. This strategy is designed both to win shareholder confidence and to drive up the price of the stock.
3. Repurchase shares—with surplus cash or even borrowed funds. This will tend to drive up the market price and reduce the number of shares in 'nervous' hands.
4. Secure outside assistance—either from consulting firms or other firms in the industry who may be anxious to prevent the bidder from increasing his market share.
5. Launch a publicity campaign—to encourage stockholders not to sell at an 'unfair' tender price.
6. Legal action—threatening to bring into bear federal anti-trust laws or simply threatening to impose law suits on the grounds that the bidder is disrupting the regular operation of business by asking for stockholders' lists and so forth. A further possibility is to create a situation where anti-trust or other regulatory statutes become a factor by acquiring a company which competes with the bidder.
7. Counteractive take-over—of a third company and paying in stock. This reduces the proportion of stock the bidder has acquired and places a large block of shares in more friendly hands.

It was decided to run the regressions twice, once in terms of the probability of being taken over and again in terms of the probability of experiencing a take-over bid (both successful and unsuccessful).[8] The valuation ratio for those firms experiencing unsuccessful take-over bids was calculated in the same way as it was for those actually taken over.

With respect to the two measures of the valuation ratio and the inclusion of a regression with take-over bids, it seems reasonable on grounds of statistical methodology where no single method of measurement suggests itself, to let the data identify the best method according to the fit. For this reason, a third measure of the valuation ratio was constructed from a combination of the two columns of data. For firms experiencing a take-over bid (either successful or unsuccessful), the lowest valuation ratio was used, while for firms not taken over, the lowest annual mean valuation ratio was applied.

The model was constructed on the assumption of a linear relationship between stock market valuation and the probability of take-over because there is no basis with which to justify a curvilinear term. The addition of other variables to act as 'shifters' such as the rate of growth, profitability, the liquidity ratios and the retention ratio was considered, but on the basis of the theory developed above we would expect their effects on the probability of experiencing a take-over bid to be felt via the valuation ratio and not on their own. For this reason they were not included. There is, however, the possibility that the size of a company may affect its probability of experiencing a take-over bid. For example, one might expect small companies to be swallowed up even though their valuation ratios were not dangerously low, while with very large companies, no matter how low their valuation ratio, there might not be a bidder available with sufficiently large supplies of finance to make an offer. On this reasoning, the size of a company, calculated from balance sheet data, was added to the basic relationship as a 'shifter'. The final functional relationship that is to be tested is of the form:

$$Y_i = a + bV_i + cS_i + u_i$$

where V_i is the relevant measure of the valuation ratio; S_i is the size 'shifter'; u_i is the stochastic error term; and Y_i is the dummy variable indicating the occurrence or non-occurrence of either a take-

[8] The inclusion of take-over bids in the dependent variable could be handled by allowing the dummy to take on three values. But this requires the ability to assume a system of weighting take-overs, take-over bids and non-take-overs, according to various different valuation ratios. Since there is no *a priori* reason to assume that whatever enables a firm to avoid take-over once it has been bid for will necessarily be reflected in the pre-bid level of the valuation ratio, allowing the dummy to take on arbitrary values such as 0, 1, 2, or 0, 1, 10 would be without theoretical justification.

over or a take-over bid. The subscript i relates to observations in the sample of firms where $i = 1, 2, \ldots, 250$. The choice of the length of the sample period is critical to the interpretation of the parameters of this model. The longer the period of observation, the greater will be the probability that a firm will experience some sort of take-over threat during that period. The sample of firms was examined over the 6½-year period January 1961 to June 1967.

In the following section we will present an account of the empirical analysis of the model, including a discussion of the practical problems encountered with the collection and interpretation of the data, a description of the estimational procedure, an analysis of the results and some suggestions on how this test might be improved upon.

III. ANALYSIS AND RESULTS

The Data

A stratified sample of 250 firms quoted on the London Stock Exchange was generated with the use of tables of random numbers. Such types of securities as Banks, Investment Trusts and the assorted foreign mining and agriculture were excluded so that the population can be regarded as what is basely termed 'Commercial and Industrial'. The sample was taken from the *Financial Times*, January 2nd, 1961, from a total of 1153 quoted companies. This source is somewhat unsatisfactory because the 'Commercial–Industrial' classification in the *Financial Times* is itself an approximately 40 per cent sample of the total number of Commercial–Industrial quoted companies. The other 60 per cent are typically small companies (less than £1 million assets). Their omission may significantly affect the importance of the size 'shifter' in our model. There is, however, no other available source from which companies in existence in 1961 could be sampled. Twenty-two of the firms were replaced from the original sample for various reasons, including disappearance through wind-up, steel nationalization, and take-over previous to 1961, where some shares were still outstanding on January 2nd, 1961. The final sample of 250 firms which made up of 199 firms who had not experienced a take-over bid and 51 which had, of which 38 were successful. While it was not too difficult to identify successful take-over bids, there was no systematic means available with which to uncover unsuccessful take-over bids. Those unsuccessful bids that do appear in the sample data were discovered by examining past issues of the *Financial Times*, *Investors Chronicle* and the *Stock Exchange Gazette*. It is recognized that this is an uncertain means of obtaining the required information and as such there is no guarantee that the list of unsuccessful take-overs is complete. The time period over which the 250 firms were examined ran from January 2nd, 1961, to June 30th, 1967.

The valuation ratios were computed in the manner described in Section II above. In all cases the denominator was the net assets per ordinary share for the relevant year, while the numerator was either the low or mean share price for the same year. The variable for size was derived from balance sheet data representing the book value of the company net of depreciation and current liabilities. All statistical data were extracted from *EXTEL Ordinary Service and Auxiliary Service* cards.

Some interesting features emerge from a cursory examination of the data. First of all, as might be expected, the mean value of the valuation ratios for all companies centres approximately on unity. For the valuation ratios computed of the 6½-year lows the mean was 0.8994; for the lowest annual mean value, the mean was 1.1760; and for the combined data (i.e. lowest annual mean for non-take-over bids and lowest value for take-overs plus take-over bids) the mean was 1.1260. Secondly, it appeared to be possible for companies with very low valuation ratios to survive for a 6½-year period. Ten firms' valuation ratios had dipped to below 0.3 without experiencing a take-over raid and the valuation ratio of fourteen firms had persisted for a year or more at less than 0.5, apparently without experiencing a take-over bid. Thirdly, only two of the thirty-eight take-overs had valuation ratios greater than the mean for the sample, while in three of the eleven unsuccessful take-over bids the valuation ratios exceeded the sample mean.

Estimational Procedure

Twelve single equation, least-squares regressions were run using the alternative measures of the valuation ratio, with and without the variable for size, against the dependent variable, first including only take-overs and secondly with both take-overs and unsuccessful take-over bids. The definitions of the variables are set out below.

$Y1_i$—a dummy variable taking the values zero for the non-occurrence of a successful take-over and unity for the occurrence of a successful take-over.

$Y2_i$—a dummy variable taking the values zero for the non-occurrence of a take-over bid and unity for the occurrence of a take-over or an unsuccessful take-over bid.

S_i—a variable for size defined as the book value of the company net of depreciation and current liabilities.

$V1_i$—the valuation ratio measured at its lowest level during the period for those companies not experiencing a take-over bid and its lowest level in the year previous to the bid for those companies which experienced a take-over bid.

$V2_i$—the valuation ratio measured at the lowest mean value for those companies not experiencing a take-over bid, and at its mean value in the year previous to the bid for those companies which experienced a take-over bid.

$V3_i$—the valuation ratio measured at the lowest annual mean value for those companies not experiencing a take-over bid and at its lowest value during the year previous to the bid for those companies which experienced a take-over bid.

Results

The results of the various formulations of this model are set out in Table I and Table II. Taking as a rough measure of statistical significance that the parameter estimate must be at least twice its standard error,[9] all formulations of the model indicated a significant inverse relationship between the valuation ratio ($V1_i$, $V2_i$ and $V3_i$) and the probability that a firm will experience a take-over bid ($Y2_i$) or actually be taken over ($Y1_i$) during the $6\frac{1}{2}$-year sample period. In no equation does the size variable (S_i) emerge as significant, though it consistently takes on the expected negative sign. In comparing Tables I and II, S_i is shown to be larger than its standard error when only take-overs are used as the dependent variable, but becomes smaller than its standard error when unsuccessful take-overs are included. Thus, the results may indicate that while size is an unimportant influence on the probability that a firm will experience a take-over bid, it may be important in determining whether or not the bid will in fact be successful. One may conclude from this that the size of a firm is related to its ability to take defensive action against a raider. It also may be true that the larger the firm bid for, the more likely the bid will be foiled by counter-bids from other firms in the industry seeking to prevent the raider from increasing his share of the market. Furthermore, because the sample was obtained from a truncated size distribution in which the smaller quoted companies were excluded, it may be that the parameter estimate of S_i of the 'true' population of all quoted companies would prove to be significant. That is, it seems likely that the exclusion of small companies from the sample was at least partially responsible for the effects of company size not having an important impact on the probability of take-over.

[9] This approximately corresponds to the 5 per cent probability level.

In none of the regression equations was the explanatory power of the valuation ratio very impressive. The highest R^2 achieved was just over 10 per cent in the equation relating $V3_i$ and S_i with the probability of experiencing a take-over bid. That is, at best, variations in the valuation ratio and size explained only 10 per cent

TABLE I
REGRESSION EQUATIONS EXPLAINING THE CONDITIONAL PROBABILITY OF TAKE-OVER ($Y1_i$)

Equation	*Constant*	S_i	$V1_i$	$V2_i$	$V3_i$	R^2
1	0.2578	−0.0004932 (0.000365)	−0.1081 (0.04039)			0.0351
2	0.2516	−0.0005079 (0.0003661)		−0.07719 (0.03246)		0.0293
3	0.3124	−0.0005078 (0.0003568)			−0.1347 (0.03088)	0.0781
4	0.2491		−0.1080 (0.04046)			0.0279
5	0.2417			−0.07631 (0.03252)		0.0217
6	0.3031				−0.1342 (0.03094)	0.0705

Note: Figures in parentheses indicate the standard errors of the associated coefficients.

TABLE II
REGRESSION EQUATIONS EXPLAINING THE CONDITIONAL PROBABILITY OF EXPERIENCING A TAKE-OVER BID ($Y2_i$)

Equation	*Constant*	S_i	$V1_i$	$V2_i$	$V3_i$	R^2
1	0.3374	−0.0002978 (0.0004085)	−0.1426 (0.0452)			0.0407
2	0.3324	−0.0003178 (0.0004099)		−0.1045 (0.03634)		0.0344
3	0.4110	−0.0003173 (0.0003953)			0.1790 (0.03421)	0.1016
4	0.3322		−0.1426 (0.04516)			0.0386
5	0.3263			−0.1040 (0.03630)		0.0320
6	0.4051				−0.1787 (0.03419)	0.0992

Note: Figures in parentheses indicate the standard errors of the associated coefficients.

of the total variation in the dependent variable. $V3_i$ proved to be the superior measure of the valuation ratio as the R^2 associated with $V2_i$ and $V1_i$ were approximately a third of the R^2 associated with $V3_i$. The inclusion of unsuccessful take-over bids only marginally improved the R^2 between Table I and Table II.

The size of the intercept term is as was expected from an examination of the data. We already noticed that no matter how low their valuation ratio, some companies were not taken over, or bid for. The interpretation of a constant term of .4110 (Table II, equation 3) is that at a zero valuation ratio a company has a 41 per cent probability of experiencing a bid, or nearly a 60 per cent chance of avoiding the disutility of a take-over bid—as measured in the sample period.

Other Variables

Judging from the low R^2 in all the above regressions it is obvious that other factors are influencing the probability that a firm will be raided. One obvious candidate is the industry classification of the firm. In industries such as breweries, machine tools, food shops, soft drinks, small electricals, and motor components, take-overs have been proceeding at a swift pace, while in others they have been virtually unknown. The rationale for including such a variable would be either that some industries had a greater supply of raiders than others or that a technical innovation within the industry had recently made large-scale operation more profitable. One way to specify a variable for the industry is to include a string of dummy variables in the functional form. This was not possible, however, in this study because the sample was too small to give enough observations to each dummy for sensible industry classifications. Using something like the Standard Industrial Classification would be unsuitable because of its excessive generality.

Another possibility is to attempt to include the industry effect in the equation by way of concentration ratios; such that the greater the concentration and hence the supply of raiders, the more likely that a take-over would be attempted. A variable of this sort would be superior to a dummy because of the interpretative power that could be attached to it. Again, this was not possible because of the limitations imposed by the size of the sample.

A third possibility is to specify a yearly time 'shifter' in dummy variable form. While there is little evidence to support the commonly held belief that the incidence of take-overs varies with the trade cycle,[10] such a variable might still prove significant if it picked up other influences such as changes in Government policy towards business.

[10] For a summary and analysis of the evidence for the cyclical behaviour of mergers see J. W. Markham, 'Survey of the Evidence and Findings on Mergers', in *Business Concentration and Price Policy*, National Bureau of Economic Research, Princeton University Press, 1955, pp. 146–54.

Finally, one could explicitly specify those variables which, under our theory, are supposed to affect the valuation ratio, such as the retention ratio, the liquidity ratio, profitability and the rate of growth. If our object was simply to predict the occurrence of take-overs, then the inclusion of these variables would be justifiable. To do this here, however, would represent a departure from the central purpose, which is to test the validity of the hypothesis within the theoretical context of utility maximization.

All the above hypotheses are being examined with respect to all quoted U.K. companies in a study currently in progress. The primary emphasis will be to construct an econometric model of take-overs, disaggregating to the industry level, in an attempt to explain the occurrence of take-overs in the light of the industrial structure. In addition, the characteristics of raiders, the factors which determine whether or not a bid will be successful and the effect take-overs have had on the industrial structure will be examined.

V. CONCLUSIONS

Because the results of this enquiry are rather tentative, the scope of the concluding remarks must be somewhat limited. Nevertheless, I think several things have been accomplished. In particular, the results have tended to confirm the Marris hypothesis that the firm's valuation on the stock market, which is itself to some extent the result of the firm's financial policies, is likely to have some feed-back as managerial behaviour via the security component of the managerial utility function. As such, our study lends confirmation to the increasing body of data supporting the validity of the behavioural revisions to the theory of the firm.

The low explanatory power of the valuation ratio was almost bound to result from the sort of cross-section sampling that was employed because spatial variations are typically more pronounced than, for example, variations through time. It would be overly optimistic to expect any theory describing a wide spectrum of behaviour to do much more than suggest important influences on that behaviour. This, as has been shown, the theory has accomplished. Furthermore, the probabilities of take-over which have been generated, are objective probabilities based on the historical occurrence of an event. If managers are 'mini-maxers' they may associate a much higher subjective probability of take-over with a given valuation ratio because of the regret attached to being taken over. In essence, though the 'objective' probability of take-over may be linearly related to the valuation ratio, the subjective probability, reflecting its effect on managerial utility, may be curvilinear. Thus the low R^2

associated with the objective relationship may actually underestimate the subjective effect low valuation ratios can exert on managerial utility. Furthermore, if managers regard the other objective influences on the probability of take-over as random, unknown, or unalterable (as the industry classification reflecting the supply of raiders or the degree of concentration) they are likely to see their security as dependent upon the one variable they do have the power to influence—the valuation ratio.

THE UNIVERSITY OF WARWICK

BIBLIOGRAPHY

BAUMOL, W. J., *Business Behaviour, Value and Growth*, New York: Macmillan & Co., 1959.

BULL, G. and VICE, A., *Bid for Power*, London: Elek Books Ltd., 1958.

COHEN, K. J. and CYERT, R. M., *Theory of the Firm: Resource Allocation in a Market Economy*, Englewood Cliffs, N.J.: Prentice-Hall Inc., 1965.

HAYES, S. L. and TAUSSIG, R. A., 'Tactics of Cash Take-over Bids', *Harvard Business Review*, March–April 1967.

JOHNSTON, J., *Econometric Methods*, New York: McGraw-Hill Book Company Inc., 1963.

MARKHAM, J., 'Surveys of the Evidence and Findings on Mergers', *Business Concentration and Price Policy*, National Bureau of Economic Research, Princeton University Press, 1955.

MARRIS, R. L., 'Incomes Policy and the Rate of Profit in Industry', *Manchester Statistical Society*, December 1964.

MARRIS, R. L., *The Economic Theory of 'Managerial' Capitalism*, London: Macmillan & Co. Ltd., 1961.

ORCUTT, G. H., GREENBERGER, M., KORBEL, J. and RIVLIN, A. M., *Microanalysis of Socioeconomic Systems: A Simulation Study*, New York: Harper & Row, 1961.

WAREHAM, W. S., ed., *The Stock Exchange Official Yearbook*, vol. 1, 1967, and vol. 2, 1966, London: Thomas Skinner & Co.

WILLIAMSON, O. E., *The Economics of Discretionary Behaviour: Managerial Objectives in a Theory of the Firm*, New Jersey: Prentice-Hall Inc., 1964.

TESTS OF MARKET SHARE STABILITY IN THE CIGARETTE INDUSTRY 1950–66

by THOMAS HAVRILESKY AND RICHARD BARTH

I. INTRODUCTION

MICROECONOMIC theory predicts that the market shares of firms in differentiated, highly concentrated oligopoly should be stable. Yet, if the conventional assumption of fixed consumer tastes is relaxed this prediction may be modified. This paper tests the share-stability prediction for firms in the heavily differentiated, highly concentrated cigarette industry, during periods when it was reputed to have experienced notable variations in consumer tastes.

The prediction that the firm's market share is stable in heavily differentiated,[1] highly concentrated[2] oligopoly is rather thoroughly accepted in the literature. Market shares could be stabilized by either strong buyer allegiance, a concomitant of product differentiation, or by nonprice interdependence or collusion which are hypothetical results of high concentration. However, when exceptional, autonomous shifts in buyer tastes are introduced, knowledge of and/or concern for rival reactions may be expected to diminish firm interdependence and nonprice rivalry could increase.[3] Either the shift in demand or the resulting increase in rivalry could disturb market share stability.

Casual observation of conditions and experience in the cigarette industry could confirm *either* case. First, the cigarette industry possesses degrees of product differentiation and concentration which support the inference of market share stability.[4] Yet in recent years, the industry has displayed shifts in buyers' preferences. What *might*

[1] Generally, it is felt that buyer attachment to a firm's differentiated products (reinforced by large selling cost outlays) weakens the effectiveness of the sales-promotion and product-variation strategies of its rivals. Joe S. Bain, *Industrial Organization* (New York: John Wiley, 1959), pp. 216–17.

[2] In heavily concentrated industries, the speed of nonprice retaliation assures the potential wayward firm that gains from embarking upon independent action and ignoring either collusive agreements or rival reaction would be transitory. Joe S. Bain, *Industrial Organization*, pp. 317–24; *Price Theory* (New York: John Wiley, 1952), pp. 305, 332–5; *Barriers to New Competition* (Cambridge: Harvard University Press, 1965), pp. 179, 287.

[3] Firms in a highly concentrated industry would rarely appear to be very uncertain of or purposely unconcerned with rival reaction. Hence, it is expected that product and sales promotion policy would not be independent enough to alter market share stability over an extended period. However, a distinct stimulus to relatively independent conduct might be autonomous changes in buyers' tastes which curb brand allegiances. Bain, *Barriers*, p. 287.

[4] The cigarette industry is heavily differentiated. Relatively large levels of total sales-promotion outlays as well as recent high levels of physical product variation obviously support this classification. For instance, total measured advertising expenditures in the industry have averaged 5–6 percent of sales for many years. Bain, *Barriers*, p. 179.

be classified as intense nonprice rivalry may have stemmed from these shifts.[5]

Whether these shifts in demand and the apparent rivalry which ensued actually stimulated share instability is an empirical question. The stability of market shares will be examined through various statistical tests. Then, results will be compared to the share-stability prediction. If test results make it necessary to qualify the share-stability prediction, evidence of both rapid shifts in interindustry and intraindustry consumer preferences and concomitant increases in nonprice competition will be sought.

Data limitations in the oligopolistic sector of the economy often impede investigation of such interesting problems. For the 1950–66 period considerable data for the cigarette industry have been obtained; this includes data for the market shares of the six leading firms; data on brand volume are available but incomplete for this time period.

II. TESTS OF MARKET SHARE STABILITY

In order to examine statistically market share stability over time, three separate tests were performed with the market share data for firms in the cigarette industry. First an analysis of variance tests the stability of market shares over the entire 1950–66 period and for certain sub-periods; then a Mann-Whitney non-parametric test was used to isolate possible sub-periods of extreme instability; finally, as a further check on sub-period stability an index of instability, following Hymer and Pashigian,[6] was constructed.

The following model was used for the first analysis of variance: $E(Y_{ij}) = \mu + t_i$ where Y_{ij} is the absolute change in market share by the jth firm over the ith year; μ is the overall mean market share change over one year and t_i is the difference between the ith year change in mean market share and the overall yearly change in mean market share. The share-stability prediction suggests the test hypothesis that there are no differences in the change in mean market

[5] There is a possibility that the sizable intraindustry taste changes stemming from the cigarette 'health scare' of recent years may have disturbed market shares and/or temporarily shocked firms into a state of active share rivalry or reduced significantly the degree of nonprice collusion to the extent that market shares then reacted strongly. Whether this shift in demand and the increase in nonprice rivalry it may have stimulated was strong enough to provoke market share instability over an extended period is highly problematic. The proliferation of the industry's new cigarette brands added (6 in 1964 and 12 in 1966 compared to 2 in 1960) and the wide fluctuation in firm advertising (especially in the 1950s) suggests that substantial noncooperative, nonprice behavior was occurring and was reflected in market share instability. See Lester Telser, 'Advertising and Cigarettes', *Journal of Political Economy* (October 1962), pp. 473, 495–6, 498–9.

[6] Stephen Hymer and Peter Pashigian, 'Turnover of Firms as a Measure of Market Behavior', *Review of Economics and Statistics*, XLIV (February 1962), p. 85.

share over time; i.e., that $t_i = t_2 = \ldots = t_i = 0$. Index i extends over the sixteen year, 1950–51 to 1965–66, period. Index j covers the six leading cigarette firms. Table I presents the changes in market share.

TABLE I

CHANGE IN MARKET SHARE BY FIRM: 1950–66
(All changes in market share are in absolute value and multiplied by 1000)

Firm number	*1*	*2*	*3*	*4*	*5*	*6*	$\bar{Y}_i$	$\sum_j Y_i^2$
t = 51–t = 50	23	116	56	34	46	40	53	21,993
52–51	53	8	100	14	27	33	39	14,887
53–52	19	107	12	12	94	65	52	25,159
54–53	157	26	136	72	48	280	120	129,709
55–54	88	72	40	67	26	122	69	34,577
56–55	178	80	92	135	92	31	101	74,198
57–56	81	42	4	253	223	18	104	122,403
58–57	10	136	7	227	416	64	143	247,326
59–58	195	85	14	48	34	8	64	48,970
60–59	178	88	2	47	69	32	69	47,426
61–60	166	71	19	8	24	75	60	39,223
62–61	81	90	2	11	31	23	40	16,276
63–62	51	7	21	58	45	27	35	9,209
64–63	105	9	21	49	104	132	70	42,188
65–64	40	95	54	21	28	134	62	32,722
t = 66 – t = 65	50	28	61	86	9	89	54	22,403
							1135	928,669
							$\bar{Y} = 71$	

Source: Market volume (by firm in billions of cigarettes, John Maxwell, Jr. *Historical Trends In the Tobacco Industry*, Montgomery, Scott & Co., 120 Broadway, New York, 1967.

TABLE II

ANALYSIS OF VARIANCE
Period: 1950–66

Source	*Sum of squares*	*D.F.*	*Mean square*
Years	22,599	15	9,039
Residual	651,699	80	8,146
Mean	141,376	1	
Total	928,669	96	

Mean square ratio: 1.11.
Value of F. (0.05) for 15 and 80 degrees of freedom: 1.81.

The results of the test of stability for the 1950–66 period are presented in Table II. The mean square ratio is not significant at the 0.05 level; therefore, we cannot reject the hypothesis that there are no differences among changes in mean market share over the 1950–66 period when each year is taken as a separate group.

Although the period 1950–66 was seen to exhibit relative market share stability, casual observation of firm product variation and advertising data revealed that certain sub-periods may have exhibited much higher levels of nonprice competition among firms. This may have been caused by the health scares in the industry. Either of these phenomena may have produced market share instability.

Dividing the sample into four sub-periods, 1950–53, 1954–57, 1958–61 and 1962–65, an analysis of variance was used to determine whether there was a significant difference in stability attributable to these sets of years. The results of this test are presented in Table III. The mean square ratio was significant at the 0.05 level, thus the hypothesis that there is no 'year group' effect on market share stability must be rejected.

TABLE III

ANALYSIS OF VARIANCE FOR SUB-PERIODS 1950–65

Source	*Sum of squares*	*D.F.*	*Mean square*
Year groups	40,920	3	13,640
Residual	409,346	86	4,760
Mean	466,560	1	
Total	906,266	90	

Mean square ratio: 2.87.
Value of F. (0.05) for 3 and 86 degrees of freedom: 2.49.

This sub-period instability in market share may be explained by strong evidence of nonprice competition[7] among cigarette firms in the 1954–57 period. Product variation and measured advertising expenditures increased sizably in these years. For example there were 18 separate physical product variations (filter, size, package, and menthol changes) in the industry during the 1954–57 period, more changes than any other four-year block in the 1950–65 period. In

[7] As a general example of the influence of advertising outlays on market share the following equation was estimated by ordinary least-square regression analysis using yearly data for 6 firms for the 1950–65 period:

$$S = -0.06054 + 1.35805\,A + \mu$$
$$(0.01824)\ (0.10361)$$
$$\bar{R}^2 = 0.673 \qquad \delta = 2.49$$

where S = market share, A = firm advertising as a percentage of industry advertising, $\bar{R}^2$ = the coefficient of determination, the bracketed term is the standard error, and δ = the Durban-Watson Test statistic, the estimate is significant at the 1 percent level of significance.

While this test is not intended as an exhaustive treatment, the results show that as the firm's advertising outlays as a percentage of industry advertising increases by 1 percent, market share systematically increases by 1.3 percent. This result roughly conforms to the *a priori* predictions of Bain in *Barriers*, p. 289, and *Theory*, p. 309, and William J. Baumol, *Economic Theory and Operations Analysis* (Englewood Cliffs: Prentice-Hall, 1961), pp. 199–201. Compare this simple result to the interesting discussions of Telser, *op. cit.*, and 'Advertising and Competition', *Journal of Political Economy*, LXXII (December 1965), pp. 537–62. Source of advertising data: *Advertising Age*, 1950–65, advertising expenditures for brands with sales volume exceeding one billion units on network radio and TV and in newspapers, magazines and Sunday supplements.

addition total measured industry advertising on brands with sales over a billion units increased from $72 million in 1954 to $123 million in 1958.[8] By 1962 this outlay had reached only $138 million.

The possible acceleration of nonprice competition may have resulted from rapid changes in consumer tastes which in turn stemmed from the first major cigarette 'health scare' (first noted in Britain, 1952, but not generally publicized in the United States until 1953–54).[9] The assumed change in *interindustry* tastes is supported by a decline in industry sales in the 1953–55 period.[10] It is quite likely that concomitant *intraindustry* taste changes occurred. This would have initially altered market shares. Both changes may have reduced the firm's knowledge of and/or concern for retaliation by rivals to the point that relatively independent, nonprice conduct and hence open, nonprice warfare ensued, and persisted for a few years.

In order to inspect further for the years of greatest share instability a simple non-parametric test was used. Coefficients of variation of the market share of firms were computed for four-year periods from 1950 to 1966 and a comparison between pairs of the sub-periods was made. A variation of this test was used by Schneider in his comparison of market share stability between homogeneous and differentiated oligopoly.[11] With the exception of 1954–57 the hypothesis that the coefficients of variation for firms between two four-year periods came from the same population could not be rejected at the 0.05 level.[12] However, the hypothesis that the 1954–57 coefficients of variation for firms came from the same population as any other four-year group was rejected at the 10 per cent level, thus supporting the finding that 1954–57 was a period of instability in the industry.

Finally, using a variation of the Hymer–Pashigian index of instability[13] a comparison was made for the four-year periods. The following values of the index were obtained:

Years	*Index value*
1950–53	889
1954–57	1288
1958–61	1055
1962–65	971

[8] Ibid.

[9] This reasoning would also indicate a second period of market share instability following the post–1964 series of cigarette health pronouncements. At this time data are insufficient to examine stability in this second period.

[10] Direct evidence of the 'health scare' is the sizable decline in industry sales during 1953–55. See any *Moody's Manual* or Maxwell, op. cit.

[11] Norman Schneider, 'Product Differentiation, Oligopoly, and the Stability of Market Shares', *Western Economic Journal*, V (December, 1966), p. 61.

[12] For a description of the test see Sidney Siegel, *Non-parametric Statistics* (New York: McGraw-Hill, 1956), pp. 116–20, 271.

[13] Hymer and Pashigian, op. cit., p. 85.

The index was computed as follows: $I = \sum_{l=1}^{n} [S_{i,t} - S_{i,t-1}]$.

Where n = number of firms in the industry, $S_{i,t}$ = market share of ith firm at time t. Thus the larger I is, the greater the level of instability. This test substantiates the previous tests concerning the 1954–57 period.

III. CONCLUDING COMMENTS

Test results suggest that market shares have been stable in the cigarette industry for all years of the 1950–66 period except for 1954–57. This would generally tend to confirm the hypothesis that heavy product differentiation (and concomitant buyer allegiance) and intense concentration (and resulting firm aversion to independent nonprice strategy) militate against considerable nonprice rivalry and, as a predictable consequence, stabilize market shares.

Shifts in demand and a more rivalrous nonprice competition appear to have been the causes of statistically significant market share instability during the 1954–57 period. More intense nonprice rivalry is felt to have followed the first cigarette health scare after 1953. This is revealed by sizable increases in physical product variation and advertising in the 1954–57 period.

The test results suggest that given strong shifts in buyer preferences (such as those currently manifest in the cigarette industry), more intensive nonprice competition could emerge with physical product variation and advertising outlays being the predominant tools.[14]

UNIVERSITY OF MARYLAND,
BUREAU OF LABOR STATISTICS

[14] Further direct tests of the competitive and collusive influences on advertising outlays and physical product variations are being made by the authors.

THE ORGANIZATION OF THE CERAMIC INDUSTRY AROUND THE NAGOYA AREA OF JAPAN*

by TSUTOMU NAKAMURA

I. INTRODUCTION

THE DIVISIONS of the ceramic 'table-ware' industry into different production subgroups and the flow of finished products into various markets are indicated in the chart below.[1] 'Body' is here used as the shaped but unpainted piece.

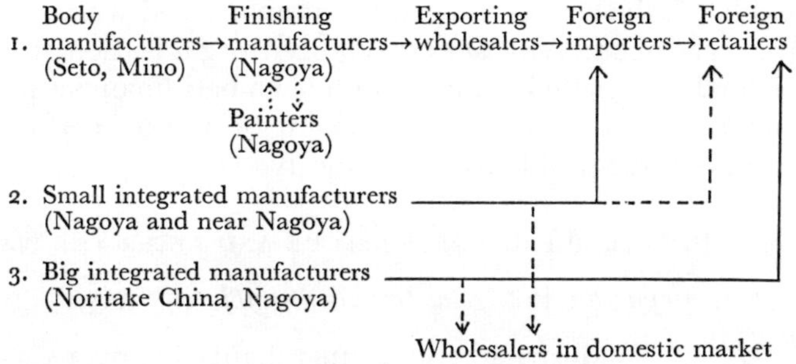

1. No specialized body manufacturing concern employs more than 1000 persons. Between 30 and 300 persons (depending upon plant size) are employed by each finishing manufacturer.
2. Each of the small integrated manufacturers employs between 300 and 1000 persons. Painting is mostly the domestic work of housewives now.
3. There are about 3000 persons in the employment of the Noritake China company, and it is in a special class.

The following topics will be treated in this paper. (1) Some problems of finishing manufacturers: Before the war, they were a kind of merchant employer (*toiya*) and had a predominant power over body manufacturers and painters. This was indicative of the backwardness of Japanese economy. After the war, the characteristic of *toiya* disappeared; but the *toiya* still retain the characteristic of being merchants and have acquired that of manufacturers. We have to analyze their characteristics, why they have changed, and what form they have acquired. This will be done in Section II and the Appendix.

* A grant was given for this study by the Ministry of Education in Japan.

[1] Nagoya city and Seto city are in Aichi Prefecture. Mino district, which includes Takiro, Ena (Table I) and other places of ceramic production, is in Gifu Prefecture. Gifu Prefecture is next to Aichi Prefecture. Both are in central Japan, and the largest center of ceramic production. The dotted line shows weak relation.

(2) Noritake China has an overwhelmingly predominant position in this industry. The prices of its products are about twice as high as those of others. Still it manages to sell, and therefore ranks very favorably *vis-à-vis* others. On the other hand, the other manufacturers are competing very keenly with each other. We will treat their market behavior and performance in Section III.

(3) The Specialized production (which means the division of production processes among finishing manufacturers, body manufacturers and painters, as expressed in the above chart) still exists even though the merchant-employer system has disappeared; but it seems to have backward characteristics compared to integrated manufacturers. However, the financial position of integrated manufacturers is worse than those of firms that specialize. The only exception is Noritake China, which is the largest integrated company and whose financial position is very good. Why does specialized organization still exist? Why are small integrated manufacturers in a bad financial position? Is this good or bad from the standpoint of market performance? We will study these problems in Section IV.

II. FINISHING MANUFACTURERS BEFORE AND AFTER THE WAR

1. *Before the War—the 'merchant-employer'* (toiya)

At the outset of industrialization, a merchant-employer system was introduced. The merchants performed the functions of selling products, supplying raw materials, and providing financing for domestic cottage manufacturers. They exerted influences originating outside the production process and gradually controlled the small manufacturers and had most of the bargaining power in their hands. Small manufacturers were only concerned with production, and their income was very much the same as that of wage earners. Most of the profit went to the merchants.

The above description of the merchant-employer system is applicable to the ceramic industry in Aichi and Gifu Prefectures, Japan, before the war. The manufacturing of ceramic bodies was on a small scale; and thus the merchants got an overwhelming advantage over the body manufacturers because of their superior financial position. The body manufacturers entered into a contract with the merchants, and as a result of this contract they were assured a minimum level of production; however they had to pay for it by accepting low prices. The merchants also had a strong hold over the small painting manufacturers. Since design is very important for pottery, merchants wished to have control over the painters, and they did so easily because of their power. They were called toiya (merchant-employer).

2. *Change after the War*

The painting (i.e. finishing) of bodies by merchants themselves, which had already been partially tried since 1935, developed much more after the war. Such concerns called themselves 'fabricating and finishing manufacturers' since about 1933, though it was chiefly as a counter-measure against the governmental policy which favored manufacturers over finishers. Merchants lost their position and wealth due to restrictions, which forced mergers and closures during the war, and since then body manufacturers have become relatively larger and freer from the controlling power of the merchants. What has happened to the 'merchant-employer'?

It seems to me that the detailed investigation of this problem is important for clarifying the peculiar characteristics of the development of Japanese industry. But it may be somewhat troublesome for foreign readers who are not familiar with some of the peculiar problems of Japanese industry. So this will be treated in the Appendix.

III. BIG BUSINESS AND SMALL BUSINESS—COMPETITION AND MONOPOLY IN PRICING

1. *Facts about the Market*

The output of the ceramic tableware industry was worth 65.6 million dollars in Japan in 1965. Three-fourths of it was produced in Aichi Prefecture and Gifu Prefecture, the center of which is Nagoya City. Seventy-six percent of it was exported, and the biggest export market was and still is the United States of America, the share of which is 52 percent. The markets in America are subdivided as follows:

The first is the market for medium-quality products, and it is composed of Noritake China (Japan), West German and English ceramic manufacturers. This is an international oligopolistic market.

The second is the market for low-quality products. The suppliers in this market are the Japanese integrated manufacturers except Noritake China, and fabricating and finishing manufacturers.

The third is the highest-quality market, supplied by English and American manufacturers. This is also an oligopolistic market. Due to high wage rates, the American ceramic industry is at a disadvantage as far as the production of thin porcelain of high quality is concerned because in its production there is a limited capacity for automation. Hotel ware made of thick earthenware is chiefly produced by means of automation in America.

The domestic market for western style ceramic tableware has been increasing recently. Noritake China provided 16 percent of export and 26 percent of domestic demand in this industry in 1964. Noritake China was the only company in this industry which then ranked among the 394 biggest businesses in Japan as recorded by the Bank of Japan survey. Nevertheless, its total assets are 0.3 billion dollars and total sales are 0.2 billion dollars, which is only one-fourth the average for these big manufacturers in Japan.

2. *Market Behavior—Facts About Price Competition*

First, the gap between the price of Noritake China and the prices of other manufacturers is very large. The factory price of the standard 93-piece dinner set exported to America is about 30 dollars for Noritake China and about 17 dollars for other producers.

Secondly, the main competitors against Noritake China in American markets are West German manufacturers. The retail prices of a standard dinner set are 90–200 dollars in the case of Noritake China, 100–200 dollars for West German ceramics, and 500 dollars for the highest quality American ceramics. The prices of other Japanese porcelains are only 60–90 dollars. Noritake China dominates the market where the price range is 90–150 dollars, whereas West Germany puts emphasis on goods priced more than 150 dollars. The form of competition of Noritake China with foreign firms is chiefly in quality, the design and planning of new products. There are few explicit price competitors among them; but we cannot overlook the fact that price still has an important role to play in competition. There is no collusion among foreign firms.

Thirdly, the price gap between Noritake China and other integrated manufacturers is not so large in the Japanese domestic market as in America. Noritake China, five other integrated firms, and two main finishing firms supply about 60 percent of the total domestic demand, but there is no oligopolistic behavior among them. Recently, the larger manufacturers seem to have hesitated to step into the domestic market any more because they cannot follow frequent changes in style and in combinations of pieces which are characteristic of the domestic market.

What is the effect of price competition on their financial position?

3. *Market Performance*

(1) *The difference of financial positions among firms by group*

Table I indicates the financial positions of the ceramic industry for western tableware. This table includes the following categories: Noritake China, finishing and integrated manufacturers in Nagoya, and manufacturers in Seto, Takiro and Ena. Manufacturers in Seto, Ena and Takiro chiefly produce bodies, although fully integrated and finishing producers are also included to some extent. The table shows: first, that the financial position of Noritake China is far superior to the others; secondly, that integrated and finishing manufacturers around the Nagoya are in a strikingly contrasting position; and, thirdly, that body manufacturers around Seto and Gifu ranking between the two, show quite fair profit rates.

(2) *The causes of the differences of financial positions by group. (a)—Noritake China and small manufacturers*

What is the cause of the difference in financial position? First, the difference in costs must be observed. The cost of a standard 93-piece dinner set may be estimated at 27 dollars in Noritake China and at 17–20 dollars in small manufacturers, which are based on the above prices and profit rates. As far as quality differences are concerned, they certainly exist, though the difference has been decreasing to some extent since the war. Noritake China has the advantages of access to high-quality materials, monopolistic acquisition of rare raw materials, the use of precise models, employment of specialists in the fields of shape and design, and the uniform and continuous color and shape of the dinner-set based on its integrated production. Noritake was and still is the pioneer of the development of technology in this field. Other manufacturers have customarily imitated it. However, we cannot compare the costs of products, because there are quality differences between them. Other factors must therefore be considered.

As for productivity, Noritake China is the only one which satisfies the requirements for mass production because it can connect an individual order with ongoing production. It seems to have achieved the results of good quality, mass production and low costs. But the problem is the balance of wage differences among firms and the extent of automation. As Table I shows, the wages in Noritake are twice as high as in others. On the other hand, capital equipment per employee is only half as much as the average of all large manufacturers, although it is much more than that of others in the ceramic industry. It is a labor intensive industry. Thus, labor cost as a percentage of sales in Noritake is higher than that for other ceramic manufacturers and especially higher than that of the average of large manufacturers (Table I). Noritake has no cost advantage over small manufacturers which employ cheaper labor, because mechanization is limited in this industry.

Thus the main cause of the difference of financial positions rests on the difference in price. The cause of the difference in price rests on, first, the brand name 'NORITAKE CHINA'. This is also based on the continuous efforts for the improvement of quality, design and sales value. Both these sets of factors interact to promote the sales of Noritake China. It also has a well organized distribution system which supports the brand.

We must not overlook that the 'big' scale has some role in this context. The big scale is necessary both for the establishment of the distribution system abroad, which is one of the requisites of the product differentiation and for the enforcement of effective integrated production. The scale has an important role for the product differentiation, too, which is characteristic in this industry.[2]

(3) *The causes of the differences of financial positions by group. (b)—Integrated, finishing, and body manufacturers*

The causes of bad financial positions of small integrated manufacturers are listed as follows: (i) the prices of their products are much lower than Noritake; (ii) the character of the production process of the body is different from that of painting, and it is rather difficult for small manufacturers to coordinate these two from the point of view of production management; (iii) labor cost is higher in this group than in the finishing industry or body manufacturing; (iv) overhead costs are rather high, especially for very fine quality china; (v) the share of separate dinner wares has been increasing in the export market, which may handicap integrated manufacturers in comparison with body manufacturers which are more flexible; (vi) market production[3] cannot be pursued by integrated manufacturers, but it can by body manufacturers during bad times.

Finishing and fabricating manufacturers are in the midst of excess competition and cannot shift the loss to body manufacturers because

[2] The types of product differentiation may be classified into three according to the scale. The first is the group where the 'differentiated oligopoly' and the 'concentrated oligopoly' coexist as mentioned by Sylos-Labini (Sylos-Labini, *Oligopoly and Technical Progress*, 1962). The automobile industry is typical of this.

The second is the group where the scale of firms has an important role and some degree of concentration can be seen. But this group is not as a whole the concentrated oligopoly, but the differentiated oligopoly. Noritake China is typical. The third is the group where the product differentiation is not very strong, and the ratio of concentration is low. Noted products such as local types of pickle or cake are typical. The group equilibrium which E. Chamberlin analyzed may be most applicable to this case.

The significance of this classification is to clarify the difference in entry barriers, and of monopolistic power. The automobile industry in which a strong distribution system and advertisement are tied up with high technology, supported by huge capital, has the highest barriers. The barrier to entry of the second group, which is represented by Noritake China, ranks in between the two, based on the fact that the difference in scales and in technologies have some effect on the product differentiation. It seems to me that a fountain-pen industry can be also included in this group.

[3] Market production is manufactured for stocks, not for orders.

TABLE I

FINANCIAL RATIO, 1964 (IN PERCENTAGES)

		Nagoya[2]		*Body manufacturers*[2]			*Average all manufacturing*[3]	
					Gifu prefecture			
	Noritake China[1]	*Finishing firms*	*Five integrated firms*	*Ceramic exporting firms in Seto*	*Takiro*	*Ena*	*Big business*	*Small business (50–299 persons)*
Net profit before tax as percent of sales	10	1.3	Δ7.8	5.2	2.5	7.5	5.2	3.1
Net profit before tax as percent of sales (firms with income)	—	2.0	0.8	6.9	4.2	7.8	—	—
Net profit before tax as percent of total assets	5.2	2.9	Δ9.9	6.0	3.2	9.2	4.6	5.1
Labor cost as percent of sales	30.4	12.0	29.0	32.6	28.5	24.0	10.9	13.5
Outside order as percent of sales	1.9	8.1	5.3	2.4	6.4	32.3	—	—
Annual wages per employee (thousand yen)	535.5	271	353	324	241	249	624	373
Capital equipment per employee (thousand yen)	857	196	—	191	—	—	1970	535
Total equity as percent of total assets	31.6	17.8	36.3	26.5	19.7	29.3	27.6	21.4
Surplus (profit) as percent of total assets	23	8.9	13.3	—	—	—	10.9	12.8

Δ = Loss.

Sources: [1] Report on valuable securities.

[2] Japan Ceramic Trade Association, Nagoya, Japan.

[3] *Managerial Analysis of Small Manufacturers*, The Bank of Japan.

the position between them has been reversed. The basis of profit for body manufacturers is that they do not have as difficult production management problems as do the integrated manufacturers and that their form of production seems to be fairly appropriate from the standpoint of present Japanese small business.[4]

(4) *Other indicators of market performance*

Emphasis has been put on the price–cost margins and profit rates in market performance in this paper because it seems to be most closely connected with the market structure in this industry.

As for other factors, Table II may furnish some information. Growth of output, total value added, and also growth of output and fixed assets per capita from 1956 to 1962 has been considerably slower than in total manufacturing and electric industry, which has developed most rapidly. But it seems to me that this is little connected with market structure, but rather with market demand. Japanese industry has developed very much during this period owing to private domestic investment. Ceramic goods, chiefly exported, were outside the demand of this kind. Ceramic manufacturers have been suffering rather badly from the increase of wages owing to the labor shortage because of its labor intensity. It is not evidence of growth, but because of the increase in wages that the value added per worker in this industry exceeds that of total manufacturing.

[4] *On the theory of the specific oligopoly price*. The behavior of this particular type of oligopoly has to be considered in connection with relevant price theories. This may be the preliminary stage for the theoretical abstraction about its peculiar behavior which I would like to pursue later. It is true that a general abstract theory cannot explain the behavior of the particular industrial type without an intermediate analysis, but the problem is whether the theory involves the logic by the application of which the behavior can be explained.

A question on differentiated oligopoly is that the scale problem is not explicitly treated by either E. Chamberlin or J. Robinson, though it may be implicitly the starting point of their arguments. Is it not necessary to include the differences in technologies, cost, capital powers, distributing powers, etc., between the case of the big market, big scale, and few firms and the case of the small market, small scale, and few firms much more in the theory? J. Bain, however, includes the problem of scale in his writings. There is no discussion on the product differentiated theory in Marxism. The theory of the concentrated oligopoly price by Sylos-Labini, based on technological discontinuity, cannot be applied to this industry, for it is a labor intensive industry and Noritake China cannot get productivity high enough to offset the wage difference.

As regards the relation between Noritake China and small manufacturers, Vatter's hypothesis on the conflict between groups—between the centripetal stabilization policy by the core of oligopolists and the centrifugal split policy by small enterprises—is very applicable to this case. (H. Vatter, *Small Enterprise and Oligopoly*, 1955).

Both the excess competition among small enterprises and the non-collusive competition among a few concentrated enterprises in the domestic market show the characteristics of Japanese industry. My following papers are some approaches to these phenomena: T. Nakamura, 'Excessive Competition', The Economic Review (Hitotsubashi University), Vol 20, 1969; 'Economic Concentration in Japan', Economic Concentration pt. 7, 1968, U.S. Senate Subcommittee on Antitrust and Monopoly. I think excess competition among small firms is caused by the fact that big firms occupy growing prosperous industries, and that they establish high barriers to entrants.

As for technology, new equipment has been introduced to some extent since 1955, but the speed of adaptation to new technology has not been as rapid as the average for other manufacturing. Competition among small manufacturers resulted in new techniques; even techniques of Noritake have spread to small manufacturers despite the fact that Noritake wanted to keep them secret.

Though there is the problem of overproduction in the background, this industry has been working at full capacity. When business is not good, small manufacturers don't limit their production, but run into excess competition, cutting down on prices. And there was no period when export demand fell sharply for the past ten years.

TABLE II

GROWTH OF OUTPUT, VALUE ADDED AND INVESTMENT

	1962		*1962*			*1964*
	(billion yen)		*Per worker (thousand yen)*			
	Output	*Value added*	*Output*	*Value added*	*Investment fixed assets*	*Outstanding fixed assets*
Table and kitchen pottery	33	17	704	377	38	
All manufactures	20,560	775	2,434	788	220	
Electric machinery	1,920	6,657	2,397	968	205	
GROWTH:	1962 ÷ 1956 (%)		Per worker, 1962 ÷ 1956 (%)			
Table and kitchen pottery	159	184	151	176	216	306
All manufactures	243	262	169	171	248	909
Electric machinery	491	541	182	206	321	598

Source: MITI, JAPAN: *Statistics of Manufacturing*, above 4 employees.

IV. THE MODERNIZATION OF THE INDUSTRIAL ORGANIZATION—THE JAPANESE CHARACTERISTICS

Now the basis and significance of the existence of the types classified at the beginning of this paper has to be considered from the viewpoint of the development of industry. The improvement of the quality and productivity should be pointed out as an indication of the development of industry.

The basis of the specialized production, at the core of which are the finishing manufacturers, was originally in the merchant-employer system itself. However, why does the specialized organization continue to exist in a new dress after the putting-out system has disappeared? Is it an incentive for, or restrictive of, industrial development?

Integrated production seems to be a more developed form of industrial organization than specialized production. The reason is as follows: (1) integrated production has the advantage of uniformity and continuity in the production of a dinner-set; (2) integrated manufacturers can have more refined senses of style because they have their own painting process; and (3) integrated manufacturers have a greater capability for comprehensive innovation.

However, integrated manufacturers are actually often at a disadvantage, as mentioned above. The disadvantages are also pointed out from the standpoint of the specialized organization. (1) There are few body manufacturers who can produce good white bodies for export, which reduces competition. And the lack of uniformity in a dinner-set has been decreasing owing to technological consultation among them. (2) There is little discontinuity of quality, because finishing manufacturers buy bodies continuously. (3) The productivity of body manufacturers can be high, based on the concentrated production of specialized pieces; and (4) they have made efforts for the modernization of equipment.

The specialized production as mentioned above possesses factors which are useful for the improvement of quality and productivity. It also has characteristics which conform to conditions of demand, as seen in the export of separate pieces out of a set. It seems to me that the specialized production of the ceramic industry in Japan is not always an inefficient form of industrial organization. One of the bases of the existence of small business might be seen here.

However, why are all ceramic manufacturers in England integrated? Why is the basis of specialized production in Japanese ceramic-making very strong? Why cannot the basis of integrated production be strengthened?

One of the reasons is the adaptability of specialized production to the Japanese economy as mentioned above. We have to point out other reasons for the stagnation of small integrated manufacturers, too. First, they involve factors making for inefficiency, namely: (1) The scale of the firms is not big enough to develop new technology; their research capacities are relatively poor compared with Noritake. Low prices and meager profits make it difficult for the firms to expand and adopt new technology and to strive for improvement of quality, which again hinders them from getting reasonable prices and profits. At first sight it seems to be something like a vicious circle. (2) They cannot have a well-balanced mass production system because they cannot get the orders suitable for continuous mass production. (3) The distribution system is still insufficient. (4) There is a big gap between small integrated manufacturers and Noritake in price. In short, the first reason is that the small integrated manufacturers do not have enough scale and accumulation to develop their capacity, notwithstanding they have the prospect of technological development more than have specialized firms.

The second set of reasons is the high barriers of Noritake China to entry into the market, which is related to the first reason. This seems to be a decisive factor. Small integrated manufacturers could overcome the above difficulties more easily but for the establishment of Noritake's high product differentiation. Of course, this does not mean Noritake has played a restrictive role in industrial development. The reverse is the case. We just say small integrated manufacturers should make painstaking efforts to improve their own position in the industry where such a market structure has been established.

APPENDIX

THE CHARACTERISTICS OF FINISHING MANUFACTURERS

We referred to the change of the character of 'merchant-employer' (*toiya*) in Section II, and asked what had happened to the 'merchant-employer'. It should be investigated here.

1. *Aspects as Manufacturer*

(*a*) The painting process is by nature part of the fabricating production.

(*b*) The painting process represents a high percentage of total production cost.

The cost of raw materials is only 54 percent of total cost of finishing manufacturers, resales being excluded, according to the Trade Association data. The share of painting cost is 36 percent in integrated ceramic manufacturers. If half of the overhead and transporting costs are added, the share becomes 45 percent.

(*c*) High sales turnover and low fixed assets per employee, which are characteristic of the position of merchants, are also the characteristic of *small* manufacturers. If resales are excluded, the sales turnover rate is appropriate to that of the average small manufacturer.

2. *Aspects as Merchant*

Main functions of finishing manufacturers in the ceramic industry are now, first, to decide the design and, secondly, to collect bodies.

The fundamental industrial properties of ceramic goods are the color, shape and solidity. Though the design may be part of the last production process, it is also very much related to the sales promotion. Thus the painting process has a strong commercial element, although by nature it belongs to production.

Secondly, although assembling of parts is the core of the production process in such an industry as the automobile, in ceramics painting is a secondary production process and partly belongs to the sales process. It has the commercial aspect of collecting much more than the manufacturing aspect of procuring parts. Furthermore, we cannot overlook the fact that they buy ready-made goods as wholesalers for further resale. If we take the value of the purchased semi-finished goods for painting as 100, the value of the ready-made goods for re-sale is approximately 94 according to the data of Trade Association. Thus the function is commercial.

Thus, those who fabricate and finish may be defined as manufacturers if we focus our attention on their industrial activities. But according to their function, they might be defined as merchants. We might say that a kind of production process in which commercial factors are included to a considerable degree, and which may be regarded as secondary in point of production, protrude into the distribution process through their assembly function. I think the merchanting description is more appropriate. It points to the peculiar character of Japanese small business in it.

NANZAN UNIVERSITY
JAPAN

PUBLICATIONS RECEIVED

An Approach to Short-term Business Forecasting, by James Morrell, The Administrative Staff College, March 1968.

Appraising Capital Works, by E. J. Broster, Management Studies Series, September 23rd, 1968, 63s.

Le Aziende Elettriche, by Ferdinando Canaletti, Pubblicazione Serie 1 Monografie.

Basic Mathematics, by R. G. D. Allen, Macmillan & Co. Ltd., September 26th, 1968.

Behaviour in the Working Environment, by E. Andrew Life, Basil Blackwell & Mott Ltd.

The Brazilian Capital Goods Industry 1929–1964, by Nathaniel H. Leff, Harvard, Oxford University Press, April 3rd, 1969, 52s. 6d.

British Coal, A Review of the Industry, its Organisation and Management, by John Platt, An Administrative Staff College Monograph, Lyson Grant and Green, 1968, 28s.

British Made, by Patricia Millard, Kenneth Mason, February 27th, 1969, 42s.

Business Economics, by Cadman, November 7th, 1968, 42s.

A Century of Pay, by E. H. Phelps Brown, January 16th, 1969, 105s.

Commercial Banking Arrangements, by Henry G. Homel and Francis J. Walsh Jr. A survey by the Conference Board, Managing the Financial Function No. 3.

Concentration and Price Cost Marginsin Manufacturing Industries, by N. R. Collins and L. E. Preston, Cambridge University Press, published on behalf of University of California Press, September 12th, 1968, 54s. 6d.

The Consumer in the Soviet Economy, by Hanson, Macmillan & Co. Ltd., November 28th, 1968, 65s.

Contemporary Agricultural Marketing, Edited by Irving Dubov, The University of Tennessee Press, May 20th, 1968, $5.95.

Demand for Fuel; Programme for Growth, by Richard Stone, K. Wigley, Chapman & Hall, December 5th, 1968, 30s.

Denazification, by Constantine FitzGibbon, Michael Joseph Ltd., March 10th, 1969, 35s.

Depreciation Accounting and Economic Analysis, by Shinkichi Minemura, The Society of Business and Commerce, Keio University (Tokyo, Japan).

Development Prospects of Pakistan, by Ole David Koht Norbye, Universitetsforloget, August 1968, 44s. 6d.

Doctoral Dissertations on Transportation 1961–1967, A Bibliography, Transportation Centre, Northwestern University, $2.00.

Economic Aspects of Antitrust, Readings and cases, by Henry Adler Einhorn and William Paul Smith, Random House, $4.95.

Economic Geography for Professional Students, by John Inch Pitman, Basil Blackwell and Mott Ltd., November 15th, 1968, 35s.

Economic Problems of Agriculture in Industrial Societies, Proceedings of a Conference held by the International Economic Association at Rome, Edited by Ugo Papi and Charles Nunn, April 24th, 1969, £7.

The Economics of Soviet Oil and Gas, by Robert W. Campbell, Oxford University Press, Basil Blackwell & Mott Ltd., February 27th, 1969, 81s.

The Employment of Young Workers, by Nancy B. Keene, B. T. Batsford Ltd., March 27th, 1969, 50s.

Estimated Annual Variations in Gross National Product 1789–1901, by Thomas Senior Berry, University of Richmond, The Bostwick Press, 1968.

Federal Funds for Research, Development and other Scientific Activities, Fiscal Years 1967, 1968, 1969. Volume XVII, Surveys of Science Resources Series, National Science Foundation, NSE 68–77.

Foreign Collaboration in Indian Industry, Survey Report, Reserve Bank of India, Bombay Center of Planning & Econômic Research, 1968, 8s.

The Gold-dollar System: Conditions of Equilibrium and the Price of Gold, by Milton Gilbert, Essays in International Finance, Department of Economics, Princeton University.

Graduate Study and After, by Ernest Rudd and Stephen Hatch, October 17th, 1968, 55s.

A History of the Zinc Smelting Industry in Britain, by Edward Hohn Cocks and Bernhardt Walters, George G. Harrap & Co. Ltd., May 9th, 1968, 55s.

Hemisphere West: El Futuro, Edited by William F. Gleuck, Bureau of Business Research, The University of Texas at Austin.

Industrial Relations Contemporary Issues, by B. R. Roberts, November 7th, 1968, 90s. *Information Agreements, Competition and Efficiency*, by D. P. O'Brien & D. Swann, January 9th, 1969, 75s.

International Finance Intermediation Deficits Benign and Malignant, by George N. Halm, International Finance Section Department of Economics, Princeton University.

An Inter-sectoral Analysis of the Missouri Economy 1963, by Floyd D. Hamston, Research Centre School of Business and Public Administration, University of Missouri, 1968, $2.00.

An Introduction to Econometrics, by A. A. Walters, Macmillan & Co. Ltd., October 10th, 1968, 35s.

Is Scientific Management Possible?, A Critical Examination of Glaziers' Theory of Organization, Joe Kelly, October 28th, 1968, 63s.

The Knowledge Revolution, by D. N. Charafas, George Allen & Unwin Ltd., November 21st, 1968, 30s.

Leasing in Industry, Studies in Business Policy No. 127, A Research Report, National Industrial Conference Board, Price—Associates $3.50, Non-Associates $17.50.

Management Information; a Systematic Approach, by P. L. Cloot, The Administrative Staff College, January, 1968.

Missouri Economic Study, An inter-sectoral analysis of the Missouri Economy 1963, by Floyd K. Harmston, Research Center School of Business and Public Administration, University of Missouri, 1968.

Management Glossary, by H. Hohannson and A. B. Robertson (Edited by E. F. L. Brech) Longmans Green & Co., September 23rd, 1968, 30s.

The Money Game, by '*Adam Smith*', Basil Blackwell & Mott, 42s.

The Movement of Manufacturing Industry in the United Kingdom 1945–65, by Board of Trade, London H.M.S.O., September 11th, 1968, 8s. 6d.

New Techniques in Railroad Rate Making, Study No. 44 by George E. McCallum, Bureau of Economic and Business Research.

A Note on Advertising and Uncertainty, by Ira Horowitz, Core Discussion Papers No. 6907, Center for Operations Research & Econometrics, February, 1969.

PRICING PIONEERING PRODUCTS

by JOEL DEAN

I. INTRODUCTION

PRICING pioneer products is one of the most important and puzzling of marketing problems. The high proportion of new products which fail in the market place proclaims the difficulty of pricing them correctly.

A pioneer product is here defined as one which incorporates a major innovation. Its market is therefore, at the outset, ill-defined, since potential applications cannot be foreseen with precision. Pricing decisions usually have to be made recognizing wide margins of error in the forecasts of demand, cost, and competitors' capabilities.

The difficulty of pricing new products is enhanced by the dynamic deterioration of the competitive status of most new products, which decay is speeded by today's high rate of innovation. This makes the life cycle of a new product's economic status a strategic consideration in practical pricing.

This paper is concerned with the level of price of the new product not its price structure. For example, the average price per pound of a new plastic, not the structure of price differentials depending on quality-spreads, order-size, distribution-channel, geographical location, etc.

II. DYNAMIC COMPETITIVE SETTING

A product which is new to the world, as opposed to being merely new to the company, passes through distinctive competitive stages in its life cycle. The appropriate pricing policy is likely to be different for each stage.

New products have a protected distinctiveness which is doomed to progressive degeneration from competitive inroads. As new competitor products enter the field, and as their innovations narrow the gap of distinctiveness between your new product and its substitutes, your zone of pricing discretion narrows. Your distinctive 'speciality' fades into a pedestrian 'commodity' which is so little differentiated from other products that the seller has limited independence in pricing, even if rivals are few.

Throughout the cycle, continual changes occur in promotional and price elasticity and in costs of production and of distribution. These changes may call for adjustments in price policy.

Appropriate pricing over this 'competitiveness cycle' depends on three different aspects of maturity, which usually move in approximately parallel time paths:

1. Technical-maturity, indicated by declining rate of product development, increasing standardization among brands, and increasing stability of manufacturing processes and knowledge about them.
2. Market-maturity, indicated by consumer acceptance of the basic service idea, by widespread belief that the products of most manufacturers will perform satisfactorily, and by enough familiarity and sophistication to permit consumers to compare brands competently.
3. Rivalry-maturity, indicated by increasing stability of market shares and price structures.

III. MONOPOLY PRICING

New product pricing, if the product is truly novel, is in essence monopoly pricing. Stark monopoly pricing, which is the core of new product pricing, considers only what the traffic will bear—the price which will maximize profits taking into account the price-sensitivity of demand and the incremental promotional and production cost of the seller. What the product is worth to the buyer, not what it costs the seller is the controlling consideration.

The competitive setting of the new product has, however, peculiar features that modify monopoly pricing. The monopoly power of the new product is (1) restricted (i.e., buyers have alternatives in the form of products that compete indirectly), (2) ephemeral (i.e., subject to inevitable erosion by imitation and obsolescence) and (3) controllable (i.e., capable of some degree of expansion and prolongation by actions of the seller).

For example, Quanta Welding's new diffusion bonding system, based on a millisecond shaped power pulse is a patented monopoly. But its pricing power is restricted by alternatives. For supersonic aircraft, these are resistance-welding, or rivetting, which are candidate pricing benchmarks. The market-power of Quanta's superior metals-joining process will be eventually eroded. Solid state devices may make obsolete the mercury vapor tube that supplies the controllable massive pulses of electrical energy on which the process depends. Penetration pricing might discourage this competitive entry.

The peculiarities of the new product monopoly introduce dynamism and uncertainty which call for modifications of monopoly pricing:

1. Substitute ways to get the service set limits on the market power of a new product and hence serve as benchmark for pricing it.

2. The perishability of the new product's wanted distinctiveness makes the timing of price, promotion and capacity competition crucial (e.g., choice between skimming and penetration pricing).

3. The ability to influence the amount and the durability of the new product's market power in some degree by your own pricing and promotion actions gives added weight to the effect of today's pricing upon tomorrow's demand.

IV. DEMAND: SENSITIVITY OF VOLUME TO PRICE

Maximum profit monopoly pricing of a new product, even with these dynamic competitive modifications, requires estimates of how price will affect sales. This relationship can be explored in two steps: (1) find what range of price will make the product economically attractive to buyers: (2) estimate what sales volumes can be expected at various points in this price range.

Price range

The price range is determined by the indirect competition of substitutes, which set limits to the monopoly power of the new product. No product serves needs that are totally new; the most novel product merely plugs an abnormally large gap in the chain of substitutes. This gap marks out the potential range of its price.

For industrial products, quick and cheap ways to find this range usually feed on the wisdom of people experienced in looking at comparative product performance in terms of buyers' costs and requirements, for example, distributors, prime contractors and consulting engineers, as well as purchasing analysts and engineers of prospect companies.

For consumers' goods, different methods are needed. In guessing the price range of a radically novel product of small unit value, the concept of barter equivalent can be useful. For example, a manufacturer of paper specialities tested a dramatic new product this way: a wide variety of consumer products totally unlike the new product were purchased and spread out on a big table. Consumers selected the products they would swap for the new product.

Price–Volume relationship

The effect of the price of the new product upon its volume of sales is the most important and most difficult estimate in pricing. We know in general that the lower the price, the greater the volume of sales and the faster its rate of growth. The air freight growth rate is about 18 percent; priced higher, it will grow slower. But to know the precise position and shape of the price–quantity demand schedule or how much faster sales will grow if the price is 20 percent lower is not possible. But estimate it some way we must.

The best way to predict the effect of price on sales volume for a new product is by controlled experiments: offering it at several different prices in comparable test markets under realistic sales conditions. For example, frozen orange juice was thus tested at three prices. When test marketing is not feasible, another method is to broaden the study of the cost of buyers' alternatives and include forecasts of the sales volume of substitutes (and other indications of the volume of customers of different categories). This approach is most promising for industrial customers because performance comparisons are more explicit and measurable and economics more completely controls purchases. When buyers' alternatives differ widely in service value, the difficulty of translating this disparity into superiority-premiums adds to the imprecision of this method of estimating price-volume relationships.

V. PRICING BENCHMARKS: BUYERS' ALTERNATIVES

The buyers' viewpoint should be controlling in pricing. For every new product there are alternatives. Buyers' best alternatives are usually products already tested in the market place. The new product will, presumably, supply a superior solution to the problem of some categories of buyers. The superiority differential over existing products differs widely among new products. The judgement of degree of superiority over substitutes usually also differs widely among buyers.

Benchmark alternatives

The prospective buyer of any new product does have alternatives. These indirectly competitive products are the benchmark for the buyers' appraisal of the price-performance package of your new product. This comparison with existing products determines its relative attractiveness to potential buyers. This kind of analysis [of demand] can be made in the following steps:

1. Determine the major uses for your new product. For each application, determine your product's performance characteristics.

2. For each important usage area, specify the products that are the buyer's best alternative to your new product. Determine the performance characteristics and requirements which buyers view as crucial for their product selection.

3. For each major use, determine how well your product's performance characteristics meet the requirements of customers compared with the performance of these buyers' alternative products.

4. Forecast the prices of alternative products in terms of transaction prices, adjusted for the impact of your new product and translated into units of use. Estimate from the prices of these benchmark substitutes the alternative costs of the buyer per unit of the new product. Real transaction prices (after all discounts) rather than list prices, should be the benchmark, in order to reflect market place realities. Prices should be predicted, after the introduction of the new product, so as to reflect probable competitive adaptation to the new product. Where eventual displacement of existing substitutes appears likely, short run incremental costs supplies a Jeremiah forecast of defender's pricing retaliation.

5. Estimate your superiority premium, i.e., price the performance differential in terms of what the superior solution supplied by the new product is worth to buyers of various categories.

6. Figure a 'parity price' for your product relative to the buyers' best alternative product in each use, for major categories of customers. Parity is a price which encompasses the premium a customer would be willing to pay for your comparative superiority in performance characteristics.

Pricing the superiority differential

Determining this price premium over benchmark products which the new product's superiority will most profitably warrant, is the most intricate and challenging problem of new product pricing.

The value to the customer of the innovational superiority of the new product is surrounded by uncertainties: whether the product will work, whether it will attain its designed superiorities, what its reliability and durability performance will be, and how soon it in turn will become obsolete. These uncertainties influence the price a customer would pay and the promotional outlay to persuade him to buy. Thus, customers' uncertainties will cost the seller, either in price or promotion.

In essence, the superiority premium requires translation of differential performance characteristics into dollars, based on value analysis from the buyer's viewpoint. The premium will differ among uses, among alternative products and among categories of customers. For some, it will be negative. Unless it proves practical to segment the market by application and to have widely discriminatory prices, the new product is likely to be priced out of some applications.

A simplistic, single-point premium reflecting 'what the product can command in the market place' will not do. The customer response-pattern that is needed is the relationship between (1) a series of prospective superiority premiums and (2) the corresponding potential volumes.

What matters is superiority as buyers value it, not superiority as calibrated by technicians' measurements or by the sellers' costs. This means that more and better promotion can raise the premium-volume schedule and make a lower superiority premium achieve the same sales volume or rate of sales growth as would a higher premium without the promotion. This premium-volume schedule will be kicked about by retaliatory pricing of displaceable substitutes as well as by the imitative and innovative new-product-competition of rivals.

The optimizing premium, i.e., the price that would maximize profits in any specified time period will depend upon your future costs as well as upon the hazy and dynamic demand schedule. It will be hard to find. Uncertainty about the future thus makes the appropriate pricing strategy for the long run a matter of sophisticated judgment.

VI. RATE-OF-RETURN PRICING

Application of these principles of economic pricing is illustrated by rate-of-return pricing of new capital equipment. Investment goods are sold to businessmen in their capacity as profit makers. The technique is different for a producer's good (e.g., a truck) than for pricing a consumer's good (e.g., a sports car).

The difference is caused by the fact that the essential service purchased if your product is a producer's good is added profits. Your product represents an investment by your business-man customer. The test of whether or not this investment is a desirable one should be its profitability to the customer. The pricing guide that this suggests is rate-of-return on the capital your customer ties up by his investment in your product.

Rate-of-Return on customer's investment

Rate-of-return pricing looks at your price through the investment eyes of the customer. It recognizes that your upper limit is the price which will produce the minimum acceptable rate-of-return on the customer's investment. The added profits obtainable from the use of your equipment differ among customers and among applications from the same customer. Cut-off criteria of required return also differ, so prospective customers differ in the rate-of-return which will induce them to invest in your product. Thus, the rate-of-return approach opens up a new kind of demand analysis for industrial goods. This analysis consists of inquiry into: (a) the costs of buyers from displaceable alternative ways to do the job; (b) the cost-saving and profit-producing capability of your equipment in different applications and for different prospects; and (c) the capital budgeting policies of your customers, with particular emphasis on their cost-of-capital and their minimum rate-of-return requirements.

The rate-of-return analysis just outlined is particularly useful in the pioneering stages of new products, when you compete only with obsolescent ways of doing the job. At more mature stages in the life cycle of a new product, competitive imitation improves your prospective customers' alternatives. These rival investment alternatives must then be taken explicitly into your analysis.

One way is to use your competitor's product as the benchmark in measuring the rate-of-return which your product will produce for specified categories of your prospects. The profitability from your product is measured in terms of its superiority over the best alternative new equipment offered by rivals, rather than by its superiority over the customer's old equipment. Rate-of-return pricing translates your competitive superiority into dollars of added profit for your customer, and relates this added profit to the added investment. In effect, you would say: 'To be sure, buying my competitor's product will give you a 25 percent rate-of-return and that is better than keeping your old equipment; but buying my product will give you a 30 percent rate-of-return.' For each customer category, rate-of-return analysis reveals a price for your product that makes it an irresistably good investment to your customer in view of his alternatives, but a price which at the same time extracts from your customer all that you can safely demand.

Investigation of (1) the productivity of the buyers' capital investments that you sell in your new product and (2) the required rate-of-return of your prospective customers has proven a practical way to predict the demand for some industrial goods. It must be coupled with forecasts of your costs to find the most profitable price, immediately and with considerations of competitive strategy, for the longer run.

VII. ROLE OF COST

To get maximum practical use from costs in new product pricing, three questions of theory must be answered: (1) whose cost? (2)

which cost? and (3) what role? As to whose cost, three are important: (1) the costs of prospective buyers, (2) the costs of existent and potential competitors and (3) the costs of the producer of the new product. Cost should play a different role for each of the three and the pertinent concept of cost will differ accordingly.

1. *Buyer's cost*

How should costs of prospective customers be used in setting the price of a new product? By applying value analysis to prices and performance of alternative products to find the superiority-premium that will make the new product attractive from an economic standpoint to buyers of specified categories. Rate-of-return pricing of capital goods illustrates this buyer's-cost approach, which is applicable in principle to all new products.

2. *Competitors' costs*

Competitors' costs is usually the crucial estimate in appraisal of their capabilities.

Costs of two kinds of competitive products can be helpful. The first is products already in the market place. The purposes are to estimate (1) their staying power and (2) the floor of retaliation pricing. For the first purpose, the pertinent cost concept is the competitor's long-run incremental cost. For the second, short run incremental cost.

The second kind is the unborn competing product that could blight your new product's future or eventually displace it. Forecasts of competitors' costs for such products are not necessarily wild and can help assess the effectiveness of a strategy of pricing the new product so as to discourage entry. For this purpose, the cost behavior to forecast is the relationship between unit production cost and plant size as you and your rivals move from pilot plant to small scale test production plant to large scale mass production. The cost forecasts should take into account technological progress and should be spotted on a time scale that reflects the potential headstart cost advantages that you could attain under a policy of penetration pricing and under a policy of skimming pricing. Estimates of cost of unborn competitive products are necessarily rough but evaluation of major differences between competitors' costs and your costs can nevertheless be useful. Thus cost estimates can help formulate a defending product's retaliation-pricing and an invading product's conquest-pricing.

3. *Producer's cost*

The cost of the producer plays several roles in pricing a new product. The first is birth control. A new product must be pre-priced provisionally early in the research and development stage and periodically as it progresses toward market. Forecasts of production and promotional costs at matching stages should play the role of forecasting its economic feasibility in determining whether to continue product development and to ultimately commercialize. The concept of cost relevant for this birth-control role is a prediction of full cost at a series of prospective volumes and corresponding technologies. It should encompass imputed cost of capital on intangible as well as tangible investment.

A second role is to establish a price floor which is also the threshold for selecting from candidate prices that which will maximize return on a new product investment over the long run. For both jobs, the relevant concept is future costs, forecasted over a range of volume, production technologies, and promotional outlays in the marketing plan.

Two categories of cost require separate forecasts and have quite different impact on new product pricing:

a. Production costs (including physical distribution).
b. Persuasion costs, which are discretionary and rivalrous with price.

The production costs that matter are the future costs over the long run that will be added by making this product on the predicted scale (or scales) *vs.* not making it. You should estimate the added investment necessary to manufacture and distribute the new product. Investment should include intangibles like R & D, promotion and launching outlays as well as increased working capital. Then you should estimate the added costs of manufacturing and selling the product at various possible sales volumes. Calculate total costs (rather than unit costs) with and without the new product. The difference can then be assigned to the new product. Ignore present overhead that will be the same whether you go ahead with the addition to your product line or not. Future additions to overhead caused by the new product are alone relevant in pricing it. Build up two sets of cost and investment figures—one showing the situation without the new product, and the other showing the situation with the new product added to your line and at several possible volumes. High costs of pilot plant production and of early small scale production plants should be viewed as intangible capital investment rather than viewed as the current operating costs. The losses of a break-in period are part of the investment on which a satisfactory return should be made.

Long-run future incremental costs, including costs of equity capital, (i.e., satisfactory return on the added investment) supply the baseline above which contribution profits of a new product should be maximized—not an impenetrable floor, but a calculation benchmark for optimization.

VIII. STRATEGY CHOICES

A major strategy decision in pricing a new product is the choice between (1) skimming pricing and (2) penetration pricing. There are intermediate positions but the issues are made clearer by comparing the two extremes.

Skimming pricing

Some products represent a drastic improvement upon accepted ways of performing a service or filling a demand. For these products a strategy of high prices with large promotional expenditure in the early stages of market development (and lower prices at later stages), has frequently proven successful. This I call a skimming price policy. There are four main reasons for its success:

1. Your sales of the product are likely to be less sensitive to price in the early stages than when the product is 'full-grown' and competitive imitations have appeared. In the early stages, the product usually has so few close rivals that cross-elasticity of demand is low. Promotional sensitivity is, on the other hand, quite high, particularly for products with high unit prices, since it is difficult for the customer to value the service of the product.

2. Launching a new product with a high price is an efficient device for breaking the market up into segments that differ in price elasticity of demand. The initial high price serves to skim the cream of the market that is relatively insensitive to price. Subsequent price reductions tap successively more elastic sectors of the market. This pricing strategy is exemplified by the systematic succession of editions of a book, sometimes starting with a $50 limited personal edition and ending up with a 25-cent pocket book.

3. A skimming policy is safer, or at least appears so. Facing an unknown elasticity of demand, a high initial price serves as a 'refusal' price during the stage of exploration. How much costs can be reduced as the market expands and as the design of the product is improved by increasing production efficiency with new techniques is difficult to predict.

4. High prices frequently produce a greater dollar volume of sales in the early stages of market development than are produced by low initial prices. When this is the case, skimming pricing will provide you with funds to finance expansion into the larger volume sectors of your market.

Penetration pricing

Despite its many advantages, a skimming-price policy isn't always the answer to your new product problems. Although high initial prices may maximize profits during the early stages of product introduction, they may also prevent sales to many of the buyers upon whom you must rely for a mass market. The alternative is to use low prices as an entering wedge to get into mass markets early. This I call penetration pricing. This approach is likely to be desirable under these conditions:

First, when sales volume of the product is very sensitive to price, even in the early stages of introduction.

Second, when you can achieve substantial economies in unit cost of manufacturing and distributing the product by operating at large volume.

Third, when your product faces threats of strong potential competition, very soon after introduction.

Fourth, when there is no 'elite' market—that is, no class of buyers willing to pay a higher price to obtain the newest and the best.

While a penetration pricing policy can be adopted at any stage in the product's life cycle, you should always examine this pricing strategy before your new product is marketed at all. This possibility should be explored again as soon as your product has established an elite market. Sometimes a product can be rescued from premature death by adoption of a penetration price after the cream of the market has been skimmed.

One important consideration in your choice between skimming and penetration pricing at the time you introduce your new product is the ease and speed with which competitors can bring out substitute products. For products whose market potential looks big, a policy of low initial prices makes sense because the big multiple-product manufacturers are attracted to mass markets. If you set your initial price low enough, your large competitor may not feel it worthwhile to make a big investment for slim profit margins.

The speed with which your product loses its uniqueness and sinks from its sheltered status to the level of just another competitive product depends on several factors:

a. Its total sales potential: A big potential market entices competitive imitation.
b. The investment required for rivals to manufacture and distribute the product: A big investment barrier deters invasion.
c. The strength of patent and know-how protection.
d. The alertness and power of competitors.

Although competitive imitation is almost inevitable, the company that introduces a new product can use price to discourage or delay the introduction of competitive products.

Pricing in maturity

To determine what pricing policies are appropriate for later stages in the cycle of market and competitive maturity, the manufacturer must be able to tell when a product is approaching maturity. Some of the symptoms of degeneration of competitive status toward the commodity level are:

1. Weakening in brand preference—this may be evidenced by a higher cross-elasticity of demand among leading products, the leading brand not being able to continue demanding as much price premium as initially without losing position;
2. Narrowing physical variation among products as the best designs are developed and standardized—this has been dramatically demonstrated in automobiles and is still in process in television receivers;
3. The entry in force of private-label competitors—this is exemplified by the mail-order houses' sale of own-label refrigerators and paint sprayers;
4. Market saturation—the ratio of replacement sales to new equipment sales serves as an indicator of the competitive degeneration of durable goods, but in general it must be kept in mind that both market size and degree of saturation are hard to define (e.g., saturation of the radio market, which was initially thought to be one radio per home and later had to be expanded to one radio per room);
5. The stabilization of production methods—indicated by slow rate of technological advance, high average age of equipment and great uniformity among competitors introduction technology.

IX. PROMOTION AND DISTRIBUTION

Promotion

Initial promotion outlays are an investment in the product that cannot be recovered until some kind of market has been established. As the innovator, you shoulder the burden of educating consumers to the existence and uses of the product. Later imitators will never have to do this job; so, if you, the innovator, do not want to be simply a benefactor to your future competitors, you must make pricing plans to earn a return on all your initial outlays before your pricing discretion evaporates.

Your basic strategic problem is to find the right mixture of price and promotion to maximize your long-run profits. You can choose a relatively high price in pioneering stages, together with large advertising and dealer discounts, and plan to get your promotion investment back early; or you can use low prices and lean margins from the very outset, in order to discourage potential competition when the barriers of patents, and investment in production capacity, distribution channels, or production techniques become inadequate.

Channels of distribution

Choice of channels of distribution should be consistent with your strategy for initial pricing and for promotional outlays. Penetration pricing and explosive promotion calls for distribution channels that promptly make the product broadly available. Otherwise you waste advertising or stymie mass-market pricing. Distribution policy also concerns the role you wish the dealer to play in pushing your product, the margins you must pay him to induce this action and the amount of protection of territory and of inventory required to do so.

Estimation of the costs of moving the new product through the channels of distribution to the final consumer must enter into the pricing procedure, since these costs govern the factory price that will result in a specified final price. Distributive margins are partly pure promotional costs and partly physical distribution costs. Margins must at least cover the distributors' costs of warehousing, handling, and order taking. These costs are similar to factory production costs in being related to physical capacity and its utilization, i.e. fluctuations in production or sales volume. Hence these set a floor to trade-channel discounts. But distributors usually also contribute promotional effort—in point-of-sale pushing, local advertising, and display

—when it is made worth their while. These pure promotional costs are more optional.

Distributors' margins are best determined by study of distributors' alternatives. This does not mean that your distributor gross margin must be the same as rival products. It should instead produce a better rate of return on the distributors' investment (in inventory, shelf space and sales capacity).

X. SOME PRICING PRECEPTS

Pricing new products is an art. The important determinants in economic pricing of pioneering innovations are complex and interrelated and hard to forecast. Experienced judgment is required in pricing and repricing the product to fit its changing competitive environment. This judgment may possibly be improved by some pricing precepts suggested by the preceding analysis:

1. Be clear about corporate goals. Pricing a new product is an occasion for rethinking them. In this article I have assumed the overriding corporate goal is long-run profit maximization, e.g., making the stock worth most.

2. Pricing a new product should begin long before its birth. Prospective prices, coupled with forecasted costs, should play the decisive role in product birth control.

3. Pricing a new product should be continuing process of bracketing the truth by successive approximations. Rough estimates of the relevant concepts are preferable to precise knowledge of historical irrelevancies.

4. Costs can supply useful guidance in new product pricing, but not by the conventional wisdom i.e., cost-plus pricing. Costs to three persons are pertinent: the buyer, the seller, and his rivals. The role of cost differs among the three, as does the concept of cost that is pertinent to that role: different costs for different purposes.

5. The role of your cost is to set a reference base for picking the most profitable price. For this job the only costs that are pertinent to pricing a new product on the verge of commercialization (i.e., already developed and tested) are your incremental costs: the added costs of going ahead, at different plant sales. Costs of R & D and of market testing are now sunk and hence irrelevant.

6. Recognize the pricing implications of the changing economic status and competitive environment of your product as it passes through its life cycle from birth to obsolescence. This cycle, and the plans you make to influence it, are of paramount importance for your pricing policy.

7. Look at your product through the eyes of your customer and price it just low enough to make it an irresistable investment, in view of his alternatives as he sees them. To estimate successfully how much your product is worth to your prospect is never easy; but it is usually rewarding.

8. Customers' rate of return should be the main consideration in pricing novel capital goods. Buyers' cost savings (and other earnings) expressed as a return on his investment in your new product is the key to predicting the price-sensitivity of demand and to pricing profitably.

9. The strategic choice between skimming and penetration pricing should be based on economics. The skimming policy, i.e., relatively high prices in the pioneering stage, cascading downward thereafter, is particularly appropriate for products whose sales initially are comparatively unresponsive to price but quite responsive to education. A policy of penetration pricing, i.e., relatively low prices in the pioneering stage in anticipation of the cost savings resulting from an expanding market, is best when scale-economies are big, demand is price-sensitive, and invasion is threatened. Low starting prices sacrifice short-run profits for long-run profits and discourage potential competitors.

JOEL DEAN ASSOCIATES, INC.,
HASTINGS-ON-HUDSON

SOME MANAGERIAL INFLUENCES ON A FIRM'S PRICING POLICY*

by A. J. Burkart

We propose to discuss certain factors influencing a firm's pricing policy, which arise more from the way a firm is run than from the way it reacts to changes in its market. We argue that these managerial influences tend to militate against a flexible pricing policy, and by this we mean a policy that recognizes and indeed seeks opportunities to vary, upwards or downwards, the prices of the firm's products. (We have in mind producers of consumer goods and services rather than manufacturers of capital goods or services mostly used by other firms.)

A firm will determine, for what it makes, a price which seems to it appropriate, and an estimate of market demand will be only one consideration. Indeed, the market demand is quite rarely considered in itself, at least explicitly, and when it is, such phrases as 'charging what the market will bear' tend to be used. The use of this kind of language itself signifies a preoccupation with demand which has for the time being overridden other considerations.

At any one time, a firm's appropriate prices will be set at a given level, arrived at in practical terms by successive adjustments from previous historical levels. The current determination of these prices therefore will quite possibly have been made without overmuch explicit consideration of market demand (except in the unproven case of a new product), because there will be sufficient current experience of the market to guide the firm. Interest lies therefore in how price changes are eventually made, how the need for changes are signalled, and what prevents changes and adjustments to prices being made more frequently, or, to put the matter the other way round, why are firms reluctant to adjust their prices?

To take first the case where falling demand may suggest the need for lower prices, the early signals will be physical in character, for example, low volumes moving ex-factory, or sluggish traffic over retailers' counters announced by a retail audit. *Per contra*, the possible need for an upward revision of prices may first be signalled by increasing overtime working or lengthening delivery dates. Apprehensions about the activities of competitors will induce a firm at least to try to hold its current prices, despite indications that

* This article was written while the author was an honorary research fellow, University of Lancaster, and grateful acknowledgement is made to Professor P. W. S. Andrews and his colleagues in the Department of Economics for much discussion of the topics herein.

a higher price is appropriate and thus to accept some pressure on trading margins. Conversely, anticipated rises in costs may lead a firm to condone a price higher than is evidently justified in the market, in the optimistic belief that all will be well in the end. Indeed, generally rising costs are a more potent factor in the raising of prices than is buoyant demand. Given continuing inflation of course, a firm may expect that its rivals will likewise be under pressure from continually increasing costs, and all firms know this and know that all will have to raise their prices sooner or later. If within, say, the United Kingdom, all firms in an industry will be subject to the same degree of inflation, it might be expected that in respect of export prices, a greater flexibility might be found, on the grounds that rival firms in overseas markets would not be experiencing the identically same inflationary experience. A distinction should be made here between acceptance of lower export prices (and perhaps reduced profit) and willingness to be more flexible in pricing. If firms are more flexible in export pricing, it might be urged that they simply have less control over their marketing abroad and that the managerial influences discussed below bear less convincingly in the export case. Probably firms are willing to accept a lower profit margin in the export case, but give considerable latitude in pricing to the importer. The latter in his turn may display his own variety of inflexibility, which may be different in degree but similar in kind from that of his exporting principal. What perhaps it amounts to is that a degree of inflexibility will be displayed appropriate to each particular market, but differing as between markets. In the last resort, the only justification for reluctance to adjust or vary prices is the assumption of a particular degree of elasticity (not necessarily a correct assumption) in demand in a particular market, and this will rarely be identical between markets. We now discuss certain managerial influences tending to incline a firm to keep intact its current prices and price structure.

THE UTILIZATION OF PLANT

Firms are dominated in their corporate thinking by the factory, by their plant, even when they match this preoccupation with considerable emphasis on the marketing function. In the short run at least, marketing is about disposing advantageously of what the factory can make, for that period while the firm is locked in to its present plant. For most firms, their plant accounts for the bulk of their physical assets, and attendance at the plant engages by far the larger part of their labour force. Consequently, the full utilization of the plant is rightly a major objective of management. For plant capable of very great productive capacity, like a fleet of vehicles, the absolute gain to be secured by marginal improvement in utilization can be very great. Moreover, the plant will contribute together with its attendant labour force a very large and fairly invariant component to final costs; it is tangible and daily visible, its problems can be seen on the shop floor, and its smooth operation creates a kind of affectionate pride in watching management—in shipping, and perhaps in all transportation, the vehicle is invested with nearly human qualities, but other forms of productive enterprise do not escape a fair amount of emotional involvement with their plant. The effect of this is to lead to a conviction that the market will certainly demand the quantities the firm wishes to make, that the firm will be able to sell more of its production than in the event it will do, for how can managements believe that such a valued plant produces something which is not really wanted?

BUDGETING

The practice of cost–revenue budgeting, especially if conducted on an annual basis and without frequent up-dating, subtly reinforces managerial orientation towards production. In budgeting, a firm will be able in the immediate future to estimate costs with acceptable accuracy: costs of materials, the effect of wage agreements, the annual cost of the plant, etc., can all be estimated with reasonable precision, and an allowance made for possible inaccuracies or mis-estimates. Perhaps the only major element for which no estimating procedure is available is a change in taxation. Estimating revenue for budgetary purposes is, however, altogether a different kind of thing. Present trends may be extrapolated, and market and other research used in aid, but unless there exists a number of substantial forward contracts, the revenue estimates cannot be invested with the same kind of certainty as costs. The fundamental basis of revenue budgeting is the examination of alternative hypotheses about the future, and the selection of one as the most probable outcome.

The difference in quality between the cost estimates and the revenue estimates, however, is liable to be blurred when the entire budget is brought before a firm's management, and while a cost budget may reasonably be represented as a decision of the firm to trade in a particular way, the revenue budget is not a decision at all, but simply a chosen hypothesis which has been preferred to the available alternatives. If costs are tending to inflate, as will have been the experience of most U.K. firms during the past two decades, a firm's revenue-earning departments will be under some pressure to 'improve their budget' and the quantities they claim to be able to sell will be overstated. On the assumption that the revenue budget or hypothesis has been made honestly in the first place, to ask for an improvement is to choose a second-best alternative hypothesis. Either the original estimate was dishonestly made, or the asked-for improvement has a lesser likelihood of being attained. The logical thing would appear to be to ask whether prices can be raised, or lowered, without decreasing total revenue or better still increasing it. But this would introduce a new complication, and a revenue department's instinct will always be to go for the higher physical quantity at the existing price.

The effect of both preoccupation with plant utilization and of conventional cost–revenue budgeting is to lead firms to believe that they can sell more than in fact they will and they can sell that quantity at a price rather higher than they originally deemed appropriate. Despite the contradiction in this attitude, firms behave as if they believe that if they raise their prices, they will sell as much as before or that if they lower prices, increased demand will not appear. In other words, firms intuitively judge demand to be relatively inelastic, when in fact it may be rather elastic, and at the same time display reluctance to vary prices.

ADMINISTRATIVE DETERRENTS

There are a number of deterrents to greater flexibility in pricing which are administrative in character. Price lists, packs and outers of all kinds, and often promotional material have to be printed and distributed with the new information at every price change. Oil companies and transport undertakings, whose products are not elaborately packaged, may have relatively few complications here, but timetables will still need amending and prices on the forecourt pumps need changing. The cost of printing and distributing new material, the wastage of existing material and the direct costs of notifying the change, could conceivably exceed the advantages of making a price change at all. In a number of industries there may exist a tradition of pricing, in round or exact prices, and a firm may be very reluctant to depart from these. It may be that this influence was to be felt more strongly before the virtually complete abandonment of retail price maintenance, and certainly one's impression is that the exact or the conventional price operates with far less force to-day than was previously the case.

Increasingly complex legislation in the weights and measures and labelling areas may involve adjustments not merely to price but also to pack size, and in some cases where the logical way of increasing or reducing prices would be to make small adjustments to pack size or contents, current legislation prevents this option.[1] There is a sense in which such consumer protection legislation may well distort or amplify price adjustments, and although such legislation is drawn in in consultation with manufacturers to mitigate the cruder effects, this is perhaps no substitute for permitting more sensitive changes in price to be made by manufacturers who are already reluctant to do so. In this context, it should be recalled that not all price changes are made upwards. The administrative complications of price adjustment produce thus further obstacles to flexibility in pricing which, coupled with a time lag between the decision to make a change and its date of implementation, tends to reinforce a firm's desire to maintain its current price level.

RETAILERS' REACTION TO PRICE CHANGES

Retailers, particularly stockholding retailers, do not welcome price changes. After all, they introduce an element of confusion into the day to day business of shopkeeping. Reductions in price are seen as erosions of retail margins, increases as likely to reduce demand across their counters. Increases may accelerate the effect of retailers' fears of reduced demand, by making them unwilling to stock brands the subject of price increases or unwilling to give such brands prominent display. Retailers are acutely sensitive to the possible effects of price changes on local demand, and are aware that while high prices are likely to be deterrents, lower prices are not necessarily incentives to the consumer to buy. Apprehensions of retailers' reactions to changes in price are likely to weigh heavily on a firm and conspire again to keep prices unaltered.

IRRATIONALITIES

A firm may cherish irrationalities which work to prevent greater flexibility in pricing policy. Its natural pride that its own product is different from and better than those of its competitors, may lead a firm to feel that its product 'ought' to command a higher price. However, a more complex irrationality may arise from the 'share of

[1] There are numerous examples of this type of legislation: in the U.K. for example, tea may not be sold in packets less than $\frac{1}{4}$lb in weight. To achieve fractional price changes, a manufacturer cannot make minor adjustments to weight. I am indebted to Mr P. A. Robinson, of the Board of Trade, for drawing my attention to this point.

the market' concept. Devised originally to assist, especially in the short term, in measuring a firm's performance *vis à vis* its competitors and to serve as a measure of efficiency, it can too easily deteriorate into a goal in itself as if trading were a war to be won and a competitor an enemy to be forced to yield territorial acquisitions. This attitude is the more prevalent when share of the market is measured in physical terms rather than in terms of the revenue each is getting out of the market. Management is more readily afflicted by a sense of failure if its physical share is not maintained and is correspondingly more reluctant to experiment with price adjustments which might nevertheless yield more revenue from the market. Of course firms are reluctant to engage in vigorous price competition, and as an alternative, may well seek to enlarge market share by merging with or taking over a weak competitor. Recent restrictive practices legislation and the operation of the Monopolies Commission have limited effectively the opportunities for collusive action to predetermine market shares and to stabilize prices, a procedure which can be rationalized by asserting the merits of combination to expand the total market rather than each firm competing for an increasing share. Even when such practices are forbidden in law, they do re-appear occasionally in the guise of industry-wide cooperative advertising promoting the whole class of products rather than individual brands. While in the U.K. so-called institutional cooperative advertising on behalf of whole industries seems to be less frequently met with than was the case some years ago (one thinks of campaigns to promote the drinking of relatively homogeneous products like beer or milk), a more subtle form has perhaps arisen in the newspaper supplements devoted to a single industry such as holidays abroad or central heating.

THE NEW PRODUCT CASE

By contrast with the foregoing, the launching of a new product offers an opportunity to be less rigid in pricing. Here the market will have been thoroughly researched, the opportunity for the new product assessed, but still in this case firms will keep their initial prices low. In the first place, lack of experience in the market can be explicitly recognized, and allowed for in pricing. Secondly, maximum penetration of the market will be sought initially, even if some subsequent contraction is envisaged. Thirdly, since retailers count physical quantities too, a fast initial flow through the market is required, to established retailer confidence, to ensure good display, and to promote re-ordering. Fourthly, a low price provides a dramatic theme for advertising and promotion, and finally it may well be acceptable not to make a financial profit in the early years of a product's career—a best-selling physical success may be thought to be more likely to establish the new product for the longer term. Typically, the physical sales of a new product may rise sharply to an early peak, declining later to perhaps only a third of the early quantity. At this point, with demand stabilized, a price increase may be sought, and the initial launching period may well be defined as the period between the new product's first appearance and the first increase in its price.

CONCLUSION

The factors we have described as inhibiting flexibility in pricing reinforce the inherent entrepreneurial optimism of managements. At its simplest, this optimism produces a state of euphoria that makes it seem inconceivable that budgets will not be met, that cash flow will not be adequate, and that profits will not accrue. That the cost budget and the revenue budget are of quite different provenance is masked by the firm's optimism, and much time may be wasted in analysing shortfalls in revenue or in physical sales, as if revenue budget figures were actual measurements rather than hypotheses adopted for the purposes of budgeting.

The factors described above tend to make a firm reluctant to alter its prices at all and conspire towards a status quo in pricing, but they are less of a deterrent to raising prices than to lowering them. Even when a firm recognizes the need for a reduction in prices, it will prefer methods which do not unduly disturb a stable system of price quotation and which makes it possible to revert to original prices as soon as possible. In practice, any one firm will operate a range of prices, low prices for large quantities, surcharges for small, seasonal variations, short-term reductions for advertising purposes and the like.

We must distinguish in conclusion between the absence of flexibility in pricing, and the tendency to keep prices high, or a reluctance to reduce them. Both are, we submit, important attitudes. We are asserting firstly that there are a number of administrative or organizational influences which make for rigidity, that lead firms to feel that the more sensitive adjustment of price is simply too difficult. But we are also saying that firms frequently and habitually think that the demand for their product is a good deal more inelastic than is really the case. Granted the real difficulty of judging elasticity of demand, the practical problems of revising prices reinforce this managerial optimism that an increase in price will be readily absorbed without affecting sales. We think that this unwillingness to be more flexible, to accept that sales are often rather more sensitive to price changes than the firm believes, leads to an undetected but steady deterioration in revenue.

ROMSEY, HANTS

THE U.S. TANKER INDUSTRY: A STRUCTURAL AND BEHAVIORAL ANALYSIS*

by RAN HETTENA AND HIRSCH S. RUCHLIN

IN MOST of the last decade the U.S. tanker industry has been characterized by unsatisfactory performance. In this article we investigate the strategic economic variables which—within a given legal and institutional framework—have adversely affected the industry's performance. We do so by first describing the extent of deterioration sustained by the industry, which we will follow with a brief analytical outline of the industry and its environment. Next, we analyze the structural and behavioral patterns, draw the necessary implications, and present empirical evidence to support our conclusions. In the process we derive cost and supply functions which are uncommon—if not unique—in the unregulated sector of the economy. We establish the existence of monopsony exercised, paradoxically, by a U.S. government agency presumably interested in promoting the industry's development.

THE INDUSTRY IN ITS ENVIRONMENT

The unsatisfactory performance of the industry is indicated by physical deterioration, loss of capital, lack of profitability, and freight rate instability. The U.S. share of the world's tanker fleet declined from 18.9 per cent in 1956 to 8.3 per cent in 1966. The average age of the U.S. fleet in 1966 was 14.9 years compared with 7.6 years for the world fleet. Between 1962 and 1966 the average age of the world fleet remained unchanged while the United States' increased by almost 2 years. Only 7.6 per cent of the world tanker fleet was constructed prior to 1946 and as much as 36 per cent during 1963–66 as opposed to 46.9 per cent and 7 per cent respectively for U.S. tankers.[1] Trends in new tanker construction also confirm the relative decline of U.S. tankers: in 1964, the U.S. accounted for 1.8 per cent of completed tanker tonnage and 1.2 per cent of tonnage on order; in 1966 these figures were down to 0.3 per cent and 0.1 per cent

* We are indebted to Professor Benjamin J. Katz of New York University and Professor Donald Dewey of Colombia University for their valuable comments on an earlier draft of this paper. We are, however, wholly responsible for whatever errors of fact and interpretation remain.

[1] Sun Oil Company, Economics Department, *Analysis of World Tank Ship Fleet*, 1962–66 editions.

respectively.[2] The lack of new tanker construction over the last decade and the consequent increase in U.S. tankers' average age clearly indicate a net capital outflow in that more capital is being consumed through depreciation than is flowing into the industry by way of new construction. Lack of industry profitability is verified by our profitability estimates for 1961–65, reported in Appendix A, which show that industry profitability was overwhelmingly negative for most years and for most tanker classes with losses substantial for 1961, 1962 and 1965. Finally a considerable degree of freight rate instability is revealed by Fig. 1. Even after seasonal adjustment freight rate variations of 20 per cent or more over a few months are common and still greater variations not infrequent.

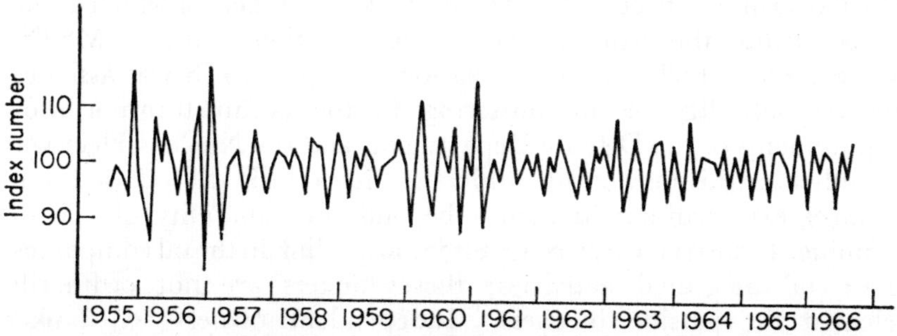

Fig. 1. Irregular Component Index, Single Voyages, U.S. Gulf East Coast, Clean Trade (ATRS flat = 100).*

*The American Tanker Rate Schedule (ATRS specifies freight rates for the full range of U.S. tanker voyages computed in such a way as to ensure that a typical tanker is guaranteed the same daily return irrespective of the particular voyage it performs. Fluctuations in tanker market rates are expressed in the percentage above or below ATRS (ATRS ± %).

The industry is defined as the aggregate of U.S. flag tankers in clean and dirty petroleum transportation qualified to carry domestic and government-sponsored cargoes (including military) exclusively reserved for U.S. vessels under a body of U.S. laws and regulations.[3] U.S. tankers also carry grant-in-aid grain in bulk under P.L. 480 but resort to this trade only when petroleum freight rates are depressed or when the vessel's physical deterioration makes the cost of petroleum transportation prohibitive. The U.S. tanker market is simultaneously protected from foreign competition by U.S. laws and isolated from international markets by the considerably higher cost of construction and operation of U.S. tankers.

[2] OECD, *Maritime Transport* (Paris: OECD, 1966), Tables XXX, XXXI. Although at the end of 1967 there were 16 tankers under construction in U.S. yards, these were the result of the surge in tanker rates caused by the Vietnam war and the closing of the Suez Canal in June 1967.

[3] Merchant Marine Act of 1920, Military Act of 1904 as amended, and Cargo Preference Act.

As of December 1966 the U.S. tanker fleet consisted of the following.[4]

Owned by	No. of ships	Deadweight tons (DWT)	Percent of total DWT
Oil companies (industrial carriers)	152	3,766,000	44.0
Non-oil companies (independent carriers)	118	2,987,000	35.0
Total privately owned	270	6,753,000	79.0
U.S. Government	117	1,797,000	21.0
Total U.S. fleet	387	8,550,000	100.0

The Government fleet includes some 75 Navy tankers of which about 30 constitute the Military Sea Transportation Service (MSTS) Nucleus Fleet. Following its formation in 1949, MSTS was assigned the responsibility of administering to the ocean transportation requirements of the Defense Department, and the Nucleus Fleet was provided for this task on the understanding that it will be used only to meet extraordinary demands beyond the capability of private shipping. Industrial carriers are essentially a link in the oil companies' chain of integrated activities; these tankers are not ordinarily released for outside business.[5] Independent owners sell tanker services for a living by chartering out their tankers on the open market. For purposes of analysis, then, the independent tanker market is the relevant market. It operates in a manner not unlike commodity exchanges except that it is much smaller. Tankers are offered largely on the basis of size and date of readiness. Commercial charterers report their tanker needs (and shipowners their vessels' availability) to brokers who then attempt to match supply and demand. MSTS circulates its requests for bids directly with shipowners; it usually 'counteroffers' to the lowest bidder at a lower rate which, if rejected by the shipowner, is offered to another. If there are no takers, the order is withdrawn until the next invitation to bid.

STRUCTURE

The following structural analysis seeks to portray the competitive posture of the tanker industry and to compare it with the competitive norm. We will use the term competition in the sense used by J. M.

[4] Sun Oil Company, Economics Department, *op. cit.*, 1966 edition, pp. 8, 15–16; U.S. Department of Commerce, Maritime Administration, *Employment Report of the U.S. Flag Merchant Fleet*, MAR-560-13 Series. Washington, D.C. (February 1967), Table IV.

[5] When they are, they act as independent carriers.

Clark and as formulated by the Attorney General to define workable or effective competition.[6]

Competitive requirements are met on the supply side of the U.S. tanker market. Product differentiation does not exist; advertising and sales promotion are rare; no effort is made to acquaint buyers with differences in vessel specifications; no firms exist by their ability to attract a special class of customers. Differences between vessels affect only the cost of transportation, not the nature or homogeneity of the service. There are no obvious overall administrative and financial economies of scale.[7] Multi-tanker firms are subject to roughly constant returns to scale over a wide range from as few as two to as many as fourteen vessels.[8] No elaborate administrative superstructure is needed to operate efficiently. The tanker employment scale (crew) is low, ranging from 35 to 50 persons. The average flexible optimum tanker size is about 0.0045 per cent of private U.S. tanker capacity, and even the largest vessel in the trade is itself less than 1 per cent of private capacity.[9]

Neither are construction costs a barrier to entry: the cost of construction of the flexible optimum scale tanker is under $10,000,000,[10] and long-term financing of 87.5 per cent of construction cost is available at a low interest rate through U.S. Government Title XI Mortgage Insurance. Tanker mobility substantially reduces the cost of exit from any geographic market thereby serving to equalize demand and supply.[11]

Seller concentration is fairly low. With tanker firms defined in the broadest sense as the group of tanker-owning companies under single control, we find a total of 33 independent controlling groups with the largest four accounting for 18.6 per cent and the largest eight 35.5 per cent of the tankers owned.[12] Seller concentration is

[6] J. M. Clark, 'Toward a Concept of Workable Competition', *American Economic Review*, Vol. XXX, No. 3 (June 1940), pp. 241–56; J. M. Clark, *Competition as a Dynamic Process* (Washington, D.C.: The Brookings Institution, 1961); *Report of the Attorney General's National Committee*, March 31st, 1955 (Washington, D.C.: U.S. Government Printing Office, 1955).

[7] Zenon S. Zannetos, *The Theory of Oil Tankship Rates* (Cambridge, Mass.: The MIT Press, 1966), pp. 178–9.

[8] Allen Ferguson *et al.*, *The Economic Value of the United States Merchant Marine* (Evanston, Ill.: The Transportation Center at Northwestern University, 1961), p. 289.

[9] The optimal tanker for maximum flexibility is about 30,000 DWT; and for maximum productivity at a 35 ft draft or less, the optimum scale is about 50,000 DWT. The 108,400 DWT tanker *Manhattan* has seldom operated in the U.S. tanker trade on account of its size.

[10] U.S. Department of Commerce, Maritime Administration, *Commerce News*, MA-NR-68 Series, Washington, D.C. (April 15th, 1968).

[11] Zannetos, *op cit.*, pp. 179–80.

[12] H. Clarkson and Company Limited, *The Tanker Register, 1967* (London: Author, 1967; Terminus Publications, Ltd.; *Tanker and Bulk Carrier World Directory*, 1967 (London: Author, 1967); Maritime Association of the Port of New York, *Lloyds Shipping Index* (New York: Author, U.S.A. edition, September 1967).

therefore somewhat less than in Bain's Type V, low–moderate, concentration.[13] (Concentration ratios for industrial carriers are considerably higher and typical of oil companies' oligopoly.) Furthermore, the sellers' concentration ratios we have cited appear to overestimate the effect of concentration in the relevant market: first, because we have excluded imports;[14] second, because we have narrowly defined the industry by excluding industrial tankers and pipelines;[15] and third, because we have broadly defined the firm as the group of tanker companies under single control. Indeed if we had —as Zannetos—defined the firm as the single tanker,[16] seller concentration in the relevant market would not be far from atomistic. Contrary to the sellers' case, buyers' concentration is high. Our analysis of 1657 tanker fixtures (charters) concluded during 1961–66 as reported by the tanker brokerage firm of C. D. Mallory and Co., Inc., reveals the following concentration patterns (in percent).

PERCENT OF TOTAL FIXTURES ATTRIBUTED TO VARIOUS CHARTERERS

Year	*MSTS*	*Amoco*	*Gulf*	*Hess*	*Humble*	*Shell*	*Sinclair*	*All* others*	*Largest 4 charterers*
1961	30.3	6.3	6.0	12.8	7.8	3.2	2.1	31.5	57.2
1962	27.9	11.2	3.1	6.4	3.4	3.5	3.1	41.4	48.9
1963	14.8	8.1	1.7	6.4	9.8	4.3	1.5	53.4	39.1
1964	21.7	9.5	1.1	4.5	3.5	2.9	1.6	55.2	39.2
1965	40.0	5.6	2.3	4.0	1.8	7.6	0.8	37.9	51.4
1966	52.6	6.9	1.5	1.6	2.9	2.0	2.5	30.0	64.0

* The composition of the 'All others' category typically includes over twenty firms.

Averaged out over the six-year period, MSTS, the largest charterer by far, accounted for 33 percent, and the largest four charterers for 50 percent, of all fixtures. Measured monthly, concentration ratios for the largest four exceed 65 percent in at least one-third of the entire period thus falling into Bain's Type II classification of highly concentrated industries.[17]

While the exclusion of petroleum imports and the narrowness of the industry definition tend to reduce the effect of the concentration ratios on the supply side, these same factors tend to produce the opposite effect on the demand side. Tanker sellers are restricted to

[13] Joe S. Bain, *Industrial Organization* (New York: John Wiley & Sons, Inc., 1959), pp. 32, 131–2.

[14] George Stigler, 'The Extent and Basis of Monopoly', *American Economic Review*, Supplement, Vol. 32, No. 2 (June 1940), pp. 1–22; and U.S. Congress, Senate, Committee on Judiciary, Subcommittee on Antitrust and Monopoly, *Concentration Ratios in Manufacturing Industry*, 1958, 87th Congress, 2nd Session (Washington, D.C.: U.S. Government Printing Office, 1962), p. vi.

[15] *Ibid.*, p. iv.

[16] Zannetos, *op. cit.*, pp. 182–3.

[17] The monthly ratios can be provided upon request.

dealings only with U.S. tanker charterers; buyers have access to competing industries, such as pipelines and imported oil, in at least some trades. To the extent that import quotas are held or purchased, foreign oil may be substituted for domestic oil and foreign tankers for U.S. tankers.[18] Furthermore, taking account of the size of the U.S. tanker fleets owned by the oil companies and MSTS and lumping them together with the chartered tonnage would materially increase the buyers' concentration ratios.

A last—and often neglected—structural feature is the inelasticity of demand. The demand for U.S. tankers derives principally from the demand for refined products or crude oil whose elasticity has been estimated by Koopmans as ranging from 0.2 to 0.5.[19] Furthermore, as a corollary of the derived demand principle, the influence of tanker rates on final product is minor unless rates are abnormally high. Finally, the elasticity of tanker demand is further and materially decreased by the tendency of stability inherent in oil company pricing policy and the fact that the volume of MSTS demand is determined by military and not economic considerations.

Cost and Supply Conditions

The composition of the average total cost of transportation per ton mile (AC) between fixed (AFC) and variable (AVC) cost components varies with vessel size. Predictably, the AFC (financial charges and overhead) of a modern (larger) tanker constitutes a greater proportion of AC than for an older (smaller) tanker for which AVC (vessel plus voyage expense) constitutes a substantial proportion of AC. Layup cost (C_L), the cost of maintaining a vessel in layup status, is of particular relevance because, contrary to AFC and AVC which are stable throughout the operating period, C_L varies inversely with the actual duration of the layup, ranging from 100 percent to 10 percent of vessel expenses. Hence, C_L is a function of time: $C_L = C_L(t)$.[20]

[18] The magnitude of these alternative means is substantial. In the first eleven months of 1967 Gulf/East Coast shipments averaged 1,802,000 b/d (barrels a day) for tankers compared with 1,154,000 b/d for pipelines; crude and product imports by tanker averaged 1,739,000 b/d for the same period.

[19] T. Koopmans, *Tanker Freight Rates and Tankship Building*, Netherlands Economic Institute (London: P. S. King and Sons, Ltd., 1939), pp. 28–9.

[20] We calculate the relationship between C_L and duration for a U.S. tanker to be roughly as follows.

Duration of layup	*Cost of layup as a percentage of vessel expenses*
Under 10 days	100
10–29 days	50
30 days and over	20–10

We may now define the short-run average variable cost (SAVC) for a given tanker as the average variable cost (AVC) minus layup cost, $C_L(t)$: SAVC = AVC$-C_L(t)$.[21] Designating the market rate, P_M, which equals a particular vessel's SAVC as the reservation rate P_R[22] and assuming the shipowner minimizes his losses, when $P_M > P_R$ the vessel operates; when $P_M < P_R$ the vessel lays up. When rates decline below AVC, the shipowner's P_R will depend on his *expectation* of the duration, t, of the fall in P_M since his expected $C_L = C_L(t)$. But as t is inversely related to $C_L(t)$, the shorter the t period, the

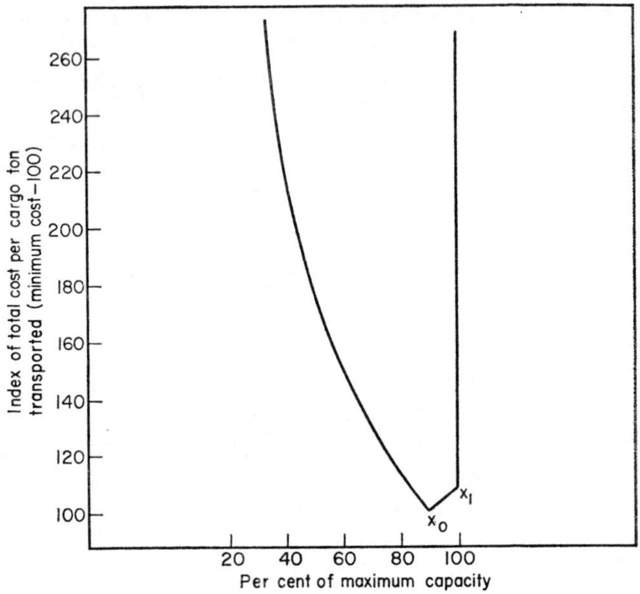

Fig. 2. Index of Unit Cost of Transportation 33000 DWT U.S. Flag Tanker at Various Output Levels.

lower the P_R, and P_M may fall well below the total cost of the marginal vessel before the available tonnage supply is reduced. The total cost curve, AC, tracing out the relationship between average unit cost and percentage of tanker capacity utilization is shown in Fig. 2[23] for a typical 33,000 DWT tanker. The characteristically V-shaped

[21] Theoretically, the shipowner may either (*a*) operate or (*b*) lay up or scrap. Operationally, in the short run, layup costs are compared to operating costs rather than scrappage and we have adopted this formulation.

[22] P_R is analogous to Koopmans' *laying-up rate*; see Koopmans, *op. cit.*, p. 109.

[23] Method of estimation based on H. B. Benford, 'Engineering Economy in Tanker Design', *Transactions*, Society of Naval Architects and Marine Engineers, Vol. 46, 1956; also D. M. Mack-Forlist and R. Hettena, 'An Economic Feasibility Study of United States Bulk Carriers', *Marine Technology*, Vol. 3, No. 2, April, 1966, pp. 137–40. Computation details will be furnished by the authors upon request.

curve is significant in tanker operations because the cost/output relationship will always impel the tanker owner to operate at, or close to, full capacity or not to operate at all. AC declines rapidly as the quantity of cargo carried increases and until X_0 (normal capacity) is reached. Beyond X_0, AC rises rapidly to maximum capacity, X_1, and thereafter vertically.[24] The V-shaped AC curve—and AVC curve as well since FC is constant—arises from the fact that a tanker cannot be 'used' more or less intensely except within exceedingly narrow limits. Only a very minor speed variation beyond normal output is possible, and the marginal cost (MC) of carrying additional cargo is virtually zero until the cargo load reaches maximum practical capacity. Since any reduction from maximum capacity produces no significant cost reduction, and since revenue is always proportional to the quantity of cargo carried, whenever a tanker operates, it will always do so at, or close to, 100 percent of practical capacity.

The distinctly V-shaped AC tanker cost curve—and by abstraction the SAVC and short-run MC curves as well—constitute a distinguishing characteristic of tanker operations.[25] This feature is not common in other, unregulated, industries. For in manufacturing at least, average costs are invariant over a substantial portion of the output range. And as long as shifts in the demand and marginal revenue curves are restricted to the area of marginal cost constancy, price will not change if demand retains its elasticity as the curves shift.[26] Under these conditions firms can adjust output without materially affecting profit margins.

But assumptions of MC constancy are inconsistent with the conditions underlying tanker firms. Here MC rises steeply beyond the point of normal output; tanker output is zero at all freight levels below minimum SAVC and virtually invariant at all levels above it. Hence, no supply elasticity can be expected from variation of tanker output: contraction of tonnage supply can occur only through total shutdown of a part of the tanker fleet.

[24] The right leg of the curve will not rise completely vertically because at high enough freight rates it may pay to postpone repairs or incur extra costs by 'pushing' the vessel to her maximum speed, although the extra output thus obtained is of a very limited scope and time span.

[25] The V-shaped cost curve is more pronounced for a tanker than for a dry cargo liner and other ocean-going vessels for which cargo handling costs make up a greater proportion of variable cost.

[26] Joel Dean, *Managerial Economics* (Englewood Cliffs, N.J.: Prentice Hall, Inc., 1951), pp. 272–96; Roy F. Harrod, *Economic Essays* (New York: Harcourt and Brace, Inc., 1952), pp. 154, 170; Richard B. Heflebower, 'Full Cost, Cost Changes and Prices', in *Business Concentration and Price Policy*, (Princeton: Princeton University Press, 1955) p. 370; J. Johnston, *Statistical Cost Analysis* (New York: McGraw-Hill Book Co., Inc., 1960), Chapters II and V; P. J. D. Wiles, *Price, Cost & Output* (Oxford: Basil Blackwell, 1961), Chapter III Appendix.

Economies of scale are the principal determinant of unit cost of transportation. For purposes of evaluation a closely substitutable service was obtained by considering all tankers operating at a draft of 35 ft or less as close substitutes irrespective of the quantity transported by any single unit. Furthermore, tankers in the 15,000–30,000 DWT range (called 'handy size' in the trade) may be taken, generally speaking, as providing a homogeneous service. Unit cost of transportation for various vessel sizes was then calculated for the dominant (Gulf/East Coast) trade and shown in Fig. 3. Relation-

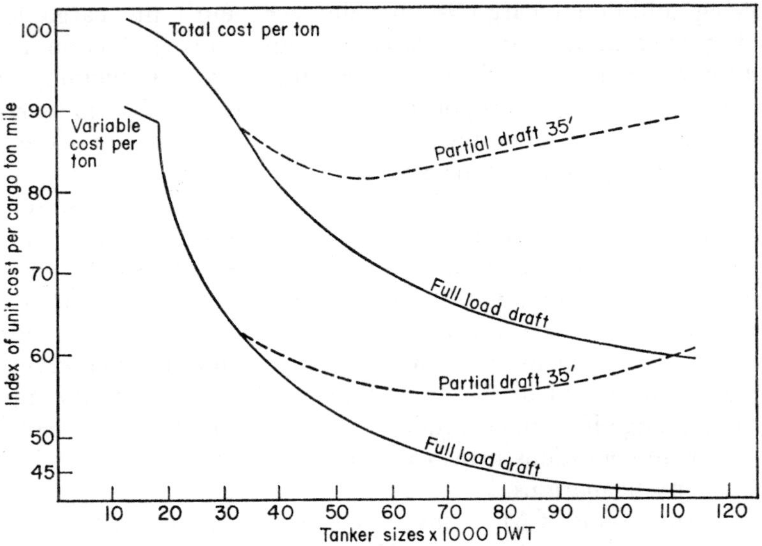

Fig. 3. Unit Cost of Transportation with and without Draft Restriction, Various Size Tankers, U.S. Gulf East Coast.

ships indicate significant economies of scale. At a maximum draft of 35 ft (closely substitutable tanker services) economies of scale begin to level off at about 30,000 DWT reaching their optimum at about 50,000 DWT.

The approximate industry supply schedule may be constructed by multiplying the AVC per ton-mile for each vessel size by the number of vessels in each size category. An idealized smoothing of the AC and AVC curves drawn against corresponding tanker size classes are presented in Fig. 4.

Since $C_L(t)$ is a function of time, SAVC cannot be treated along with these static curves. Very generally, SAVC will tend to lie below and roughly parallel to AVC. We may construe the SAVC curve—and by proxy the AVC curve—as being approximately the industry supply curve representing at any moment in time the set of alternative combinations relating each market freight rate to the corresponding supply of tonnage called forth at that rate.

The supply schedule $SAVC = AVC - C_L(t) = P_R$ was so far treated as a function which—given t—uniquely relates the quantity supplied, Q, to the freight level, P_M. This approach was followed by Koopmans and others.[27] But in tanker operations—given t—the unique relationship between P_M and Q will not hold irrespective of the directional movement of market rates, i.e. the sign of dP_M/dt. When freights decline ($dP_M/dt < 0$), P_R will depend also on the (random) timing of certain periodical events which do not affect $C_L(t)$ but which affect AVC in the immediate future. For instance if expenses such as unexpired insurance premiums or completed annual repairs have been paid up or accrued, the P_R for the remaining period will be reduced by the extent of such expenses. For parallel reasons if the vessel is already in layup because P_R exceeds P_M, the latter now rising, it will not be reactivated until P_M reaches the vessel's SAVC now inflated by impending periodical expenses. In short the P_R of an operating vessel is lower than the P_R of a laid-up vessel, and a *supply band* rather than a single supply curve would be a more accurate diagrammatic representation of supply conditions.[28] Furthermore, by retarding tonnage withdrawal during declining rates and tonnage offering during advancing rates, this effect further increases supply inelasticity thus intensifying freight rate fluctuation. It may also partly explain the wide dispersion in Koopmans' (single) laying-up rates he used in deriving his international tanker supply curve.[29]

This cost structure carries important implications with respect to tanker freights behavior. Because by virtue of the structure—and particularly the V-shaped tanker cost curve—when demand increases, short-run supply cannot increase significantly beyond reactivation of laid-up vessels. Hence, supply conditions shown in Fig. 4 are characterized by rising MC throughout and particularly in the relevant range.

Let us note the short-run effect of shifts in demand, d, on the market rate, P_M, first, under competitive and, second, under monopsonistic demand conditions.[30] Figure 4 shows that when $d \geq Q_0$ then

[27] Koopmans, *op. cit.*, chart 7.2, p. 114; Ferguson, *op. cit.*, pp. 439–57; it must be noted that the discussion in this latter study is in terms of dry cargo vessels; no attempt is made at the empirical derivation of the supply curve.

[28] For a similar formulation see Charles C. Holt *et al.*, *Planning, Production, Inventories and Workforce* (Englewood Cliffs, N.J.: Prentice-Hall, Inc., 1960).

[29] Koopmans, *op. cit.*, chart 6.5, pp. 80–4.

[30] The figures in the remainder of this section are approximations based on the construction of Fig. 4 and are intended for illustration only.

$P_M \geqslant P_0$, where Q_0 is 100 percent of capacity and P_0 is 100 on the freight index. All vessels cover total costs and larger vessels make a profit. When $P_M < P_0$ some high-cost tankers lay up. When $d = Q_1$ (95 percent of capacity), $P_M = P_1$ (85 on the index): 5 percent of uncommitted tanker tonnage concentrated amongst the 16,000–18,000 DWT marginal class lays up. A 5 percent fall in tanker demand has caused a 15 percent fall in freights.[31] But under com-

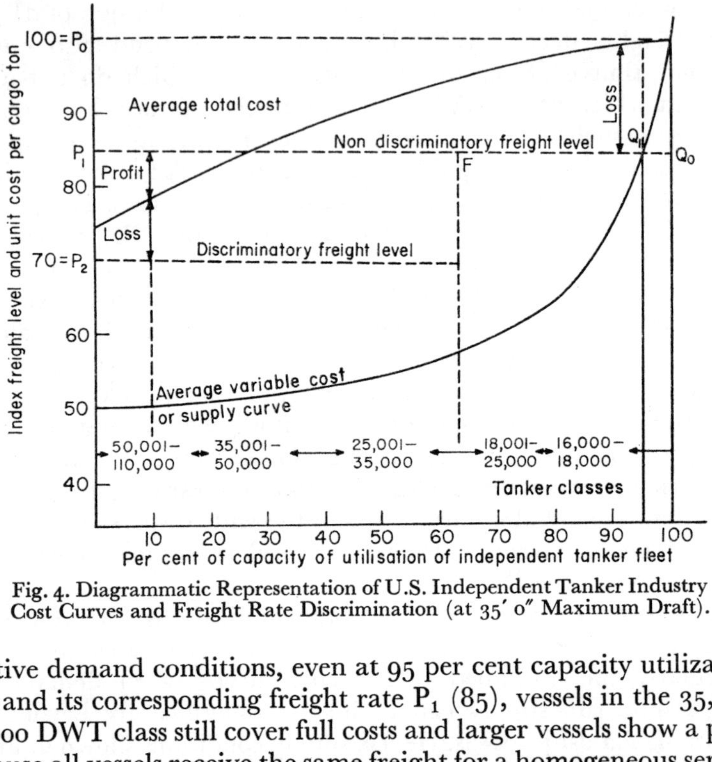

Fig. 4. Diagrammatic Representation of U.S. Independent Tanker Industry Cost Curves and Freight Rate Discrimination (at 35′ 0″ Maximum Draft).

petitive demand conditions, even at 95 per cent capacity utilization, Q_1, and its corresponding freight rate P_1 (85), vessels in the 35,000–50,000 DWT class still cover full costs and larger vessels show a profit because all vessels receive the same freight for a homogeneous service. And if shipowners expect P_1 to persist, larger vessels could be built profitably. New construction tends to move the supply curve to the right and thus expand industry capacity, reduce reactivation chances of laid-up tonnage, accelerate scrapping of high-cost tankers already in layup, and above all reduce freights.

Let us now assume that a monopsonist can decide what the freight rate shall be for each tonnage category. Let us further assume that Q_1 (95 percent of capacity) is still demanded for which P_1 (85) is paid

[31] This analysis assumes, of course, that demand is independent of price. We have shown that demand is highly inelastic in the short run.

to all vessels FQ_1 of less than 25,000 DWT and P_2 (70) to all vessels P_1F of 25,000 DWT and over. Under these conditions all tankers P_1 Q_1 remain in operation because in each case $P_M > P_R$. Vessels Q_1 Q_0 lay up since in each case $P_1 < P_R$. All vessels now sustain losses of varying degree.

In the following section we argue that this type of monopsonistic discrimination does in fact occur in the U.S. tanker industry.

BEHAVIOR

Even in the absence of a completely atomistic structure on the supply side of the market, competitive conditions prevail. First, no substantial degree of seller concentration appears to exist. But even if it did exist, it would constitute a necessary but not sufficient condition for the exercise of oligopolistic power. Secondly, the data presented indicate that a few owners could control the market *if they behaved accordingly* since supply elasticities would permit anyone owning 4–6 percent of capacity to exercise price leadership. This, however, does not happen because no one has all his vessels in the market at any one time. Owners deliberately space or 'rotate' their vessels in the market to reduce the risk of unemployment; and the concentration of ownership of vessels operating in the market at any moment of time is small with no-one owning more than 2 percent of available capacity.[32]

As for the market behavior of U.S. tanker charterers, even though major oil companies are large enough to engage in oligopsonistic chartering, they do not ordinarily do so for three main reasons. First, tanker transportation affects only a fraction of U.S. petroleum demand—accounting only for 6.4 percent of total U.S. and 21.6 percent of East Coast consumption in 1966. Second, tanker freight rates constitute only a very small fraction of refined products price and cost: a 25 percent reduction in coastwise freights leads only to a $2\frac{1}{2}$ percent reduction in the cost of the transported product which itself only applies to 6.4 percent of the total market. Third, a depressed tanker market gives a competitive advantage to independent oil companies who do not own tankers and who charter spot tonnage. To independents, low freight levels mean transportation costs lower than the long-run based rate of the tanker owning majors which permits independents to shade their product prices thereby eroding the majors' market shares and causing them losses outweighing average transportation costs savings.

[32] See Zannetos, *op. cit.*, pp. 174–5.

In contrast to the competitive chartering incentives of the major oil companies, MSTS is motivated to, and in fact does, exert its market power to depress freight rates. MSTS is obligated to minimize costs by unequivocal directives from the Department of Defense; and being a branch of the government, it is not constrained from the exercise of market power by antitrust legislation. MSTS's monopsony power derives from three main sources: first, from its sheer size in relation to sellers', MSTS having at times accounted for as much as 60 percent of the entire market; second, from the existence of the MSTS nucleus fleet which enhances MSTS's ability to control the market by adding to the supply of tonnage where and when desired; and third, from the temporal monopsony power arising when more than one tanker seek at a given time and place one cargo controlled by a large charterer[33] who is then able—even when competition is open over longer periods—to extract a monopsonistic charter rate.[34] Naturally, the longer the idle period the shipowner faces, the greater the monopsony power. Whether this power is used depends on the motive of the charterer who possesses it.

In light of these factors how will MSTS use its power? Under direction of the Defense Department to obtain tonnage at the 'lowest sound price', MSTS will attempt to: (1) depress the overall rate structure by engaging in price leadership and (2) modify the internal rate structure by exercising rate discrimination against low-cost vessels. As MSTS is the dominant concern, we may infer that it serves as the industry's price leader who is then followed by other charterers, the process made easier by the 'perfect knowledge' of wide circulation immediately following the conclusion of every fixture.

Price leadership also permits MSTS to achieve its second-cost minimizing objective by exercising rate discrimination of a type analogous to Machlup's *get-the-most-from-each-group* type[35] and which we call *pay-the-least-to-each-group*. Although this type of discrimination has few illustrations in industrial pricing and occurs mostly in publicly regulated utilities, it is suspect and in danger of being construed as unlawful whenever it is practiced by a private enterprise.[36]

[33] Such temporal monopsony power is also enjoyed by large charterers such as major oil companies.

[34] The classic case of monopsony power is a deliberate curtailment of one's own output to get lower factor prices. Here in fact, MSTS—and to a degree the major oil companies—cannot reduce their cargo requirements but can only use bargaining threats or resort to foreign flag vessels. Thus our usage of the term monopsony is a modification of the classic definition and implies monopoly power from a combination of market and institutional forces.

[35] Fritz Machlup, 'Characteristics of Price Discrimination', in *Business Concentration and Price Policy*, p. 410.

[36] *Ibid.*

Finally, as a large and diversified organization MSTS can use its monopsonistic power to secure tie-in contracts. It did so in the latter part of 1966, when, on account of the Vietnam requirements, dry cargo vessels were in short supply while tankers were readily available. MSTS used its bargaining power to induce companies operating both types of vessels to tie-in tanker charters to dry cargo charters at lower rates than were being paid by commercial charterers.

Empirical Evidence

Evidence of monopsony power is implicit in the prevalence of charters of short duration. The fixture data reveal that between 1961 and 1966 fixtures were concluded overwhelmingly for spot, short, repetitive voyages. Short-term chartering entails the risk of frictional unemployment as well as longer unemployment due to depressed market conditions. Under long-term chartering both risks are borne by the charterer.[37] In this case buyers use their market power to transfer these risks to the sellers.

We have set up two tests to establish whether the theory we have advanced is validated. First, if it is true that MSTS uses its monopsony power to achieve lower freights, then the MSTS market share must be negatively correlated with the freight level. Second, amongst all large charterers, not only does MSTS have the greatest capacity to exercise rate discrimination, but it is the only large charterer clearly motivated to do it. Hence, if rate discrimination exists, MSTS must be the rate discriminator; in which case the larger the MSTS market share the higher the degree of price discrimination and the greater the rate differential between homogeneous high-cost and low-cost tankers.[38]

Using all the adjusted data from the C. D. Mallory 'Weekly Fixture Reports',[39] we correlated for each week of the period 1961–65 the proportion of total fixtures accounted for by MSTS and the average freight rate prevailing in the said week. A correlation of −0.69 was found for the dirty trades reflecting a significant negative relationship between increased MSTS chartering activity and lower

[37] Z. Zannetos, 'Time Charter Rates', in Sun Oil Company, Economics Department, *op. cit.*, 1966 edition.

[38] This second test also encompasses the first, since discrimination cannot exist without monopoly power. But for the sake of exposition both assertions are tested.

[39] Voyages concluded with options were deleted from the data since the granting of options changes the homogeneity of the 'bundle' of tanker services being traded. For consecutive voyage transactions each voyage was weighted as a single but credited to the month of actual performance. For standardization of raw data, only fixtures for the predominant trade route, U.S. Gulf/East Coast, were used. After all exclusions and adjustments there remained 1657 separate contracts (fixtures) each representing one transaction.

freight rates.[40] To test discriminatory power we computed monthly average freight rates in the clean trade for two tonnage categories delivering a homogeneous service from the charterer's viewpoint: 15,000–20,499 DWT and 20,500–30,499 DWT.[41] The monthly average rate for each tonnage category for 1961–65 were then plotted on a scatter diagram (Fig. 5) providing at least one fixture was reported for each category in the month in question. Of the 47 observations plotted, 12 were below the 45° line, 4 were on the line, and 31 were above it indicating that over the five-year period

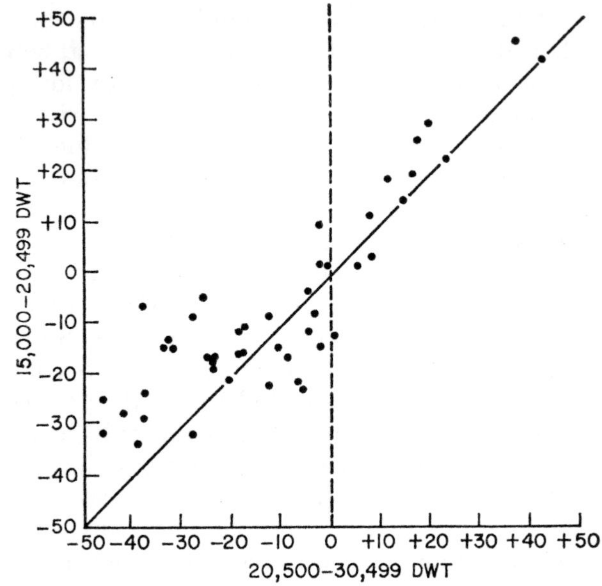

Fig. 5. Scatter Diagram. Correlation of Monthly Average Freight Rates between Tankers of 15,000–20,499 DWT and 20,500–30,499 DWT January 1961 to November 1965 (ATRS flat = 0).

the smaller tonnage group received on the average freight rates significantly higher than for the larger tonnage group. The correlation between the average monthly freight rate for the larger size category (X) and the smaller size category (Y) is given by the following least squares equation: $Y = 31.89 + 0.767\ X$.[42] This result is also consistent with our hypothesis that rate discrimination exists, and that, consequently, MSTS is the rate discriminator. Finally, the scatter

[40] A similar statistic was not uncovered for tankers in the clean trades presumably due to their greater transferability to the grain trades when petroleum rates are low.

[41] The clean trade was selected because of the higher frequency of fixtures.

[42] Correlation coefficient: $r = 0.83778$; Standard error of estimate: $S_y = 11.1075$; Least significant correlation coefficient at 95 percent level = 0.250.

diagram in Fig. 5 also shows a greater average vertical distance from the 45° line at lower freight levels. This indicates that at high freight levels the bias favoring the small size category is reduced, implying that when demand increases, monopsony power—and therefore discrimination—is correspondingly reduced. This observation is also consistent with our assertion that charterers treat all vessels in the range as providing a homogeneous service since when demand is at a high level, charterers are less able to enforce rate discrimination against low-cost sellers and are prepared to pay the same rate to both tonnage categories which provide them with the same measure of utility.

IMPLICATIONS FOR BEHAVIOR AND PERFORMANCE

Once MSTS succeeds in lowering freight rates, these will prevail over the rest of the market. While other charterers are not motivated to consciously depress freight rates, neither are they motivated to increase them. To the extent that these rates are lower than they would be under competitive demand, commercial operators also participate—though presumably unconsciously—in the confiscation of a part of the economic rent accruing to the more productive vessels. The government may claim the right to such confiscation on the grounds that these resources are being diverted from their most productive use for the taxpayer's ultimate benefit. Large commercial charterers—mainly major oil companies—may not.

Monopsony power exercised through price discrimination against the larger and lower-cost tonnage tends to discourage construction of newer, more efficient tonnage and perpetuate the existence of old, less efficient, high-cost tonnage and consequently higher overall freight levels.

Given the presence of monopsony, it may be argued that *pay-the-least-to-each-group* discrimination can be in the public interest on the grounds that although monopsonistic exploitation implies restriction in a certain group of services, the exercise of price discrimination may still cause total output to rise above the volume most profitably sold under non-discriminatory pricing. Low-cost tanker operators would not be hurt by the more favorable treatment accorded higher-cost operators so long as the rates the former receive are no lower than those they would receive in the absence of discrimination. In such a case greater capacity utilization induced by discriminatory higher rates could result in economies permitting this higher output to be delivered at lower marginal cost. This, however, does not occur in the short run. On account of low demand elasticity it is unlikely that a significantly higher output can be demanded with or without discrimination. To the extent such output is demanded, no cost economies can obtain because the V-shaped tanker cost curve precludes output expansion except by reactivation of formerly laid up, less productive units.

COLUMBIA UNIVERSITY

APPENDIX A

Profitability

As no information on tanker profitability is published it was necessary to compute it. We derived a profitability index which we define as the difference in ATRS points between the breakeven (full cost) freight rate for a given class of tankers and the corresponding average freight rate for this class of vessel for a given year.

The annual average freight rates per vessel tonnage category were derived for the predominant trade from the C. D. Mallory data previously described. The breakeven freight rate was calculated by computing fixed and variable operating cost components which were converted into ATRS scale and aggregated together. Variable costs were calculated for 1967 and de-escalated at a 4 percent per annum rate to arrive at previous years' figures.[43]

PROFITABILITY INDEX

Average breakeven rates minus average freight rates by tonnage categories, 1961–65

Profit (+) or loss (−) per class

Year	*15,000–18,499*	*18,500–20,499*	*20,500–27,499*	*27,500–30,499*	*30,500–39,499*	*39,500–59,499*
CLEAN TRADE						
1961	−3.5	−10.8	+4.5	−23.8	−6.5	+4.2
1962	−11.3	−5.1	−12.8	−17.7	−10.8	−5.0
1963[a]	+0.7	−11.2	−0.6	+3.3	+5.5	+16.1
1964	−6.7	−9.4	−8.4	−10.1	−4.5	+0.9
1965	−4.7	−25.8	−23.8	−23.8	−6.4	−16.5
DIRTY TRADE						
1961	−9.8	−10.8	−24.9	−18.1	−20.5	+4.2
1962	−12.6	−20.8	−26.3	−19.5	−23.3	−18.5
1963[a]	+6.6	—[b]	+1.0	−4.4	−2.1	+2.2
1964	−2.6	+0.2	−7.8	−7.4	−3.8	−7.1
1965	+7.0	—[b]	−15.4	−22.9	+11.7	+11.4

[a] Information incomplete from February to May.
[b] Insufficient freight rate data in vessel category to permit calculations.

[43] The precise calculations and data sources can be furnished upon request.

LINER NATIONALITY AND STEAMSHIP CONFERENCE RATE-MAKING

by John A. Walgreen*

INTRODUCTION

In a recent issue of this journal Daniel Marx, Jr., noted that many previously non-maritime, developing nations have established national-flag steamship lines in order to have a voice in the delibera-

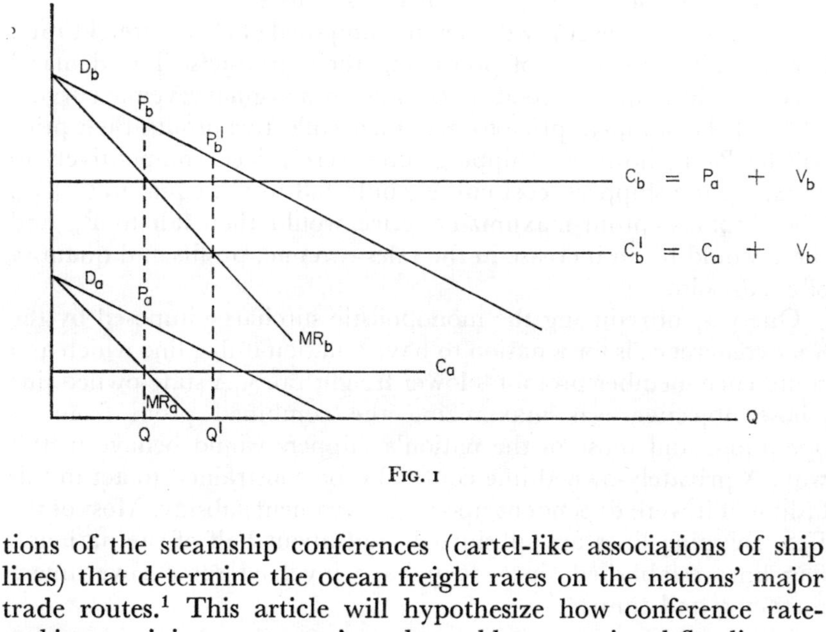

Fig. 1

tions of the steamship conferences (cartel-like associations of ship lines) that determine the ocean freight rates on the nations' major trade routes.[1] This article will hypothesize how conference rate-making can injure a country's trade, and how a national-flag line can benefit a nation by moderating conference rates.

The hypothesis will then be tested by comparing the rate-making behavior of U.S.-flag firms with that of the foreign-flag members of the same conference to see if nationality does influence firm behavior. The hypothesis is based upon nationality and not the stage of development so that the U.S. case can serve as a proxy for the case of the developing nations where the necessary data are lacking.

* The author wishes to thank Michael Mann and Alice Bourneuf of Boston College and Peter Stangl and Gopal Dorai of Wheaton College for many helpful suggestions and criticisms.

[1] Daniel Marx, Jr., 'Regulation of International Liner Shipping and "Freedom of the Seas"', *Journal of Industrial Economics* (November 1967), pp. 47–8, 54.

VERTICAL INTEGRATION AND MONOPOLISTIC EXPLOITATION

The economic theory of vertical integration[2] suggests that shipping conferences injure a nation's trade by imposing a monopolistic surcharge at an intermediate stage of the foreign trade process. This surcharge increases the delivered price of a country's goods and decreases the quantity sold, the sales revenue and the profits of the shippers. This effect is illustrated in Figure 1 where C_a represents the cost of producing liner shipping services, D_a shows the shippers' demand for these services, and MR_a is the marginal revenue curve corresponding to D_a.[3] If the shipping conference exploits its monopoly power to maximize profits, it will set price at P_a.

The shippers' cost, C_b, will then be composed of P_a, the freight rate, and V_b, all other costs of producing their products. The demand curve for the shippers' goods is D_b, and its marginal revenue curve is MR_b. If the shippers price to maximize collective profits, their price will be P_b. If, however, shipping rates were priced competitively to equal C_a, the shippers' cost curve would fall to C_b', equal to $C_a + V_b$. The shippers' profit-maximizing price would then fall to P_b', and there would be an increase in the sales revenue, profits and quantity of goods sold.

One way of reducing the monopolistic surcharge imposed by the liner conference is for a nation to have a national-flag line which as a conference member promotes lower freight rates. A state-owned line whose objective was maximizing the combined profit from its operations and those of the nation's shippers would behave in this way. A privately-owned line could also be constrained to act in this fashion if it were dependent upon a government subsidy. Most of the U.S. shipping lines are subsidized, and about half of the national-flag lines established since 1949 have involved some government financing and control.[4]

COMPARISONS OF U.S. AND FOREIGN MEMBERS OF U.S. CONFERENCES

The hypothesis that national-flag lines tend to protect a country's trading interests more than foreign-flag lines has been tested by analyzing (using the Chi-square test) the type of rate motion initiated by and the voting patterns on these motions of U.S. and foreign members of several conferences operating from U.S. Gulf of

[2] Joseph J. Spengler, 'Vertical Integration and Antitrust Policy', *Journal of Political Economy* (August 1950), pp. 347–52.

[3] Figure 1 was adapted from the figure on page 348 of Spengler's article.

[4] Marx, op. cit., p. 54.

Mexico ports to Europe.[5] The data were derived from reports of an agent of the Holland–American Line to that firm on several conference meetings in the 1950s. The reports were made public in the investigations of conference activities by the Antitrust Subcommittee of the U.S. House of Representatives.[6]

TABLE I

TYPE OF RATE MOTION INITIATED BY NATIONALITY

Rate motion	*Line nationality*		
	Foreign	*U.S.*	*Total*
Increase	26	11	37
Decrease	9	29	38
Total	35	40	75

TABLE II

MAJORITY VOTE BY NATIONALITY ON RATE INCREASES

	Line nationality		
	Majority of foreign lines	*Majority of U.S. lines*	*Total*
Vote			
For	34	27	61
Against	1	7	8
Total	35	34	69

Note: There were 37 motions to increase rates but no majority position in 2 cases for foreign lines and in 3 cases for U.S. lines.

TABLE III

MAJORITY VOTE BY NATIONALITY ON RATE DECREASES

	Line nationality		
	Majority of foreign lines	*Majority of U.S. lines*	*Total*
Vote			
For	23	33	56
Against	15	5	20
Total	38	38	76

[5] This was originally done as part of a larger study of U.S. shipping conferences, John A. Walgreen, 'The Economics of Ocean Liner Freight Conferences' (unpublished Ph.D. dissertation, Boston College, 1965).

[6] U.S. House of Representatives, Antitrust Subcommittee of the Committee on the Judiciary, *Hearings on the Ocean Freight Industry*, 87th Cong., 1st sess., 1959, Part 2.

Table I shows that U.S. lines were much more prone to initiate motions to decrease rates and less inclined to move that rates be increased than were foreign lines. The difference in the type of rate motion initiated by nationality is statistically significant at the 0.001 level. Tables II and III indicate the U.S. and foreign lines' voting on the rate motions. The majority of U.S. lines were less frequently in favor of rate increases and more frequently in favor of rate decreases than the majority of foreign lines. The difference in voting behavior between U.S. and foreign lines was statistically significant at the 0.05 level on motions to increase rates and at the 0.01 level on motions to decrease rates.

Since the lines of any one nationality are usually outnumbered by the foreign members of a conference, whether a national-flag line can have an influence on conference rate-making needs to be examined. If the outcome of decisions on freight rates was controlled by foreign members, there should be a significant difference between the relative success and failure of motions initiated by U.S. lines compared to the ones proposed by foreign lines. Table IV indicates the

TABLE IV

OUTCOMES OF U.S. AND FOREIGN LINE RATE MOTIONS

	Nationality of initiating line		
Outcome	*U.S.*	*Foreign*	*Total*
Pass	33	28	61
Fail	7	7	14
Total	40	35	75

distribution of outcomes of motions to change freight rates. Testing at the 0.05 level failed to reveal any significant difference between the passage or failure of motions initiated by U.S. and foreign conference members.

CONCLUSION

The behavior of the U.S.-flag members of conferences suggests that the developing nations may be correct in establishing national-flag shipping lines to protect their interests in ocean liner conferences. The empirical analysis supports the hypothesis that the conference rate-making activities of a national-flag line promote lower freight rates and tend to reduce the monopolistic surcharge in a conference freight rate.

Other reasons may explain the tendency for developing nations to create their own merchant marines, but this analysis indicates that protection of a country's trading interests is more than just a theoretical possibility.

WHEATON COLLEGE,
NORTON,
MASSACHUSETTS

TELEVISION STATION PROFITABILITY AND FCC REGULATORY POLICY*

by EDWARD GREENBERG

I. INTRODUCTION

THIS PAPER is concerned with the profitability of television stations as an important determinant of the programming diversity available to the public.[1] An understanding of the relation between profitability and diversity of television programs requires a brief outline of the Federal Communication Commission's (FCC) overall policy toward television.

The FCC has the task of assigning channels geographically so as to provide a nationwide system of television. These channels are assigned to licensees which are responsible for the programs transmitted over their facilities. For the most part, the FCC has chosen not to influence in a direct way the type and content of programs: it has neither attempted to censor programs nor used its power to refuse to renew the license of a station which has failed to provide the programming promised in its license application.

The Commission has tried to use other means to stimulate the industry to improve its offerings. Thus, Commissioners who are dissatisfied with programming quality—the industry's most important performance variable—frequently admonish broadcasters for their product. Ex-Chairman Newton N. Minow's addresses [11] are memorable examples. More significantly, the Commission has also

* The study resulting in this publication was made under a fellowship granted by the Ford Foundation. However, the conclusions, opinions, and other statements in this publication are those of the author and are not necessarily those of the Ford Foundation, nor of Professors H. J. Barnett, G. R. Whitaker, H. J. Levin, and a referee whose helpful comments I gratefully acknowledge. Thanks to Professors H. J. Barnett and P. O. Steiner for supplying the data used in the study, and to the Washington University Computing Facilities through NSF Grant G-22296 for part of the computations.

[1] Several empirical studies have investigated the revenues and profits of television stations and their relation to a number of station characteristics. Two of these—Alexander [1] and Steiner, Barnett, *et al.* [16]—use published FCC data in an attempt to establish breakeven revenues for stations operating in markets containing various numbers of stations; the estimated breakeven points are discussed in Section III. Since these studies appear in relatively inaccessible places, their methodology is explained in the Appendix.

Four studies, discussed in Section II, use data for individual stations or groups of individual stations: Barnett [3] was concerned with the profitability of stations in connection with the FCC's attempt to convert a number of mixed VHF–UHF markets to all UHF markets; Levin [9] attempted to account for the difference between the selling price and asset replacement value of television stations sold between 1956 and 1958; Levin directed a further study of television station sales prices, Chapter VI and Appendix H of [17], in connection with a study of the effects of group ownership of television stations; and Fisher *et al.* [6, 7] studied the effect of Community Antenna Television system competition on the revenues of stations.

taken several steps to increase the number of television stations.[2] It has continued to reserve a portion of the UHF radio spectrum for television stations in the absence of current applicants for such stations and despite the demands of non-television services. The Commission was an important force behind legislation requiring that new television sets be able to receive stations broadcasting on the UHF radio spectrum. More recently, the Commission adopted rules which have the effect of limiting the entry of Community Antenna Television (CATV) systems and their competition with potential and existing television stations, particularly new UHF stations.[3]

If an increase in the number of stations which serve a local area actually increases programming diversity, it is important to study the factors which influence what that number will be. One such factor is, of course, the number of channels assigned to the area. Another is the potential profitability of such stations, for they will not operate for long if unable to earn profits.[4] Since commercial television broadcasting is an advertiser-supported industry, revenues and profits will depend on the advertising services rendered by the broadcasters.[5] Television advertisers are primarily interested in the size of the audience exposed to their messages.

The next section of this paper contains an examination of previous and new empirical research which generally supports the view that station profitability depends primarily on audience size. In addition, station characteristics other than audience size are examined for their effects on revenues and profits. In the final section, estimates of the audience and revenues needed for a station to be viable are compared with the FCC's allocations policy.

II. EMPIRICAL STUDIES OF TELEVISION STATION PROFITABILITY

A. Review of Previous Empirical Studies

Professor H. J. Barnett utilized 1960 cross-section data for 417 network affiliated stations, placed in 107 groups in order to protect confidentiality of the individual station data [2 and 3]. Within a group, stations are approximately homogeneous with respect to a measure of audience size. In other important respects, however, the stations are not completely homogeneous (number of competitors,

[2] A rationale for improving performance by increasing the number of stations is provided by the work of Steiner [14], Rothenberg [12], and Wiles [19].

[3] See Greenberg [8] for a discussion of this rulemaking.

[4] The profitability question has been viewed in this manner by Professors Barnett and Steiner in [3], [13], and [16].

[5] A detailed analysis of television markets may be found in Barnett [3] and Levin [10].

VHF or UHF, intermixed or non-intermixed market, etc.). Barnett reports high correlations between various measures of actual and potential audience size on the one hand, and the 20-second national spot rate, network rate, total revenue and total expense.[6]

Professor H. J. Levin's study [9] is concerned with the capitalized value of television licenses. He considers the value of the franchise as '...some portion of the spread between the discounted current value of a television station's expected future income (as reflected in its sales price) and the opportunity costs of its present physical assets'. The difference between sales price and replacement costs of existing physical plant is estimated and treated as the dependent variable in a multiple regression analysis which indicates that the national spot rate (the rate paid by national advertisers ordering time directly from the stations) is the single most important variable. Levin feels that in part it is a proxy for the number of competing signals, but Barnett shows a close relationship between a measure of audience size and the 20-second national spot rates. Another variable, a measure of potential audience size divided by the number of television stations operating in the station's main counties, fails to raise the adjusted R^2 by a statistically significant amount. Other explanatory variables used by Levin were total retail sales, total effective buying income, network rate, age of station, network affiliation, and percentage of population in urban areas.

Further work done under Levin's direction (Chapter VI and Appendix H of [17]) leads to somewhat different conclusions. When sales price is used as the dependent variable (rather than sales price minus replacement costs, which are difficult to estimate), it is significantly affected by television homes covered (not divided by the number of competing stations). This later work thus confirms the importance of audience size as a determinant of station profitability.[7]

Professor F. M. Fisher's television studies [6 and 7] were undertaken to estimate the effect of CATV competition on stations in whose areas CATV's are operating. The study is confined primarily to stations operating in 1- or 2-station markets, as designated by the FCC. Station revenues are first related to a measure of audience size, using individual station data made available on a confidential basis by the FCC; this measure of audience size is then regressed on a measure of potential audience and variables representing the amount of

[6] The terms are defined below.

[7] In the more recent work, Levin finds statistically significant coefficients for age of station and type of network tie. In the case of the latter, however, an arbitrary scaling was used, making the coefficients difficult to interpret. A further problem with these results is that the sales took place over a number of years, so that the relationships may be weakened by any unusual circumstances affecting the sales in a particular year.

duplication and choice available to viewers in the area, either from other stations or from CATV systems. Fisher finds a close relationship between actual audience and station revenues. It is worth noting that Fisher does not include variables traditionally emphasized by the FCC, such as whether a station is UHF or VHF, or whether a station is a UHF station operating in a market which also contains VHF stations (inter-mixed markets). The question of whether these variables are important determinants of station revenues and profits is discussed below.

An important contribution of the Fisher paper is the way in which competition is measured in an attempt to avoid a difficulty with the FCC market classifications; the problem is that a station in a market nominally classified as a 1-station market, for example, may in fact be competing with several other stations whose signals overlap part of the station's own market. Even without direct overlap, there may be competition from CATV systems bringing in distant signals. Fisher's solution is to weight alternatives to and duplication of a station's offerings in each county within its viewing area by the number of viewers in each of these counties. These measures of competitive conditions, along with potential audience, are closely related to actual audience.

B. Additional Empirical Work

In this section I report on a regression analysis of a second set of grouped data. The three or four stations within each group are roughly comparable with respect to NWC (an audience measure defined below) and are identical with respect to the following characteristics:

1. VHF or UHF: The former are channels 2 through 13. The latter are channels 14 through 83.
2. Network affiliation status: affiliated with a particular one or more of the three major networks, or not so affiliated.
3. Intermixed or non-intermixed market: the market is intermixed if it has both VHF and UHF commercial stations.
4. Number of stations in market: approximate number of stations in competition for a particular market area.

For each group of four stations, the FCC provided totals of the following variables for 1960 and 1962 from data reported to FCC annually by the individual stations:[8]

[8] These data were supplied by FCC to Midwest Program Airborne Television, Inc., for the study by Steiner, Barnett, Greenberg and Sovereign [16]. This information is supplied to the FCC in its Form 324, and was provided on a grouped basis to insure confidentiality of individual station data.

1. Network time sales: sales of station time to networks.
2. National and regional time sales: sales of station time to national and regional advertisers.
3. Local time sales: sales of station time to local advertisers.
4. Broadcast revenues: sum of (1) and (3) minus payments to networks and commissions plus incidental broadcast revenues.
5. Broadcast expenses: sum of technical, program, selling, and general and administrative expenses.
6. Income: item (4) – item (5).

In addition to investigating relationships between profitability, audience size, and number of stations in the market, it is possible to examine the effects of such station characteristics as whether it broadcasts on the VHF or UHF, whether or not it is affiliated with a network, and whether the station operates in an intermixed or non-intermixed market.

A list of variables and symbols follows:

TVH, the most basic of the various audience measures available for this study, is the number of homes with TV sets within a station's broadcast area. The value for each station was obtained from *Television Fact Book* Nos. 32 and 33 (1961 and 1962–63 editions); the group value is the mean of the individual station values.

VHF takes the value one if the stations in the group broadcast on the VHF band and zero if on the UHF band.

NWC is net weekly circulation of a station, the number of television sets tuned to that station at least once during the week previous to the survey date. It is less than TVH since a household may be in the viewing area of a station, but fail to watch it during the survey week.

INT, the intermixture variable, is equal to one if the station is in an intermixed market, and zero otherwise.

VHFINT equals one for a VHF station in an intermixed market and zero otherwise.[9]

[9] This variable may require explanation. To capture intermixture effects, two dummy variables in addition to the VHF dummy are entered. To see how these work, suppress other variables and the intercept, and write the dependent variable, Y (revenue or profits), as a function of VHF, INT, and VHFINT:

$$Y = B_1 \text{ VHF} + B_2 \text{ INT} + B_3 \text{ VHFINT}.$$

Y then has the following values for various classes of stations:

Class of Station	*Y*
VHF in an intermixed market	$B_1+B_2+B_3$
UHF in an intermixed market	B_2
VHF in a non-intermixed market	B_1
UHF in a non-intermixed market	0

Given the values of the other variables, and assuming a UHF station facing a VHF competitor is disadvantaged (as does the FCC), we would expect $B_2 < 0$. Further assuming that a VHF station in an intermixed market is better off than a VHF station facing competition from other VHF stations, we would expect $B_2+B_3 > 0$. In the case of 4-or-more-

1STA, 2STA, 3STA, or *4STA* is equal to one if the group contains stations which are located in a 1-, 2-, 3-, or 4-or-more-station market, respectively, and zero otherwise.

IND takes the value one if the group contains unaffiliated (independent) stations and zero otherwise. The FCC market designations are such that independent stations are found only in 4-or-more-station markets.

1STATVH, 2STATVH, 3STATVH, and *4STATVH* are equal to the product of TVH and *1STA, 2STA, 3STA*, and *4STA*, respectively. Thus iSTATVH (i = 1, 2, 3, or 4) is equal to a group's average TVH if the group contains stations classified as operating in an i-station market, and zero otherwise.

ABC, CBS, and *NBC* each take the value one when a station group contains affiliates of the respective networks, and zero otherwise.

In order to see whether number of stations in the market significantly added to the explanation of profits or revenues, regressions were run which contrasted results when a coefficient was fit for TVH alone, with regressions in which 1STATVH, 2STATVH, etc., were entered.[10] Since the reduction in the error sum of squares attributed to the additional variables was significant, individual regressions for each type of market were run. Although imperfect, these categories are probably meaningful for 3- and 4-or-more-station markets, which are less likely to have overlap than other markets. Also, in 1960 and 1962, CATV was not as important as it has come to be, and is probably not a major factor in markets with more than 2 stations.

The overall regressions are presented in Table I.[11] As remarked above, the individual market category slope coefficients for TVH proved to be significant. The only other significant variable is IND; it is negative and significant in both years for both profits and revenues. While the coefficients of VHF are positive in all the overall regressions reported in Table I, given iSTATVH they are not

[10] Fisher, in the studies described above, proceeded from NWC to prime time audience per quarter hour and then to revenues. Regressions using NWC in place of TVH with the station group data yielded substantially similar results in terms of signs and significance of the remaining variables. In addition, regressions in which NWC is explained by TVH and the other variables reveal similar results. Since it does not seem to matter which measure of audience size is used, results with TVH are presented.

[11] Several groups were eliminated from the 4-or-more-station market category. These include the New York and Los Angeles network stations and the New York independents; scatter diagrams of revenue on NWC indicated that these groups were quite far removed from the others because their audiences are very much larger than the audience in other markets. Others were eliminated because information on one or more variables was missing.

---

station markets, the VHFINT variable was eliminated since there are no all-UHF, 4-station markets.

statistically significant either alone, or along with INT and VHFINT taken together. The lack of explanatory power of the VHF variable in the presence of TVH and other variables is partially confirmed by an examination of Table II. In 1-station markets, median revenues for profitable VHF stations are greater than median revenues for profitable UHF stations in 1964 and 1965, but this seems to be explained by the absence of UHF stations in the 25 markets yielding the greatest total revenues. Median revenues of UHF stations are greater than that of VHF stations, in 1964 and 1965, for the 26th–50th markets and the 51st–75th markets. The same is true for 2-station markets. Although these results do not hold for the 3-station markets, the data suggest no superiority of VHF over UHF in all situations. Moreover, regressions not reported suggest no effects of VHF, INT, and VHFINT on NWC, given TVH. The disadvantage of UHF, compared to VHF, is apparently due to a relatively smaller value for TVH; this may occur for several reasons. The FCC may not have equalized the disadvantage of operating on higher frequencies by failing to allow sufficiently high power and antennas, or it may have allocated (operating) UHF channels to areas of lower population density.

The fact that IND is negative and significant in the revenue equation is especially noteworthy since the FCC definition of affiliated stations' revenues is net of network withholdings, part of which, in effect, is a charge for network programming. For independent stations, revenue is gross of all expenses. Although a part of the advertisers' time payments is deducted from the revenues, affiliated stations still show a significantly larger revenue. Between 1960 and 1962 it appears that the position of the independent stations deteriorated relative to that of the affiliated stations.[12] Comparison of coefficients between 1960 and 1962 also reveals that the slope of TVH increases for each market category.

In general, results with the individual market regressions recorded in Tables III–VI are quite similar to those discussed previously; exceptions are the significant, positive coefficients for VHF in the revenue and profit equations for 1-station markets and 3-station markets in 1960. However, these effects are not present in 1962, suggesting that any UHF disadvantage may have become less important.

[12] The problem of independent stations is intimately tied in with the number of operating stations. If enough stations were available these could form a network, perhaps increasing programming appeal and reducing programming costs per station sufficiently to enable these stations to operate profitably. See [8] for additional comments on this possibility.

TVH continues to dominate the results; it is always positive and highly significant. There appears to be an increase in the slope of TVH for each market category for both profits and revenues between 1960 and 1962. IND is again an important variable; in 4-station markets it has a significant negative effect on profits and revenues. Between 1960 and 1962, the independent stations' relative position appears to be worsening, both for revenues and profits, based on the coefficient of IND.

Finally, INT and VHFINT are never significant, either alone or as a group. The coefficients are almost always less than their standard errors. These regressions, therefore, supply no evidence that UHF stations in intermixed markets operate at a disadvantage in the relationship between profits and revenues, given the value of TVH. But, as mentioned above, TVH for a UHF station is likely to be smaller than for a VHF station in the same market. These findings, therefore, show no statistically significant disadvantages of a UHF station relative to a VHF station, other than that reflected in its TVH and whether or not it is affiliated with a network.[13]

NUMBER OF GROUPS

Number of Stations in Market	*1960* Intermixed U	V	Non-Intermixed UHF	*1962* Intermixed U	V	Non-Intermixed UHF
1	—	—	3	—	—	3
2	2	2	2	1	2	2
3	5	4	5	4	4	5
4 or more	2	2	0	1	2	0

Groups of stations for which the network affiliation is unambiguous were used to investigate effects attributable to difference in networks. Almost all are in 3-station markets; all are VHF stations in non-intermixed markets. Table VII indicates some disadvantage to ABC affiliates in 1960, but none in 1962. Whatever may be the financial situation of the network companies, the affiliated stations do not appear to be unequal, given the magnitude of TVH.

III. BREAKEVEN POINT COMPARISONS AND CONCLUSIONS

The empirical work discussed in the previous section has demonstrated the overriding importance of audience size on the revenues and profits of stations, and the significant effect of number of

[13] Results with VHF, INT, and VHFINT should be taken as no more than suggestive in view of the small number of groups containing UHF stations and stations in intermixed markets, as may be seen from the following table:

stations in the market. These relationships are next exploited to estimate the number of stations a market can support as a function of potential audience.

To estimate this number, it is assumed that a station is viable if it has sufficient audience to avoid losses. The potential audience for which profits equal zero—the breakeven point—is determined from the regression lines for 1-, 2-, 3-, and 4-or-more-station markets. This is a rough benchmark. On the one hand it tends to overstate the number of stations, since stations are not likely to enter or remain in a market in order to earn zero profits. On the other hand, the growth of population and advertising rates and revenues may generate future profits for stations which are at a breakeven point at present. Note however that the estimated breakeven revenues and TVH, entered in Tables VIII–XI, seem fairly stable. Breakeven estimates used in this fashion permit comparisons with previous empirical work and appraisal of the FCC's allocations of channels to the several markets.

A. 1-, 2-, and 3-Station Markets

In the FCC allocations policy

> ...the 101st to 150th markets [ranked by NWC] have 3 or more unreserved assignments. Below this level the great majority of assignments have been made on the basis of one or two channels per market. (18, para. 65)

For these markets, the FCC allocations seem not unrealistic, although somewhat optimistic. TVH for the 101st–150th market ranges from about 250,000 to 130,000. Table X suggests a breakeven audience of close to 200,000. Stations in the larger markets would appear to be profitable, and Alexander's extremely conservative estimate implies that all of these markets could support three stations.

The largest 1- and 2-station markets in the FCC allocation would have about 130,000 TVH. Tables VIII and IX reveal a much lower required audience for 1-station markets and a comfortable margin for 2-station markets.[14]

[14] Steiner–Barnett used the following relations, based on Barnett's 1960 grouped data to establish the TVH entered in Table IX.

$$NWC = -3.3+0.1785\ R$$
$$TH = 42.4+1.6\ NWC \text{ or}$$
$$TH = 38.3+0.285\ R \text{ (where all figures are in thousands).}$$

A breakeven revenue of $450,000 yields total homes of 165,000 which is entered in the Table. By comparison, the 1962 grouped data used in the present study yields:

$$NWC = 15.0+0.1393\ R$$
$$TH = 9.4+2.1\ NWC$$

Taking R = $450,000, 154,000 total homes is obtained for the breakeven point. The other results in the Table (70,400 and 68,100) come from my regression of profits on TVH, which minimizes the residuals in the desired direction. The revenue estimates are obtained from the revenue–TVH equation.

B. 4-or-more-station markets

Empirical evidence on the viability of these markets is crude; there are just a few markets with more than 4 stations, and there are not many groups available for the regression analysis. Nevertheless it appears that the FCC's allocations are quite unrealistic. Its policy is summarized as:

> Thus, with minor exceptions the top 25 markets have 6 or more unreserved assignments; the 26th to 75th markets have 5 or more unreserved assignments; the 76th to 100th markets have 4 or more unreserved assignments. . . . (18, para. 65)

In 1962, the 25th market had about 800,000 TV households. The regression breakeven estimates, although subject to considerable error, suggest this to be fewer than necessary for breakeven in a 6-station market. Further three Los Angeles independent stations, with an average of 2,700,000 in 1960 and 2,800,000 in 1962 reported aggregate losses in 1960 and aggregate profits in the later year. They apparently were near breakeven, and this suggests that the FCC allocation of 6 or more stations to markets with 800,000 TVH is highly optimistic. It would appear that 800,000 TVH is too few homes to support 6 or more stations.

The 75th market has approximately 350,000 TVH, which seems to be fewer than necessary for the FCC allocation of 5 stations. This conclusion is based on the experience of three groups of independent stations, all in 4-station markets, which required approximately 800,000 TVH for breakeven operations in 1962.[15]

[15] A reader points out that curvilinearity in the revenue–TVH relationship may be responsible for the discrepancy between the breakeven based on the regressions and the breakeven of 800,000 based on the experience of the three groups, although, as he also points out, the result is inconclusive because the regressions are based on groups with stations in 4-station markets and markets with more than 4 stations. The reader further notes that curvilinearity may be responsible for the fact that the regressions yield revenues of −$900,000 for independent stations at TVH = 200,000. However, a value of 200,000 for TVH is a good deal smaller than the TVH for the smallest independent group (479,000). Moreover, for only one of 4-or-more-station groups was TVH below 200,000 (187,000), and for one other it was slightly above (259,000). The remainder range from 398,000 to almost 3 million. Thus, because average TVH for the smallest independent group was quite large in 1962, few conclusions can be drawn from using the regression line to estimate revenues for low values of TVH.

The point that the straight line cannot describe the data at very low values of TVH is well taken; however, the line may be a good approximation over the observed range of data and around the breakeven point. A more precise estimation of the form of the relationship would require the use of individual station data, providing observations over a wide range.

A closer look at the grouped data suggests that 150,000 TVH for breakeven is a bit high, since 10 of the 32 profitable stations (35 percent) had smaller audiences, while only 1 out of 7 of the losing stations (14 percent) had a larger audience. On the other hand, 70,400 appears low since 5 of the 7 losing stations (71 percent) had larger audiences and only 2 of the profitable stations (6 percent) had smaller.

C. Conclusions

In summary, it appears that the FCC's allocation policy is perhaps reasonable for 1-, 2-, and 3-station markets, but is highly unrealistic for 4-or-more-station markets. It should be noted that the Commission prefers not to think of these allocations as judgments about viability:

> . . . The above distribution of assignments should not be interpreted as a finding that markets of the different sizes mentioned can support the number of stations provided for, or that they could not support more. Additional channel requirements are expected to develop in many places not included in the table of assignments adopted herein and except where the maximum capacity of the UHF television broadcast band has been reached, such assignments can be provided as the need arises. (18, para. 65)

But agnosticism over the number of television stations which can be supported in a market is not an appropriate attitude if primary reliance for improving the industry's performance is placed on increases in the number of stations.[16]

If the breakeven estimates reported above are reasonable, markets which now have 1 or 2 stations will become 2- and 3-station markets. The new stations will very likely become affiliated with one of the major networks, enabling most areas of the country to receive the full complement of network programming. But this will not increase diversity as the term is used by Dr. David Blank [5]. He has usefully distinguished between 'diversity' (adding more '. . . serious drama, serious music, ballet, art, etc. . . .' to the light entertainment programming which currently predominates) and 'quantity' ('. . . further choice within the more restricted entertainment universe of commercial television'). An increase in diversity might occur if there were a large number of markets with more than 3 stations, but our breakeven estimates suggest that this is unlikely to happen.

The breakeven estimates discussed above can be improved by using the individual station data available to the Commission, and by making allowances for such factors as population growth, growth of advertising revenue, higher program expenses, and effects of a fourth network.[17] If such an analysis suggests that many of the

[16] See [15] for arguments that the Commission should examine the viability of television stations.

[17] A further difficulty with the breakeven points discussed above is that they are average relationships; a substantially smaller audience may serve to support additional stations under such special conditions as a large, easily identifiable minority group which is within the viewing area of a station and which advertisers wish to reach.

allocated stations are not likely to open, the Commission must consider alternative methods of reaching its goals.

A number of such alternatives are available at this time, or will be in the near future: Technological developments, especially the use of communications satellites, may reduce network interconnection charges, an important element of costs. The FCC is currently considering a rulemaking to allow a nationwide system of pay-television. If the system adopted is free of such emasculating restrictions as arbitrary limitations on the number of hours a station may devote to pay-television or on the number of pay-TV stations in each market pay-television may significantly increase diversity, at least in the larger markets. A third development, complementary to satellite transmission and pay-television, is the possibility of a television system which delivers the signal to the home over wire. There is no effective physical limitation to the number of signals which can be transmitted to the home with such a system, and it has the added advantage of freeing part of the spectrum for uses which do not have wire as an alternative. A detailed discussion may be found in [4].

Improved technology and other innovations which threaten to upset the existing order are not always welcome to regulators when the problems of industry regulation are already complex but with understanding and appropriate policy, such new developments might help solve the regulator's problems. If experience and further study reveals that new stations are not likely to be available in numbers sufficient to increase programming diversity significantly, policies which make use of these innovations will be necessary.

WASHINGTON UNIVERSITY

TABLE I

OVERALL REGRESSIONS

Independent variable	*Coefficient*	*Standard error*	*β*	*Partial* r^2
	Dependent: Revenues			
	1960			
1 STA	$-.1868 \times 10^6$	$.2934 \times 10^6$	$-.0409$	.0032
2 STA	$-.1951 \times 10^6$	$.2388 \times 10^6$	$-.0558$	.0053
3 STA	$-.3723 \times 10^6$	$.2251 \times 10^6$	$-.1175$	.0212
1 STA TVH	$.2212 \times 10$	$.1446 \times 10$	.0702	.0182
2 STA TVH	$.2924 \times 10$*	.3742	.2949	.3264
3 STA TVH	$.3822 \times 10$*	.1752	.7765	.7906
4 STA TVH	$.3231 \times 10$*	.1839	.8500	.7102
IND	$-.1901 \times 10^7$*	$.2974 \times 10^6$	$-.2026$	.2448
VHF	$.3034 \times 10^6$	$.1675 \times 10^6$	.0664	.0254
INT	$-.6907 \times 10^4$	$.2359 \times 10^6$	$-.0014$	.0000
VHFINT	$.1237 \times 10^6$	$.2950 \times 10^6$	.0184	.0014
Intercept	$.1324 \times 10^6$			
R^2	.9083			
Degrees of freedom	126			
	1962			
1 STA	$-.2536 \times 10^6$	$.2997 \times 10^6$	$-.0464$	.0061
2 STA	$-.2100 \times 10^6$	$.2454 \times 10^6$	$-.0477$	.0062
3 STA	$-.5709 \times 10^6$*	$.2292 \times 10^6$	$-.1462$	.0503
1 STA TVH	$.3028 \times 10$*	$.1510 \times 10$	.0790	.0332
2 STA TVH	$.3363 \times 10$*	.3764	.2876	.4056
3 STA TVH	$.4456 \times 10$*	.1767	.7961	.8447
4 STA TVH	$.3847 \times 10$*	.1789	.8807	.7981
IND	$-.2135 \times 10^7$*	$.3091 \times 10^6$	$-.1908$	.2896
VHF	$.1520 \times 10^6$	$.1762 \times 10^6$	.0265	.0063
INT	$-.7664 \times 10^5$	$.2643 \times 10^6$	$-.0127$	.0007
VHFINT	$.1425 \times 10^6$	$.3211 \times 10^6$	.0177	.0017
Intercept	$.2978 \times 10^6$			
R^2	.9362			
Degrees of freedom	117			

TABLE I (*continued*)

Independent variable	*Coefficient*	*Standard error*	β	*Partial* r^2
	Dependent: Profits			
	1960			
1 STA	$-.7136 \times 10^5$	$.2031 \times 10^6$	$-.3590$	.0010
2 STA	$-.1748 \times 10^6$	$.1653 \times 10^6$	$-.1149$	.0088
3 STA	$-.3569 \times 10^6$*	$.1558 \times 10^6$	$-.2588$	.0400
1 STA TVH	.4438	$.1001 \times 10$	.0324	.0016
2 STA TVH	$.1308 \times 10$*	.2590	.3031	.1683
3 STA TVH	$.1690 \times 10$*	.1213	.7887	.6064
4 STA TVH	$.1155 \times 10$*	.1273	.6980	.3952
IND	$-.1803 \times 10^7$*	$.2059 \times 10^6$	$-.4415$	.3784
VHF	$.1202 \times 10^6$	$.1159 \times 10^6$	.0604	.0085
INT	$.4481 \times 10^4$	$.1632 \times 10^6$	.0021	.0000
VHFINT	$.7521 \times 10^5$	$.2042 \times 10^6$	.0257	.0010
Intercept	$-.2449 \times 10^5$			
R^2	.7681			
Degrees of freedom	126			
	1962			
1 STA	$-.9440 \times 10^5$	$.2259 \times 10^6$	$-.0377$	.0015
2 STA	$-.2191 \times 10^6$	$.1850 \times 10^6$	$-.1087$	.0012
3 STA	$-.5179 \times 10^6$*	$.1728 \times 10^6$	$-.2895$	.0713
1 STA TVH	.7482	$.1138 \times 10$	.0426	.0037
2 STA TVH	$.1705 \times 10$*	.2837	.3182	.2359
3 STA TVH	$.2159 \times 10$*	.1332	.8419	.6921
4 STA TVH	$.1515 \times 10$*	.1348	.7568	.5190
IND	$-.1923 \times 10^7$*	$.2329 \times 10^6$	$-.3753$	.3681
VHF	$.7960 \times 10^5$	$.1328 \times 10^6$	.0303	.0031
INT	$.1392 \times 10^5$	$.1992 \times 10^6$	.0050	.0000
VHFINT	$.2616 \times 10^5$	$.2420 \times 10^6$	.0071	.0001
Intercept	$.2984 \times 10^5$			
R^2	.8274			
Degrees of freedom	117			

* Significant at 5 per cent level.

TABLE II

MEDIAN REVENUES* AND NUMBER OF STATIONS†

(Ranked by total market revenues)

# Stations in markets	Stations reporting profits				Stations reporting losses			
	1962	1963	1964	1965	1962	1963	1964	1965
1 station	373(67)	418(67)	V459(61) U251(8)	V474(57) U268(8)	100(42)	133(34)	V147(19) U247(4)	V210(17) U167(4)
Market rank								
1–25	682(24)	755(25)			556(1)	—(0)		
VHF			766(25)	761(24)			—(0)	[e](1)
UHF			—(0)	—(0)			—(0)	—(0)
26–50	373(19)	411(22)			401(6)	384(3)		
VHF			436(20)	404(18)			[e](2)	420(4)
UHF			454(3)	492(3)			—(0)	—(0)
51–75	228(18)	224(15)			190(7)	193(10)		
VHF			213(11)	245(11)			221(8)	192(8)
UHF			236(4)	247(4)			[e](2)	[e](2)
76-end[a]	80(6)	77(5)			70(28)	85(21)		
VHF			86(5)	95(4)			74(9)	86(4)
UHF			[e](1)	[e](1)			[e](2)	[e](2)
2 station	819(97)	780(95)	V849(82) U794(7)	V874(83) U820(8)	332(31)	468(25)	V324(19) U489(3)	V324(19) U [e](1)
Market rank								
1–25	1395(44)	1301(45)			616(6)	620(5)		
VHF			1145(45)	1185(42)			[e](1)	855(3)
UHF			[e](2)	912(3)			[e](2)	—(0)
26–50	676(38)	650(38)			502(12)	537(12)		
VHF			645(33)	710(35)			389(13)	329(10)
UHF			695(4)	820(4)			—(0)	—(0)
51-end[b]	393(15)	353(12)			164(13)	149(8)		
VHF			328(4)	325(6)			161(5)	138(6)
UHF			[e](1)	[e](1)			[e](1)	[e](1)
3 station[c]	1679(302)	1713(261)	V1793(168) U776(27)	V1728(170) U693(27)	459(59)	437(51)	V765(21) U308(8)	V720(15) U555(11)

TABLE II (*continued*)

MEDIAN REVENUES* AND NUMBER OF STATIONS†

(Ranked by total market revenues)

# Stations in markets	Stations reporting profits 1962	1963	1964	1965	Stations reporting losses 1962	1963	1964	1965
Market rank								
1–25	4475(95)	4369(87)			759(9)	450(7)		
VHF			3619(69)	3619(69)			e(1)	e(1)
UHF			e(2)	e(1)			—(0)	e(2)
26–50	1841(84)	1927(70)			340(18)	383(14)		
VHF			1419(59)	1496(59)			961(8)	1242(4)
UHF			1079(9)	1108(11)			—(0)	e(1)
51 end[d]	948(123)	916(104)			468(32)	476(30)		
VHF			839(40)	891(42)			424(12)	590(10)
UHF			559(16)	582(15)			308(8)	558(8)
4 or more[f]								
VHF			3709(80)	4430(86)			580(8)	677(10)
UHF			730(1)	777(12)			199(10)	267(13)
All markets								
VHF			1412(391)	1490(396)			343(67)	380(61)
UHF			596(53)	582(55)			251(25)	276(29)

* Thousands of dollars.

† In parentheses.

[a] 1962: 109; 1963: 101; 1964: 92; 1965: 86.

[b] 1962: 64; 1963: 61; 1964: 56; 1965: 58.

[c] 3 or more stations for 1962 and 1963.

[d] 1962: 91; 1963: 96; 1964: 77; 1965: 76.

[e] Not given because only 1 or 2 stations in cell.

[f] 1964: 24; 1965: 28.

— Indicates no stations in the cell.

Source: FCC 'TV Broadcast Financial Data', Table 12, for various years.

TABLE III

1-STATION MARKETS[a]

Independent variable	Dependent: Revenues Coefficient	Standard error	β	Partial r^2	Dependent: Profits Coefficient	Standard error	β	Partial r^2
1960								
TVH	$.2172 \times 10$*	.5954	.6253	.4701	.4203*	.1765	.4783	.2744
VHF	$.3030 \times 10^6$*	$.1243 \times 10^6$	.4177	.2837	$.7581 \times 10^5$†	$.3684 \times 10^5$	.4133	.2201
Intercept	$-.4683 \times 10^5$				$-.5477 \times 10^5$			
R^2	.5594				.3951			
Degrees of freedom	15				15			
TVH	$.2156 \times 10$*	.6812	.6205	.3850	.4161*	.1935	.4736	.2243
Intercept	$.2077 \times 10^6$				$.8919 \times 10^4$			
R^2	.3850				.2243			
Degrees of freedom	16				16			
1962								
TVH	$.3109 \times 10$*	.5797	.7940	.6572	.8194*	.2133	.6936	.4959
VHF	$.9991 \times 10^5$	$.1221 \times 10^6$	.1212	.0428	$.3651 \times 10^5$	$.4491 \times 10^5$	.1468	.0422
Intercept	$.7869 \times 10^5$				$-.3683 \times 10^5$			
R^2	.7164				.5782			
Degrees of freedom	15				15			
TVH	$.3285 \times 10$*	.5328	.8389	.7038	.8837*	.1960	.7481	.5596
Intercept	$.1410 \times 10^6$				$-.1406 \times 10^5$			
R^2	.7038				.5596			
Degrees of freedom	16				16			

[a] Group 3 was eliminated from these calculations because of peculiarities in the Laredo, Texas, market. It was included in overall regressions, but does not affect the results.

* Significant for 1-tail test at 5 percent level.

† Significant for 2-tail test at 5 percent level.

TABLE IV

2-STATION MARKETS

Independent variable	*Coefficient*	*Standard error*	β	*Partial* r^2
	Dependent: Revenues			
	1960			
VHF	$.1755 \times 10^6$	$.2852 \times 10^6$	.0717	.0110
TVH	$.2949 \times 10^{*}$	.2962	.8498	.7446
INT	$.6491 \times 10^5$	$.3915 \times 10^6$	.0265	.0008
VHFINT	$.2812 \times 10^6$	$.4847 \times 10^6$	.0835	.0098
Intercept	$.3035 \times 10^5$			
R^2	.7587			
Degrees of freedom	34			
VHF	$.1618 \times 10^6$	$.2071 \times 10^6$	.0661	.0167
TVH	$.2960 \times 10^{*}$	.2935	.8528	.7386
Intercept	$.6118 \times 10^5$			
R^2	.7480			
Degrees of freedom	36			
TVH	$.2993 \times 10^{*}$	.2888	.8624	.7438
Intercept	$.1983 \times 10^6$			
R^2	.7438			
Degrees of freedom	37			
	1962			
VHF	$-.2277 \times 10^6$	$.3087 \times 10^6$	−.0723	.0184
TVH	$.3361 \times 10^{*}$	.3105	.8823	.8016
INT	$-.5275 \times 10^6$	$.5168 \times 10^6$	−.1674	.0347
VHFINT	$.9216 \times 10^6$	$.6025 \times 10^6$	.2427	.0747
Intercept	$.4285 \times 10^6$			
R^2	.8102			
Degrees of freedom	29			
VHF	$-.2936 \times 10^5$	$.2590 \times 10^6$	−.0093	.0004
TVH	$.3395 \times 10^{*}$	.3131	.8913	.7913
Intercept	$.2465 \times 10^6$			
R^2	.7928			
Degrees of freedom	31			
TVH	$.3391 \times 10^{*}$	.3066	.8903	.7927
Intercept	$.2207 \times 10^6$			
R^2	.7927			
Degrees of freedom	32			

TABLE IV (*continued*)

2-STATION MARKETS

Independent variable	*Coefficient*	*Standard error*	β	*Partial* r^2
	Dependent: Profits			
	1960			
VHF	$.1519 \times 10^6$	$.1642 \times 10^6$	.1284	.0246
TVH	$.1300 \times 10$*	.1705	.7750	.6308
INT	$.1599 \times 10^5$	$.2254 \times 10^6$	.0135	.0001
VHFINT	$.1239 \times 10^6$	$.2791 \times 10^6$	.0761	.0058
Intercept	$-.2296 \times 10^6$			
R^2	.6576			
Degrees of freedom	34			
VHF	$.1514 \times 10^6$	$.1179 \times 10^6$	.1280	.0438
TVH	$.1305 \times 10$*	.1671	.7778	.6287
Intercept	$-.2223 \times 10^6$			
R^2	.6502			
Degrees of freedom	36			
TVH	$.1336 \times 10$*	.1668	.7964	.6342
Intercept	$-.9406 \times 10^5$			
R^2	.6342			
Degrees of freedom	37			
	1962			
VHF	$.7797 \times 10^5$	$.2054 \times 10^6$	.0460	.0049
TVH	$.1694 \times 10$*	.2066	.8257	.6985
INT	$-.5569 \times 10^5$	$.3439 \times 10^6$	$-.0328$	$-.0009$
VHFINT	$.2115 \times 10^6$	$.4009 \times 10^6$	.1034	.0095
Intercept	$-.1896 \times 10^6$			
R^2	.7101			
Degrees of freedom	29			
VHF	$.1058 \times 10^6$	$.1666 \times 10^6$	.0623	.0128
TVH	$.1703 \times 10$*	.2015	.8304	.6975
Intercept	$-.2099 \times 10^6$			
R^2	.7041			
Degrees of freedom	31			
TVH	$.1716 \times 10$*	.1985	.8368	.7003
Intercept	$-.1169 \times 10^6$			
R^2	.7003			
Degrees of freedom	32			

* Significant at 5 percent level.

TABLE V

3-STATION MARKETS

Independent variable	Coefficient	Standard error	β	Partial r^2
	Dependent: Revenues			
	1960			
VHF	$.3436 \times 10^6$*	$.1633 \times 10^6$	.0857	.0733
TVH	.3833 × 10†	.1227	.9579	.9457
INT	$.1379 \times 10^6$	$.2180 \times 10^6$	.0330	.0071
VHFINT	$-.1160 \times 10^6$	$.2818 \times 10^6$	−.0913	.0030
Intercept	$-.2834 \times 10^6$			
R^2	.9507			
Degrees of freedom	56			
VHF	$.2779 \times 10^6$*	$.1206 \times 10^6$	.0693	.0838
TVH	.3826 × 10†	.1204	.9563	.9457
Intercept	$-.2131 \times 10^6$			
R^2	.9503			
Degrees of freedom	58			
TVH	.3891 × 10†	.1213	.9725	.9458
Intercept	$-.7261 \times 10^4$			
R^2	.9458			
Degrees of freedom	59			
	1962			
VHF	$.3246 \times 10^6$	$.2059 \times 10^6$	.0651	.0456
TVH	.4447 × 10†	.1503	.9613	.9439
INT	$.1533 \times 10^6$	$.2891 \times 10^6$	.0293	.0054
VHFINT	$-.9308 \times 10^5$	$.3658 \times 10^6$	−.0131	.0012
Intercept	$-.4298 \times 10^6$			
R^2	.9490			
Degrees of freedom	52			
VHF	$.2636 \times 10^6$	$.1588 \times 10^6$	.0528	.0485
TVH	.4439 × 10†	.1473	.9596	.9439
Intercept	$-.3599 \times 10^6$			
R^2	.9486			
Degrees of freedom	54			
TVH	.4499 × 10†	.1449	.9726	.9460
Intercept	$-.1656 \times 10^6$			
R^2	.9460			
Degrees of freedom	55			

TABLE V (*continued*)

3-STATION MARKETS

Independent variable	*Coefficient*	*Standard error*	β	*Partial* r^2
	Dependent: Profits			
	1960			
VHF	$.1221 \times 10^6$	$.1038 \times 10^6$	.0674	.0241
TVH	$.1707 \times 10$†	$.7798 \times 10^{-1}$	.9442	.8953
INT	$.1318 \times 10^6$	$.1386 \times 10^6$	.0697	.0159
VHFINT	$-.1167 \times 10^6$	$.1791 \times 10^6$	$-.0431$	.0075
Intercept	$-.3963 \times 10^6$			
R^2	.9024			
Degrees of freedom	56			
VHF	$.5875 \times 10^5$	$.7702 \times 10^5$	.0324	.0099
TVH	$.1701 \times 10$†	$.7689 \times 10^{-1}$	.9410	.8941
Intercept	$-.3292 \times 10^6$			
R^2	.9008			
Degrees of freedom	58			
TVH	$.1715 \times 10$†	$.7450 \times 10^{-1}$	.9486	.8998
Intercept	$-.2857 \times 10^6$			
R^2	.8998			
Degrees of freedom	59			
	1962			
VHF	$.8385 \times 10^5$	$.1469 \times 10^6$	.0338	.0062
TVH	$.2177 \times 10$†	.1072	.9461	.8880
INT	$.1471 \times 10^5$	$.2063 \times 10^6$	.0565	.0097
VHFINT	$-.7920 \times 10^6$	$.2609 \times 10^6$	$-.0224$	.0018
Intercept	$-.5108 \times 10^6$			
R^2	.8950			
Degrees of freedom	52			
VHF	$.2630 \times 10^5$	$.1137 \times 10^6$	.0106	.0010
TVH	$.2169 \times 10$†	.1054	.9426	.8869
Intercept	$-.4436 \times 10^6$			
R^2	.8936			
Degrees of freedom	54			
TVH	$.2175 \times 10$†	.1012	.9453	.8935
Intercept	$-.4242 \times 10^6$			
R^2	.8935			
Degrees of freedom	55			

* Significant for 1-tail test at 5 percent level.
† Significant for 2-tail test at 5 percent level.

TABLE VI

4-OR-MORE-STATION MARKETS

Independent variable	*Coefficient*	*Standard error*	β	*Partial* r^2
	Dependent: Revenues			
	1960			
VHF	$.8967 \times 10^6$	$.1170 \times 10^7$	.1194	.0403
TVH	$.3135 \times 10$*	.4426	.9059	.7819
IND	$-.1942 \times 10^7$*	$.6890 \times 10^6$	−.3436	.3619
INT	$.1096 \times 10^5$	$.8879 \times 10^6$	.0019	.0000
Intercept	$-.2883 \times 10^6$			
R^2	.8198			
Degrees of freedom	14			
VHF	$.8877 \times 10^6$	$.8906 \times 10^6$	.1182	.0621
TVH	$.3135 \times 10$*	.4266	.9058	.7826
IND	$-.1943 \times 10^7$*	$.6551 \times 10^6$	−.3438	.3697
Intercept	−.2772			
R^2	.8198			
Degrees of freedom	15			
IND	$-.1901 \times 10^7$*	$.6537 \times 10^6$	−.3365	.3459
TVH	$.3282 \times 10$*	.4003	.9482	.8077
Intercept	$.3669 \times 10^6$			
R^2	.8079			
Degrees of freedom	16			
	1962			
VHF	$.1042 \times 10^6$	$.1073 \times 10^7$	.0115	.0007
TVH	$.3818 \times 10$*	.3809	.9885	.8777
IND	$-.2192 \times 10^7$*	$.6263 \times 10^6$	−.3225	.4666
INT	$-.3091 \times 10^6$	$.7909 \times 10^6$	−.0455	.0108
Intercept	$.4448 \times 10^6$			
R^2	.8986			
Degrees of freedom	14			
VHF	$.3603 \times 10^6$	$.8253 \times 10^6$	.0399	.0125
TVH	$.3824 \times 10$*	.3697	.9901	.8770
IND	$-.2147 \times 10^7$*	$.5982 \times 10^6$	−.3160	.4621
Intercept	$.1351 \times 10^6$			
R^2	.8974			
Degrees of freedom	15			
IND	$-.2137 \times 10^7$*	$.5825 \times 10^6$	−.3145	.4570
TVH	$.3888 \times 10$*	.3310	.1007	.8961
Intercept	$.3929 \times 10^6$			
R^2	.8961			
Degrees of freedom	16			

TABLE VI (*continued*)

4-OR-MORE-STATION MARKETS

Independent variable	*Coefficient*	*Standard error*	*β*	*Partial r^2*
	Dependent: Profits			
	1960			
VHF	$.5808 \times 10^6$	$.8795 \times 10^6$	.1537	.0302
TVH	$.1908 \times 10$*	.3327	.6305	.4377
IND	$-.1813 \times 10^7$*	$.5179 \times 10^6$	−.6375	.4669
INT	$.1217 \times 10^6$	$.6599 \times 10^6$	.0428	.0024
Intercept	$-.3967 \times 10^6$			
R^2	.5982			
Degrees of freedom	14			
VHF	$.4809 \times 10^6$	$.6702 \times 10^6$	.1273	.0332
TVH	$.1094 \times 10$*	.3210	.6280	.4363
IND	$-.1830 \times 10^7$*	$.4930 \times 10^6$	−.6434	.4788
Intercept	$-.2740 \times 10^6$			
R^2	.5972			
Degrees of freedom	15			
IND	$-.1808 \times 10^7$*	$.4845 \times 10^6$	−.6355	.4652
TVH	$.1173 \times 10$*	.2967	.6736	.4943
Intercept	$.7493 \times 10^5$			
R^2	.5834			
Degrees of freedom	16			
	1962			
VHF	$.1949 \times 10^6$	$.8847 \times 10^6$	.0450	.0035
TVH	$.1464 \times 10$*	.3141	.7897	.6083
IND	$-.1960 \times 10^7$*	$.5164 \times 10^6$	−.6007	.5072
INT	$-.1670 \times 10^6$	$.6521 \times 10^6$	−.0512	.0047
Intercept	$.2463 \times 10^5$			
R^2	.7009			
Degrees of freedom	14			
VHF	$.3333 \times 10^6$	$.6784 \times 10^6$	.0769	.0158
TVH	$.1468 \times 10$*	.3039	.7915	.6087
IND	$-.1936 \times 10^7$*	$.4917 \times 10^6$	−.5933	.5083
Intercept	$-.1427 \times 10^6$			
R^2	.6995			
Degrees of freedom	15			
IND	$-.1927 \times 10^7$*	$.4796 \times 10^6$	−.5905	.5023
TVH	$.1527 \times 10$*	.2726	.8232	.6623
Intercept	$.9574 \times 10^5$			
R^2	.6946			
Degrees of freedom	16			

* Significant at 5 percent level.

TABLE VII

NETWORK REGRESSIONS*

Independent variable	Dependent: Revenues				Dependent: Profits			
	Coefficient	Standard error	β	Partial r^2	Coefficient	Standard error	β	Partial r^2
1960								
ABC	$-.5642 \times 10^6$†	$.2141 \times 10^6$	−.1775	.1880	$-.9425 \times 10^5$	$.1378 \times 10^6$	−.0672	.0154
NBC	$-.8764 \times 10^5$	$.2445 \times 10^6$	−.0244	.0043	$.8059 \times 10^5$	$.1574 \times 10^6$	.0508	.0087
TVH	$.3410 \times 10$†	.2015	.9573	.9052	$.1429 \times 10$†	.2197	.9090	.8018
Intercept	$.3802 \times 10^6$				$-.2228 \times 10^5$			
R^2	.9076				.8034			
Degrees of freedom	30				30			
1962								
ABC	$-.4220 \times 10^6$	$.2129 \times 10^6$	−.1060	.1231	$-.1090 \times 10^6$	$.1577 \times 10^6$	−.0580	.0168
NBC	$-.2676 \times 10^2$	$.2441 \times 10^6$	.0000	.0000	$.1020 \times 10^6$	$.1809 \times 10^6$	.0474	.0112
TVH	$.4176 \times 10$†	.1985	.9796	.9405	$.1885 \times 10$†	.1471	.9357	.8544
Intercept	$.7400 \times 10^5$				$-.3418 \times 10^6$			
R^2	.9410				.8551			
Degrees of freedom	28				28			

* CBS variable omitted to avoid singular matrix. Coefficient of ABC may be interpreted as difference between coefficient of ABC and CBS; coefficient of NBC may be interpreted as difference between coefficients of NBC and CBS.

† Significant at 5 percent level.

TABLE VIII

BREAKEVEN TELEVISION HOMES (TVH) FOR 1-STATION MARKETS

	Minimum revenue $	*TVH*	*Total homes*	*NWC*
Alexander	200,000	20,000	22,000	
Steiner–Barnett (1962)	225,000	30,500[a]–58,500[a]	35,000–65,000	20,000–35,000
Steiner–Barnett method				
(1963)	223,000			
(1964)	220,000			
(1965)	245,000			
Present study				
(1960)				17,000
VHF	b	b	b	
UHF	235,000	130,000[c]	144,000[a]	
(1962)	194,000	16,000[d]	18,000[a]	

[a] Assuming 90 percent saturation.
[b] Breakeven not defined because of positive intercept in regression of profits on VHF and TVH.
[c] A 95 percent confidence interval for profits at this value of TVH is ±\$30,000. Average profits were \$60,000.
[d] A 95 percent confidence interval for profits at this value of TVH is ±\$53,000. Average profits were \$91,000.

TABLE IX

BREAKEVEN TELEVISION HOMES (TVH) FOR 2-STATION MARKETS

	Minimum revenue $	*TVH*	*Total homes*	*NWC*
Alexander	300,000	45,000[a]	50,000	
Steiner–Barnett (1962)	450,000	149,000[a]	165,000	77,000
Steiner–Barnett method				
(1963)	450,000			
(1964)	450,000			
(1965)	500,000			
Present study				
(1960)	409,000	70,400[b]	78,000[a]	
(1962)	451,700	68,100[c]	76,000[a]	

[a] Assuming 90 percent saturation.
[b] A 95 percent confidence interval for profits at this value of TVH is ±\$93,000. Average profits were \$234,000.
[c] A 95 percent confidence interval for profits at this value of TVH is ±\$122,000. Average profits were \$327,000.

TABLE X

BREAKEVEN TELEVISION HOMES (TVH) FOR 3-STATION MARKETS

	Minimum revenue $	*TVH*	*Total homes*	*NWC*
Alexander	400,000	75,000	83,000	
Steiner–Barnett (1962)	550,000	189,000[a]	210,000	100,000
Steiner–Barnett method				
(1963)		189,000[a]	210,000	
(1964)		189,000[a]	210,000	
(1965)		189,000[a]	210,000	
Present study				
(1960)	641,000	167,000[b]	186,000[a]	
(1962)	712,000	195,000[c]	217,000[a]	

[a] Assuming 90 percent saturation.
[b] A 95 percent confidence interval for profits at this value of TVH is ±$65,900. Average profits were $417,000.
[c] A 95 percent confidence interval for profits at this value of TVH is ±$89,200. Average profits were $571,000.

TABLE XI

BREAKEVEN TELEVISION HOMES (TVH) FOR 4-OR-MORE-STATION MARKETS

	Minimum revenue $	*TVH*	*Total homes*	*NWC*
Alexander	500,000	125,000	139,000	
Steiner–Barnett (1962)	550,000	315,000[a]	350,000	195,000
Present study				
(1960)	3,314,000[b]	1,477,000[b]	1,641,000[a]	
(1962)	2,132,000[b]	1,199,000[b]	1,332,000[a]	

[a] Assuming 90 percent saturation.
[b] Calculated for independent stations.

BIBLIOGRAPHY

[1] (ALEXANDER, S. S.) 'CBS says U.S. TV Limit is 600 Healthy Stations', *Broadcasting-Telecasting*, Vol. 49, No. 16 (October 17th, 1955), pp. 27–31.

[2] BARNETT, H. J., 'An Analysis of United States Television Station Markets', unpublished manuscript.

[3] BARNETT, H. J., 'Economic Report of Dr. Harold Barnett', Exhibit D of *Comments of Midwest Television, Inc. in opposition to deletion of Channel 3 from Champaign, Illinois.* Before the Federal Communications Commission in the Matter of Deintermixture of Champaign, Illinois, Docket No. 14244. February 19th, 1962 (Mimeo).

[4] —— and GREENBERG, EDWARD, 'A Proposal for Wired City Television', *Washington University Law Quarterly*, Vol. 1968 (Winter 1968), No. 1, pp. 1–25.

[5] BLANK, D. M. 'The Quest for Quantity and Diversity in Television Programming', *American Economic Review*, Vol. LVI, No. 2 (May, 1966), pp. 448–56.

[6] FISHER, F. M., *Appendix to Reply Comments of the National Association of Broadcasters: The Fisher Report*, Federal Communications Commission, Washington, October 26th, 1964 (mimeographed).

[7] —— and FERRALL, V. E., JR. in association with Belsley, David and Mitchell, B. M., 'Community Antenna Television Systems and Local Television Station Audience', *Quarterly Journal of Economics*, Vol. LXXX, No. 2 (May 1966), pp. 227–51.

[8] GREENBERG, EDWARD, 'Wire Television and the FCC's Second Report and Order on CATV Systems', *Journal of Law and Economics*, Vol. 10 (October 1967), pp. 181–92.

[9] LEVIN, H. J., 'Economic Effects of Broadcast Licensing', *Journal of Political Economy*, Vol. LXXII, No. 2 (April 1964), pp. 151–62.

[10] ——, 'Economic Structure and the Regulation of Television', *Quarterly Journal of Economics*, Vol. LXXII, No. 3 (August 1958), pp. 424–50.

[11] MINOW, N. N., *Equal Time: The Private Broadcaster and the Public Interest*, edited by Lawrence Laurent. New York: Atheneum, 1964.

[12] ROTHENBERG, J., 'Consumer Sovereignty and the Economics of TV Programming', *Studies in Public Communications*, No. 4 (Autumn 1962), pp. 45–54.

[13] STEINER, P. O., *Comments on the Proposed Deintermixture of Madison, Wisconsin by Deleting its Channel 3*. FCC Dockets No. 14239 and 14229, February 1962 (mimeo).

[14] ——, 'Program Patterns and Preferences and the Workability of Competition in Radio Broadcasting', *Quarterly Journal of Economics*, Vol. LXVI, No. 2 (May 1952), pp. 194–223.

[15] ——, *Statement before Federal Communications Commission*, January 31st, 1962 (mimeo).

[16] —— and BARNETT, H. J. in association with Edward Greenberg and Michael Sovereign, 'Comments of Economic Consultants on the

MPATI Petition', before the Federal Communications Commission, Washington, D.C., Dockets No. 15201 and 14229, April 3rd, 1964 (mimeo).

[17] UNITED RESEARCH INC., *The Implications of Limiting Multiple Ownership of Television Stations*. Report prepared for The Council for Television Development, Cambridge, Massachusetts, September 1966.

[18] U.S. FEDERAL COMMUNICATIONS COMMISSION, *Fostering Expanded Use of UHF Television Channels*, Docket No. 14229, FCC 66–137. 'Fifth Report and Memorandum Opinion and Order', adopted February 9th, 1966, Washington, D.C.

[19] WILES, P., 'Pilkington and the Theory of Value', *Economic Journal*, Vol. LXXIII, No. 290 (June 1963), pp. 183–200.

APPENDIX

A. S. S. Alexander

Professor S. S. Alexander, in his 1955 memorandum for CBS [1], concluded that 600 is an upper limit to the number of television stations the United States could support. Time has proved to be remarkably kind to his estimate: the FCC's financial data for 1965 is based on 588 stations.

Alexander utilized published data similar to those of Table II for the first quarter of 1954 to compute breakeven points for television stations. He estimated the minimum revenues necessary for profitable stations profitable operation in 1-, 2-, 3-, and 4-station markets to be $200,000, $300,000, $400,000 and $500,000, respectively. The estimates were based on the observation that profitable stations tended to earn higher revenues and stations suffering losses tended to earn lower. Total revenues per television home were then computed from various 3-and-more-station markets in 1953, yielding $16 as a reasonable upper limit.[1] Dividing $16 into $2,000,000 yielded 125,000 television homes or 139,000 homes assuming a 90 per cent saturation. 83,000 homes are necessary for 3-station markets by this analysis. On a somewhat different basis, Alexander concluded that 45,000 television homes or 50,000 homes are necessary for 2-station markets, and 20,000 television homes or 22,000 homes are necessary for 1-station markets. These results are summarized in Tables VIII–XI. Applying these cutoffs to the existing television markets (1955), Alexander found that the largest 78 markets have sufficient population for 4 stations; the next 30 can support 3 stations; 57 can support 2 stations; and 52 can support 1.

The audience estimates are qualified by the possibility that stations will not share revenues equally, requiring a larger audience in order that the marginal station may earn the necessary revenues. Other qualifying factors may have a long-run effect, according to Alexander. These are declines in minimum operating costs and increases in advertising revenue.

[1] Comparison of Revenue/TVH for those 1955 3-station markets which remained 3-station markets in 1961 revealed that $16 was still an upper limit. In fact, 6 of the 9 Revenue/TVH decreased over the period, and the only case in which Revenue/TVH was substantially higher ($36.60) fell below (to $12.51).

Alexander also argues that the limit of 600 stations is not sensitive to changes in coverage patterns. In fact, if such coverage were reduced in order to allow more stations, there would be a smaller number since each market would then be able to support fewer stations. Note here again that Alexander makes no distinction between VHF and UHF stations; in fact his computations assume that all stations are VHF stations. Any handicaps suffered by UHF stations will act to reduce further the number of operating stations.

B. P. O. Steiner–H. J. Barnett, et al.

Published FCC data for 1962 were used by Professors P. O. Steiner and H. J. Barnett *et al.* [16]. The data reveal that over three-quarters of the stations with revenues over $225,000 are profitable and more than three-quarters of stations taking in less are unprofitable in 1-station markets.[1] This suggests a revenue breakeven point around $225,000. Similar analysis of 2-station markets reveals a breakeven point between $400,000 and $500,000, leading to an estimate of $450,000. For 3-station markets, Steiner–Barnett conclude that revenue between $500,000 and $600,000 is necessary for a station to break even. This figure is based on the fact that the average per-station revenue of the 3 markets reporting aggregate losses was in that range. There is little information for markets of 4 and more stations; in the absence of sufficient data, Steiner–Barnett use figures derived for 3-station markets. Analysis of grouped station data indicates that a net weekly circulation of between 20,000 and 35,000 (35,000–65,000 homes) is necessary to achieve the revenues suggested as being necessary for 1-station markets. Another set of grouped data reveals that a net weekly circulation of approximately 77,000 and total homes of approximately 165,000 are necessary to support 2 stations in a market. For 3-station markets, a new weekly circulation of 100,000 and total homes of 210,000 appear to be suitable estimates.

These estimates are qualified to the extent that population change and a fourth network will significantly change the breakeven points. Moreover the analysis generally tends to be conservative, assuming a smaller required audience for break even than the data suggest. Of course, using breakeven as a criterion is itself conservative, since merely breaking even would not keep resources in an industry for long.

It is of interest to update the Steiner–Barnett results using FCC published data for 1963, 1964 and 1965. These are placed in Tables VIII–X and seem to agree quite well with the 1962 results. The results for minimum revenues needed for breakeven also seem consistent with the less detailed information supplied by the FCC for 1960.

[1] The numbers of stations with revenues above or below particular amounts may not be exact because the FCC rankings are on the basis of total revenues in the market, not on an individual station basis

THE COMPUTER UTILITY: MARKET ENTRY IN SEARCH OF PUBLIC POLICY*

by MANLEY R. IRWIN

I. INTRODUCTION

RECENT developments in computer hardware and programming now enable several users to share the stored information and logic capability of data processing machines. The subscriber, no longer adjacent to the computer, may access the computer's logic and memory via telephone lines tied to the data center. Indeed, the combination of data centers, communication lines, and terminal equipment form the elements of what some forecast as a new industry, time-shared services or what others call the computer or information utility. Services arising out of this industry include bibliographic retrieval, stock quotation, hotel reservations, legal indexing, market reports, banking by phone, hospital information systems, common data files, program libraries, to mention a few. Such services soon promise to be international as well as domestic in operation and scope.

Last year, the Federal Communications Commission initiated an investigation into the policy implications of computer time-shared operations.[1] The Commission seeks to determine its statutory obligations given what it terms the 'growing interdependence' of computers and communications. This paper proposes to examine one of the issues posed by the Commission's investigation. Specifically, we will (1) state the regulatory issues as the Commission views them; (2) discuss the background events that prompted the inquiry; and (3) evaluate some of the competitive issues associated with time-shared computer services. We will conclude that the ground rules for market entry are at stake in the FCC's investigation.

II. THE INVESTIGATION

The Federal Communications Commission announced its computer inquiry on November 10th, 1966. Some of the Commission's questions dealt with the adequacy of tariffs, rates, and customs practiced by the communication carrier industry. Other questions focused on the issue of privacy and telephone wiretapping incident

* This study was funded by a grant from the Office of Naval Research. The Department of the Navy is in no way responsible for its conclusions.

[1] Before the Federal Communications Commission. In the matter of regulatory and policy problems presented by the interdependence of computer and communication services and facilities. *Notice of Inquiry*, Docket No. 6979, November 25th, 1966.

to the growing concentration of information. The central if not the most controversial issue, however, settled on the question of the Commission's regulatory obligations. Specifically, the Commission asked:

> The circumstances, if any, under which any of the aforementioned services (data processing, special information services, message or circuit switching) should be deemed subject to any regulation pursuant to the provisions of Title II of the Communications Act.
> (1) when involving the use of communications facilities and services;
> (2) when furnished by an established communication common carrier;
> (3) when furnished by entities other than established communication common carriers.[2]

These questions may have caught some observers by surprise, particularly members of the computer industry. However, a review of the factors contributing to the inquiry suggests that the FCC may have had little choice in exposing these issues for public discussion. In fact, the Commission's attempt to distinguish between 'data processing' and 'communications' may prelude a more general policy search in the growing field of time-shared computer services.

III. SOURCE OF INVESTIGATION

First, what prompted the investigation? Obviously the inquiry resulted from the interplay of many factors. However, four can be identified as being singularly important: (1) the Bunker–Ramo case; (2) the IBM letter; (3) diversification efforts of Western Union, a domestic telegraph carrier; (4) diversification efforts of ITT Worldcom, an international telegraph carrier. The background of each follows.

A. The Bunker–Ramo Case

The first issue, determining the content of a communication common carrier service, erupted in a service offering by the Bunker–Ramo Corporation. Bunker–Ramo sells a stock quotation service to brokers, bankers and insurance companies. Stock information is gathered from the main Exchange floor in New York, transmitted and stored in Bunker–Ramo's regional offices. Computers in these offices then distribute this information via telephone lines to the

[2] *Ibid.*, p. 1.

firm's customers throughout the country. By means of desk units supplied by the company, subscribers query the computer for a host of market security information. Bunker–Ramo, designating its service as Telequote III, operated an information retrieval system on a real-time or instant use basis.

Under this system, Bunker–Ramo provided its subscribers with stock quotation service, desk display units, and telephone communication circuits, all as a total package. Although Bunker–Ramo owned the former two units, it obviously did not own the latter. Communication lines were necessarily secured from the communication common carrier industry and then resold by Bunker–Ramo to its customers.

As a rule, the common carriers do not lease communication lines to firms who resell them. The carriers hold such activity subsidizes their competition, dilutes revenues, and ultimately translates into higher rates for their telephone or telegraph customers. The carriers argue, moreover, that the exchange or routing of messages among or between persons constitutes the essence of 'communications' as conventionally defined. This function is obviously confined to regulated communication firms.

There are, however, exceptions to this policy. Reselling of communications is permitted under the carriers' authorized user tariff. A firm may resell circuits if the carriers determine that both the firm and its customers are engaged in the same business activity. Bunker–Ramo customers, stockbrokers, etc., qualified under the authorized user tariff. Thus, the firm acting as literally a broker between its customers and the carriers, sold leased communication facilities.[3]

The announcement of a new stock quotation service, Telequote IV, reopened not only the question of definition but also the question of circuit availability. In contrast to Telequote III, Telequote IV grafted electronic message switching to the computer's capability of data processing, message switching that permitted brokers to place, execute and confirm stock orders between their offices. The carriers agreed that the message switching element constituted a new and crucial element to Bunker–Ramo's service.

Specifically, the carriers held that the store and forwarding of information constituted a tariff violation. Stated differently, Bunker–Ramo's service embraced enough communications so as to infringe upon an activity reserved to regulated entities.[4] The

[3] Bunker–Ramo letter to Federal Communications Commission, March 12th, 1965.

[4] Letter from the Western Union Telegraph Company to the Federal Communications Commission, December 3rd, 1965.

As we understand the Telequote IV proposal, the service would be offered to the brokerage industry, the conclusion is inescapable therefore that under the proposal, implication was strong that if communications was Bunker–Ramo's intent then the firm ought to apply for a franchise of convenience and necessity. In the meantime, the denial of communication lines effectively foreclosed the operation of Bunker–Ramo's new service.

This impasse prompted Bunker–Ramo to issue a letter of complaint to the FCC. The firm granted that its message switching of administrative data might be interpreted as the transportation of communications. However,

> Such transportation rarely occurs as an incident to another primary business and although a charge is collected for the overall service, the incidental transportation is not supplied with the purpose to profit from whatever transportation service may thus be performed.[5]

In short, Bunker–Ramo invoked the primary business test.

To emphasize the incidental nature of Telequote IV's communications, Bunker–Ramo revealed a breakdown of Telequote IV; 84 percent was assigned to services of stock quotations; 10 percent assigned to orders and confirmations; 1 percent to market opinions, and 3 percent to customer accounting. The controversial segment, the routing of administrative data, consisted of some 2 percent of the entire stock quotation service.[6] Clearly, argued Bunker–Ramo, this small portion did not constitute communication activity in its generally accepted sense; and clearly such activity should not condemn Bunker–Ramo's entire service as illegal.

Ultronics Systems Corporation, a competitive supplier of stock quotation service, volunteered its observations to the FCC. Ultronics submitted that the Telequote IV service embraced enough message switching or communications so as to indict the entire service as a regulated communication activity.[7] Interestingly enough, this posi-

[5] *Ibid.*, p. 3.

[6] Bunker–Ramo letter to Honorable E. William Henry, Chairman of the Federal Communications Commission, August 23rd, 1965.

[7] Letter from Ultronics Systems Corporation to the Federal Communications Commission, January 17th, 1966.

> there would be a holding out to the general public as that term is used in the law of common carriage.

See also American Telephone & Telegraph letter to the FCC, September 29th, 1965, p. 2.

> It would appear that the transmission of communications is at the heart of its (Bunker–Ramo) proposal for 'message switching' services, which services might prove in fact a most significant element of Telequote IV. The so-called 'data processing' to the extent they exist at all in such cases might be deemed ancillary to the transmission of communications. In such circumstances, we believe a conclusion that Bunker–Ramo was not engaged in a common carrier undertaking subject to regulation under the Communications Act would be open to serious question.

tion paralleled Western Union's thesis that communication rather than data processing was actually the dominant element of Bunker–Ramo's contemplated service.

In the end, the Telequote IV dispute did not require the Federal Communications Commission to promulgate a formal ruling. Subsequent negotiations between Bunker–Ramo and the Bell Telephone System (AT&T) found room for compromise. Bunker–Ramo agreed to eliminate the 2 percent administrative segment of its service; Bell agreed to lease circuits under its authorized user tariff. As a result, the policy issues latent with this dispute were merely postponed.

B. The IBM Letter

The FCC's inquiry was also identified with an open letter submitted to the Federal Communications Commission by IBM.[8] The letter was both cautious and apprehensive. IBM began by drawing a sharp distinction between the terms 'communication' and 'data processing'. Data processing or the transformation consisted of analyzing, classifying, correlating, sorting, calculating, summarizing, and producing records and reports. By contrast, communications embraced the transportation or transmission of information by wire or radio under the Communications Act of 1934. Lest the Commission confuse the two, IBM observed:

> If intelligence is sent from A to a computer and transformed by the computer and the message then goes forth from the computer to B containing the transmitted intelligence, it is clear that there has not been transmittal of a message from A to B through a computer.[9]

The issue in the Bunker–Ramo case, however, was not solely one of determining the appropriate mix between data processing and communications. The parties generally agreed that Telequote IV embraced the electronic routing of message communications. The question, however, turned on the status of switching activity performed by a firm not licensed as a communication carrier. IBM suggested the primary business test as a guide to resolving any such determination. And if communications were indeed incidental, such activity did not qualify as regulated, limited exclusively to telephone or telegraph companies.

What about the reverse situation, the case when a regulated carrier engages in data processing? Obviously aware of Western Union's diversification into data processing services, IBM cited an FCC

[8] Letter from IBM to Federal Communications Commission, February 15th, 1966, p. 5.
[9] *Ibid.*, p. 7.

decision with respect to the telegraph company's flower service. Though part of its communication plant is so employed, Western Union does not file tariff schedules on the flower segment of the service. This policy, argued IBM, provided sound precedent for Western Union's or any carrier's move into unregulated, data processing services.[10]

In sum, IBM counseled the FCC to consider the primary business test when non-regulated firms find themselves engaged in regulated or message switching activities. By the same token, IBM submitted that data processing services supplied by regulated entities do not automatically redefine that activity as a regulated one.

C. Western Union's Diversification

Since telephone or telegraph lines are by definition critical to remote data processing services, it was perhaps inevitable that the communication carriers would find computer services an attractive source of market diversification. Indeed, Western Union's concept of a national information utility, a blending of computer and communication facilities, epitomized that diversification.[11] To this end, the telegraph company announced the computerization of its Telex switching centers, the establishment of data processing service centers, the announcement of specific data processing services—legal index, employment service, among others—and the introduction of a management information system available to commercial and government users.

Western Union's entry into information services originated with its government contracts. The Autodin contract, for example, consisted of a joint data processing and message switching system to the Defense Department. A similar service, the Advanced Record System, was also leased to the General Services Administration; a system whereby the telegraph company has been responsible for the automatic dial nationwide circuit switching system, three message switching centers, and the supply and maintenance of software and message switching capability. (The computers route multiple address messages, recognize priorities, and hold messages for specific delivery time.)

The seeds of controversy inherent in a regulated firm engaging in a non-regulated activity commenced with these government contracts. As early as August 1964, the FCC requested Western Union to justify why the data processing segment of the Advanced Record

[10] *Ibid.*, p. 6.
[11] *Western Union Annual Report 1965*, p. 10.

System was excluded as a tariffed service. The Commission wrote:

> We are advised that you do not intend to include in your tariffs on file with the Commission charges for off-line processors furnished in connection with this system. It is requested that you advise us as to what you believe to be the legal justification for furnishing this item of equipment without having charges therefor on file in your tariffs.[12]

Later, the question of tariffing and contracting arose again with Western Union's announcement of its management information system for Dun & Bradstreet and Blue Cross.[13] Finally, last year the FCC urged the telegraph company once again to explain its policy with respect to its data processing services.[14]

Western Union's response attempted to place its new activities in perspective. The telegraph company reminded the Commission that it competed directly with firms whose computers were replacing Western Union's torn-tape switching systems. Rivalry between the carriers and computer firms, explained Western Union, was immediate and direct in the GSA Advanced Record System contract; and Western Union argued that had it tariffed its service, the telegraph company would have been placed in an untenable position *vis-à-vis* its competitors.

To illustrate the need for flexibility and hence our tariff policy, Western Union recalled that its original bid to GSA had been high. A downward revision occurred through the cooperation of Univac's Division of Sperry Rand—a revision that resulted in a bid that ultimately secured the contract for the telegraph company. Western Union continued:

> GSA expressed concern that since the Western Union bid was of a tariffed nature, the quoted price was not firm for (a) tariffs would be necessarily filed months after the award of a contract, and (b) regulatory action would in effect bring about a superseding of the contract. Western Union was therefore advised that it could have a contract only on the condition that a firm fixed price contract for five years could be offered, and had

[12] *Telecommunications Reports*, August 10th, 1964, vol. 30, no. 37, p. 19.

[13] *Telecommunications Reports*, November 22nd, 1965, vol. 31, no. 51, p. 14. Western Union states:

> The type of computer equipment furnished varies according to the requirements of each customer. Depending upon the capabilities of the particular equipment furnished, such equipment may be utilized for electronic processing of business data and for electronic switching of message communications. The telegraph company also undertakes on request to provide programming of the computer equipment on an initial or a continuing basis.

[14] *Telecommunications Reports*, November 29th, 1965, vol. 31, no. 52, p. 3.

> Western Union not acceded, GSA would have made a contract award to ITT.[15]

What was true for the government sector was equally true for the private sector. To meet market competition, Western Union responded that its data processing activities need not be subject to regulation despite the fact that the company itself was a regulated carrier.

Finally, Western Union elicited restrained enthusiasm from the primary business test as a policy guide to determining the communication activities of data processing firms. The primary business test, observed the telegraph company, threatened the very concept of regulation.

> Such companies as IBM would always be in the position of furnishing a part of the communication business on an incidental basis and hence, would never be subjected to regulation. The safeguards of the utility concept would thus be eroded.[16]

In specific reference to Telequote IV, Western Union was concerned that the element of direct communication among the subscribers would persist.[17]

D. ITT Worldcom's Diversification

A third element that impelled the Commission's Notice of Inquiry was associated with developments on the international scene, the international communication carriers. Last year, ITT Worldcom, a subsidiary of International Telephone & Telegraph and an overseas record carrier, filed a tariff on a computer message switching service. The tariff, designated ARX (customer data re-transmission) excluded individual circuits and terminal apparatus. Rather, the subscriber was billed on the number of messages routed through ITT's computer switching system.

The tariff encountered opposition immediately.[18] Western Union, for example, objected that as an international carrier, ITT was diversifying into the domestic communication market competing with and eliminating Western Union's torn-tape relay switching systems, thus diluting needed revenues from the telegraph company. Western Union International Telegraph Company,

[15] Letter from Western Union Telegraph Company to the Federal Communications Commission regarding computer lease and service arrangements, March 14th, 1966, p. 10.
[16] *Ibid.*, pp. 37–8.
[17] *Ibid.*, p. 34.
[18] In the matter of ITT World Communications Inc., Tariff no. 54, June 9th, 1966.

an overseas record carrier, joined Collins Radio, a manufacturer of computer switching equipment, in voicing further objections to the ARX tariff. Western Union International asserted that the tariff was unclear and ambiguous; and Collins Radio suggested that the tariff was underpriced and hence non-compensatory.[19]

ITT Worldcom acknowledged that some of its switching systems would be located within the United States. However, as long as its customers leased one private line circuit overseas, domestic switching was permitted under the Communications Act, Section 222. (The act defines an international carrier as one whose major portion of traffic and revenues is derived from international telegraph operations.)[20]

Significantly, ITT Worldcom asserted that computerized message switching was an activity subject to the jurisdiction of the Federal Communications Commission. Indeed, since the ARX tariff had been filed under this assumption, ITT Worldcom requested that the FCC expedite its approval of the ARX service. Its customers, explained the carrier, might seek alternative suppliers of automatic switching, suppliers not subject to FCC jurisdiction. Thus, on October 1st, 1966, the Federal Communications Commission denied petitions for tariff suspension and ITT Worldcom's service took effect.[21]

As if matters were not complicated enough, RCA Communications, an international record carrier and a subsidiary of RCA, inaugurated a service called Aircon devoted to the needs of international air carriers. Aircon, a computerized message switching service, also contemplated the processing of seat reservations, inventory, accounting, data on cargo, freight information, as well as a wide variety of administrative services. RCA's service was thus directly competitive with that offered by ITT Worldcom. The difference between the two was crucial; RCA refused to file a tariff.

ITT Worldcom lost no time in urging the FCC to force RCA Communications to file an appropriate tariff schedule. As requested, the FCC asked for a statement of policy from RCA Communications. The carrier replied that its automatic information reservations service would not only be at a competitive disadvantage with those provided by Collins Radio, but filing a tariff would prejudice the issues posed in the FCC's computer inquiry which by this time had

[19] *Ibid.*; Petitions of Western Union International for suspension; Reply of Collins Radio to reply of ITT World Communications, Inc. to petitions of the Western Union Telegraph Company, Western Union International Inc., and Collins Radio, Inc.

[20] *Ibid.*; Reply of ITT World Communications, Inc. to petitions of the Western Union Telegraph Company, Western Union International, and Collins Radio, June 16th, 1960, p. 5.

[21] *Telecommunications Reports*, October 3rd, 1966, vol. 30, no. 43, p. 8.

been announced. Thus, RCA Communications observed:

> It must maintain a competitive position that would enable it to compete effectively on a meaningful basis with non-regulated entities. Beyond this, a tariff filing would afford non-regulated companies an unfair advantage by exposing the entire Aircon service offering to their scrutiny while their offerings are beyond the regulatory purview.[22]

Where is the communication–data processing situation as it now stands? First, firms in both industries do not agree as to the precise limits and hence proper jurisdiction of data processing and data switching. Second, the domestic and international carriers are split among themselves as to what constitutes the relevant market for data switching; third, the international carriers are divided as to the FCC's jurisdiction over computer switching; and finally, the question of promotional pricing, and rate levels continue to beset carriers and non-carriers alike.

IV. POLICY ISSUES

A central theme can be detected in the confluence of events that prompted the FCC's investigation; and that is the question of establishing group rules for market entry and competition. Consider this theme as it applies to three questions: (1) the leasing of communication lines; (2) carrier merger policy; and (3) joint cost allocation.

A. Market Entry and Communication Lines

To repeat the obvious, regulated entities are attempting to engage in non-regulated activities, namely data processing, non-regulated firms are attempting to diversify into what is commonly regarded as regulated activities—communications. RCA Communications and Western Union typify the former trend; Bunker–Ramo typifies the latter trend. But as the Bunker–Ramo case suggests, diversification is not a reciprocal relationship. The carriers own and supply the nation's communication circuits, clearly an activity subject to state and federal regulation. With this as a base, it may be less difficult for regulated entities to diversify into unregulated activities than vice versa. In short, the granting of franchises is slow, expensive and hardly conducive to market entry for data processing firms.

What is important is that the carriers lease circuits to a growing

[22] *Telecommunications Reports*, February 27th, 1967, vol. 33, no. 11, p. 6.

group of firms who pose as competitors as well as customers. This relationship can be expected to intensify; and as the Bunker–Ramo case testifies, market diversification poses no little problem to the Federal Communications Commission. The Commission may find that carriers deny lines to companies who engage in communication on grounds that such activity is subject to regulation. On the other hand, the carriers may refuse to file tariffs on their data processing packages on grounds of market competition. This asymmetrical relationship effectively bars market entry to major candidates who are seeking to offer computer utility services, particularly if those firms reside in the non-regulated sector of the economy. By foreclosing or conditioning market entry, the structure of this new industry obviously will be predetermined.

There is a deeper problem. RCA Communications' refusal to file a tariff on computer switching suggests a profound policy disagreement, at least within the ranks of the international carriers. At odds with both a domestic carrier (Western Union Telegraph Company) and an international carrier (ITT Worldcom), RCA Communications apparently assumes that its activities now and in the future will be competing directly with those services offered by non-regulated entities.

It is clear that the blurring of data processing and communications does not lend itself to easy solution. In this search, the primary business test is an unsettling policy guide. Communication and computer firms will obviously employ the test to their own ends, however those ends are defined. That such a test borders on the arbitrary can be seen in its application. In the eyes of Western Union, flower and data processing service are 'incidental' to communications. Yet the communications industry becomes less tolerant when the identical test is invoked by the data processing industry, to wit, the Bunker–Ramo case.

Thus, the primary business test cuts both ways; it can be employed to rationalize a movement from communication to data processing; or from data processing to communications. And if such a test is resurrected as a policy guide, it takes little imagination to visualize a backlog of adjudicatory proceedings in which the adversaries seek the magic number of 49 percent.

B. Market Entry and Merger

As noted above, non-regulated firms generally seek refuge in the primary business test as a means of avoiding 'the burden of regulation and the obligation of service'. But it is conceivable that a data processing firm may assume or perhaps even hope that its activities are a legitimate common carrier function. This may occur when a data processing firm merges with a regulated firm.

Any such consolidation poses two questions. First, does merger with a common carrier sanction the conversion of a non-regulated activity to a regulated activity. The answer is, of course, speculative. The merger, however, of the Ultronics Corporation with General Telephone and Electronics Corporation, the nation's second largest telephone carrier, suggests that this possibility is very real.[23] Indeed, it was Ultronics who argued that Bunker–Ramo's Telequote IV encroached upon a regulated communication activity.

Secondly, if movement from a non-regulated to a regulated status offers a solution to Ultronics, what options are open to Bunker–Ramo, Scantlon, and other rivals of Ultronics. Does the existence of direct competition among these firms stimulate what E. H. Chamberlin terms 'parallel integration'? And what are the implications of these activities in terms of the long-term environment for computer utility services? Merger policy, particularly the consolidation of non-regulated with regulated entities, raise provocative issues in terms of market entry.

C. Market Entry and Joint Cost

Finally, the straddling of communications and the data processing package half regulated, half unregulated, conjures major accounting problems associated with joint costs. Like any regulatory body, the Commission is not entirely unacquainted with the problems of cost separation. Although it granted the telegraph company an accounting waiver for the data processing segment of the ARX service, the announcement by Western Union of its management information systems for Blue Cross and Dun & Bradstreet prompted the Commission to inquire as to the feasibility of separating the telegraph company's communication activities. In response, Western Union observed:

> Certain non-communication activities which are now clearly incidental to communication activities are expected to become significant in the future. The whole field of computer applications and information storage and retrieval is in a state of development; more important, many matters such as the method of operation remaining unsolved.[24]

Western Union's position of incipiency hardly eases a problem that is likely to become aggravated over time. The question of cost

[23] *Wall Street Journal*, May 16th, 1967, p. 14.
[24] Telecommunications Reports, September 12th, 1966, vol. 33, no. 40, p. 16.

separation, in short, will undoubtedly command the attention of all participants in the FCC's computer inquiry.

That cost separation is no easy task is demonstrated by past experience. The carriers generally prove more receptive to discussions of rate of return rather than questions of rate structure. Even when the Commission persuades a carrier, as it did the Bell System, to calculate rate of return on fully allocated costs, the carrier tends to regard its studies as less than meaningful for purposes of public policies.[25] Thus, the search for cost separation standards within the regulatory sector is fraught with complexity. But more important, the search for standards applicable to a firm half in and half outside the bounds of regulation is equally imposing.

Yet, regulatory experience suggests that such separation is crucial. The telegraph investigation indicated, for example, that the Bell System was not above employing its monopoly markets to carry its competitive markets—all within the regulated sector.[26] No one doubts that the Telpak tariff has throttled the innovation of private microwave communication systems. If then, internal subsidization places a continual burden on regulation, the accounting hazards of a firm partly regulated and partly unregulated are no less challenging. To repeat, market structure and rate structure are inseparable. Both bear on the viability of market entry.

There is a final issue. The carriers are in one sense integrating forward, packaging communication lines together with computer services. At the same time, the carriers lease circuits to potential competitors—the computer industry. Will wholesale, retail rates distort prices sufficiently in the final product market to rule out meaningful market competition? Bluntly stated, will the carriers accord themselves internal line discounts denied their customers? And if the carriers lease circuits from themselves or from other carriers, will such transactions, now apparently residing beyond the province of FCC jurisdiction, accord the carriers competitive advantages that ultimately spell who survives in the computer services industry?[27] Again, market entry rides on these issues, no matter how premature they might appear today.

[25] Before the Federal Communications Commission. In the matter of domestic telegraph service, Docket No. 14650, Report of the Common Carrier Bureau.

[26] *Ibid.*, pp. 156–7.

[27] Amendments to Title II of the Communications Act of 1934 (Common Carrier). Hearings before the Committee on Interstate and Foreign Commerce, House of Representatives, 88th Congress, Second Session, HR 6018, a bill to amend section 203 (A) of the Communications Act of 1934 as amended with respect to the filing of schedules of charges by connecting carriers; 1965.

V. CONCLUSION

In sum, the Commission's computer inquiry is confronted with an imposing agenda of policy questions. Not the least is the issue of definition and jurisdiction; for out of their determinations rests the question of market entry and market structure. Two options are clearly open to time-shared computer services: competition or regulation. But these choices apparently assume that the firm is restricted to the either/or extreme of data processing or message switching. The imperatives of technology suggest, however, that the pure case may be the exceptional case. As the amalgam of data processing and communications continues, a third choice, namely de-regulation, may pose as a policy alternative worthy of consideration. Perhaps it is unthinkable that a government agency cut the Gordian knot of regulation with any degree of seriousness. But the solutions to the computer utility question are sufficiently urgent to warrant broadening the search for unique policy prescriptions.

UNIVERSITY OF NEW HAMPSHIRE